INSTRUCTOR'S MANUAL

for

EDWARD MC NALL BURNS
PHILIP LEE RALPH
ROBERT E. LERNER
STANDISH MEACHAM

WORLD CIVILIZATIONS

Sixth Edition

G. J. SZEMLER
Loyola University of Chicago

W. W. NORTON & COMPANY
New York   London

ISBN 0-393-95089-1

1 2 3 4 5 6 7 8 9 0

CONTENTS

PREFACE

A course in the history of World civilizations is a core requirement in many American colleges and universities. This course is the only structured history class in the academic acreer of most students, many of whom graduated from high school with little, if any, background in the subject. Consequently, instructors of these courses are provided with a great opportunity to transfer their enthusiasm for their subject to the students and, as educators, they must accept the challenge to show that contemporary experiences are not unique and awareness of the past will aid in making decisions for the present and the future.

Teaching such a course well is a difficult task. But the difficulties can be eased by the selection of a good text, the primary tool to motivate learning. The Sixth Edition of Edward McNall Burns, Philip Lee Ralph, Robert E. Lerner, and Standish Meacham's *World Civilizations*, just as the previous editions, clearly fulfills this essential requirement. The Manual, an adjunct to the text, is devised as an aid to the instructor. Following the well-proven method of Earle Field in the earlier editions, it provides the instructor with a convenient instrument to evaluate "learning" and to increase teaching efficiency. The Manual treats each chapter in its entirety and occasionally draws on material from previous chapters to assure review and to emphasize continuity.

The test questions are based on two presuppositions. It is assumed that (1) the students are thoroughly familiar with the facts and concepts in the text, either through reading assignments, lectures, or discussions, and (2) instructors are aware that overemphasis on memorization could result in mediocre teaching and, in turn, mediocre learning. The multiple-choice questions, therefore, stress understanding more than facts. They also provide the instructor with examples to test learning knowledge and critical thinking ability. The identification lists are suggested to teachers for students to provide precise definitions and brief historical comments. A series of true-and-false questions address broader conceptual issues. The essay questions comprehensively include topics that were not treated in the multiple-choice questions. Each chapter closes with a list of recommended films selected for their value as supplements to the textual treatment of various topics.

The author hopes that the Manual will help instructors, regardless of specialization, to create an atmosphere of more efficient learning in a course that is, or ought to be, a challenging and rewarding educational experience for teachers and students alike.

Samuel Knox Wilson Hall   G. J. Szemler
Loyola University of Chicago   September 1, 1981

BIBLIOGRAPHY

Cashin, W. E. "Motivating Students." *Kansas State University Idea Paper*, No. 1, Aug. 1979.

Pierson, G. W., *et al.* "The Nature of History." *AHA Newsletter*, II, 4, April 1964, 5-7.

Sergiovanni, T. J. *Handbook for Effective Department Leadership*. Boston: Allyn and Bacon, 1977, especially pp. 321-370.

Stephens, L. D. *Probing the Past: A Guide to the Study and Teaching of History*. Boston: Allyn and Bacon, 1977.

NOTE ON SUGGESTED FILMS*

The selection of the 16-mm. films listed at the end of each chapter was based upon running time, age-group ratings, and film-content quality. Further film listings or information concerning title descriptions, can be found either in the catalogue series

  · *National Information Center for Educational Media (NICEM)*, 6th ed. (University Park, Los Angeles: University of Southern California, 1977; subsequent *Update Volumes* for 1978-1979).

or in the following catalogues, whose descriptions were consulted to determine film quality:

  · Bureau of Audio-Visual Instruction, *BAVI Film Reference Guide* (Madison, Wis.: University of Wisconsin, Extension Media Center, 1979-1981).
  · R. R. Bowker Co., comp., *Educational Film Locator of the Consortium of University Film Centers and R. R. Bowker* (New York: R. R. Bowker Co., 1978). This comprehensive reference—complete with subject index, cross references, and film gradings—represents the holdings of fifty-two film libraries participating in the consortium. In addition, it contains information on the leasing policies of libraries, and each film description is accompanied by a list of member libraries that have the film in their collections.
  · University of Illinois, *History Films (1977-80)* (Champaign, Ill.: University of Illinois, 1979).
  · S. J. Parlato, Jr., *Superfilms: An International Guide to Award Winning Educational Films* (Metuchen, N.J.: Scarecrow Press, 1976).
  · Ann Seltz-Petrash, project ed. and comp.; Kathryn Wolff, man. ed., *AAAS Science Film Catalog* (Washington, D.C., and New York: American Association for the Advancement of Science, and R. R. Bowker Co., 1975).

Film distributors, not always the same as a film's producer, are noted in this manual's lists. Both producers and distributors are noted in the above reference works, as are distributors addresses. Alternate sources of availability can be found in most university media-department archives, or are noted in cooperative efforts such as the *Educational Film Locator*.

Topical slide and filmstrip listings can also be found in the NICEM catalogue series.

---

*Listings compiled by W. J. Cherf, Loyola University of Chicago, in cooperation with and under the advisement of G. J. Szemler.

PART ONE.   THE DAWN OF HISTORY

CHAPTER 1.   THE EARLIEST BEGINNINGS   3

Outline

MULTIPLE CHOICE

Choose the best response.

1.   History is

    (a)   primarily the study of change over time

  *(b)   a record of past human activities in every sphere, political, social, economic, intellectual, and aesthetic.

    (c)   the story of uninterrupted human progress from the past to the present

    (d)   a story of the social and economic institutions created by men and women, by the rich and the poor, by the rulers and the ruled alike.

    (e)   primarily a chronicle of politics, battles, treaties, laws, and decrees.

2.   Those who write history, and those who study it,

    (a)   must inquire into the causes of events and patterns of human organization and ideas, and must seek to understand the reasons for successes and failures of human endeavors.

    (b)   have to examine the past, as far as is possible, through the eyes and with the minds of those who lived it.

    (c)   must identify and discuss factors involved in the rise, growth, and decline of civilizations.

    (d)   need to look at how one event has led to another and how the entire past is a prologue to the present.

  *(e)   all of the above.

3.   Until quite recently, historians considered history to be little more than a story of

(a)   social and economic institutions that men and women have created and that have shaped their lives.

(b)   ideas and attitudes of learned men that have shaped social and economic institutions.

*(c)   "past politics," in which those whose lives were not touched by the "great books" had no determining role.

(d)   conquests of popes, kings, and various other rulers.

(e)   reaction of the conquered.

4.   The first *Homo sapiens* is to be found among

(a)   the bearers of Neolithic culture, who came from western Asia into Africa and southern Europe.

(b)   the Cro-Magnon, whose material and nonmaterial culture is nearest to that of *Homo sapiens.*

(c)   *Homo habilis*, who possessed a brain larger than apes, walked erect, and used tools.

(d)   the humanlike creatures: Peking man and Java man.

*(e)   the Neanderthal, whose distinguishing features were a receding chin, sloped forehead, and a cranial capacity slightly larger than that of a modern Caucasian.

5.   Which of the following is *not* characteristic of the earlier Paleolithic period?

(a)   Cooperation was necessary for survival; thus the crude beginnings of social institutions were introduced.

(b)   The capacity of speech enabled people of this period to communicate with their fellows.

(c)   Abstract thought is evidenced by burial of the dead with daily utensils to be used in the afterlife.

(d)   Intelligence is manifested in the use of tools; they were either selected from among natural objects or chipped from flint and other stones.

*(e)   Animal-skin clothing was sewn with the aid of bone needles.

6.   Which of the following is *not* characteristic of the later Paleolithic culture:

(a)   the use of tools, both stone implements and those made of bone, including fishhooks, harpoons, and dart throwers.

(b)   the employment of professional artists and craftsmen in the manufacture of tools and weapons of amazing workmanship and technique.

(c)   a highly developed sense of the supernatural as seen in the use of sympathetic magic and the elaborate preparation of bodies for burial.

*(d)   the discovery of a technique to fashion pottery from clay.

(e)   the building of huts of simple design that were used as houses for years at a time.

7.   Cro-Magnon people painted murals on the walls of their caves primarily

*(a)   to promote the hunters' success; by the application of the principle of sympathetic magic the painters hoped to effect a good hunt and so increase food supply.

(b)   for aesthetic pleasure, in order to beautify the easily accessible areas of their living quarters.

(c)   to ward off evil spirits.

(d)   to imitate natural details and movements of the hunt as a visual aid to train apprentice hunters.

(e)   to record human activities by depicting both animate and inanimate objects.

8.   Which of the following is *not* a reason for the disappearance of the Cro-Magnon culture:

(a)   the shift in existing climatic conditions, and retreat of the ice cover northward.

*(b)   the attack by Mesolithic and Neolithic tribes from western Asia that either exterminated the Cro-Magnon people or drove them into mountainous regions.

(c)   the disappearance of the basic food supply—the reindeer, bison, and mammoth—from the cold, icy climate of southern Europe.

(d)   the inability to adapt to different sources of food or lack of success in seeking out new sources of food.

(e)   the inability to adopt new food-production techniques.

9.   The Neolithic revolution is best represented by

(a)   the manufacture of stone tools and weapons by grinding and polishing as well as the discovery of new technical skills.

*(b)   the domestication of plants and animals, and a start of agriculture.

(c)   a permanent, settled existence, with the growth of villages and populations.

(d)   a full development of political and social institutions.

(e)   the rapid spread of Neolithic culture throughout the world.

10.   What particular development of the New Stone Age provided the foundation for civilization:

(a)   the rise of material progress and better control of the environment.

(b)   distribution of a new culture over the entire world.

*(c)   domestication of animals and development of agriculture, which together could provide reliable food resources and surplus as well as encourage a permanent, settled life style.

(d)   lasting institutions.

(e)   discovery of new tools and skills, such as knitting, weaving, pottery making, and starting fire by friction.

11.   One of the following statements is incorrect when it implies that the institution of the Neolithic family

(a)   was the smallest social unit, dominated by a male patriarch with one or more wives.

*(b)   was exclusively biological in character.

(c)   was responsible for the transmission of beliefs and customs.

(d)   acquired, maintained, and transmitted property.

(e)   was responsible for the upbringing, education, and care of the young.

12.   The institution of religion in primitive society is

*(a)   a spontaneous reaction of humans to a sense of powerless dependence on forces outside themsleves.

(b)   the formalization of human attempts to control outside forces on which humanity's physical well-being depends.

(c)   a precise determination of rites that can achieve control of outside forces.

(d)   reinterpretation of outside forces as myths, dogmas, and theologies.

(e)   all of the above.

13.   The best possible definition of the state is

(a)   a specific territory where the entire population follows similar customs, traditions, and standards.

*(b)   a specific territory under a central authority, without external control, having the power to pass laws and to preserve order by enforcing these laws.

(c)   the result of the consensus of all inhabitants to engage in expansionist military activity, but without accepting central control.

(d)   a new sovereign authority which has to be substituted for ancient regional and local customs, with or without the consensus of the population, to define rights and duties of inhabitants.

(e) a gathering of like-minded inhabitants of a region to manage their own affairs.

14. A historian can speak of civilization as an advanced stage of historical development when

   (a) location and climate create proper conditions for the development of an agricultural society.

   (b) knowledge of writing becomes extensive.

   (c) advancement in arts and sciences can be widely noted.

   (d) progress is made in social organization to conquer some of the problems of a more complex society.

   *(e) all of the above.

15. The earliest civilizations began in Mesopotamia and Egypt for all the following reasons except that the

   (a) fertile, alluvial soil deposits along narrow river valleys were suitable for agriculture.

   (b) warm climate and the annual floods were conducive to the growth of abundant harvests.

   (c) river offered a natural communication route in each region.

   (d) creation of dams and irrigation canals, and the resultant social co-operation, enhanced the development of social institutions.

   *(e) mean temperature of both areas falls between 38 and 64 degrees Fahrenheit, and their humidity averages 75 percent.

IDENTIFICATIONS

Neanderthal man	Jonathan and Richard Leakey
Arnold J. Toynbee	Solutré
7500 B.C.	Sympathetic magic
5000 B.C.	Institution
3500 B.C.	Ellsworth Huntington
First hatchet	Mesolithic
Carbon-14, and Potassium-argon method	Niaux
	Ca. 55,000 B.C.

TRUE OR FALSE

T   1. As historians examine the record of past human activities in every sphere, they have to use the tools of many other disciplines. According to need, they have to learn to use the methods of a computer scientist, a demographer, an anthropologist, a psychologist, or others.

F   2.   One of the most important lessons of history is the knowledge that our own civilization is superior to those that have come before.

F   3.   A historian is not interested in preliterate societies—those that existed before the invention of writing. The artifacts of these societies are properly of interest to archeologists or anthropologists.

T   4.   The survival of *Homo habilis* depended on cooperation. There is no evidence that they killed each other. Possibly, about a million years later humans began warring with each other.

T   5.   The greatest achievement of the Cro-Magnon people is their art, which ought to be counted among the Seven Wonders of the World.

F   6.   The later Paleolithic artists were aesthetes in the true sense of the word. The graceful lines, brillant colors, and patterns produced indicate their genius for imitating natural detail.

T   7.   Neolithic peoples were the first to fashion pottery from clay and to use mud brick to build their dwellings.

F   8.   Neolithic peoples' most important achievement was the spread of their culture over the surface of the earth.

T   9.   Geographic reasons often appear to offer the most plausible explanations for the rise and growth of civilizations.

F   10.   Recent archeological evidence clearly shows that Mesopotamian civilization was older than that of Egypt.

DISCUSSION AND/OR ESSAY QUESTIONS

1. Mesopotamia and Egypt are the oldest civilizations that emerged from the Neolithic culture. What are the causes for the rise of these two civilizations? Are these causes similar in both civilizations? Are there any differences?

2. A most important achievement of Neolithic culture was the development of lasting institutions. Discuss the role that agriculture, geography, and settled existence played in the development of particular Neolithic institutions.

3. Nonmaterial and abstract elements within cultures may be influential in a culture's progress or direction. Describe these elements in the cultures of the Neanderthal, later Paleolithic, and Neolithic peoples, comparing and contrasting the three groups. Is it possible to see a progression in these elements toward institutionalized religion?

4. If preliterate society is described as historic, what are the tools by which a historian studies such societies?

5. Present evidence for cooperation in Neanderthal, later Paleolithic, and Neolithic cultures. Is such cooperation an essential element in the development of social institutions?

SUGGESTED FILMS

Blades and Pressure Flaking. 21 min. Color. University of California, Extension Media Center (1969).

Continents Adrift. 15 min. Color. American Educational Films (1971).

Digging for the History of Man (3000 B.C.-600 A.D.). 55 min. Color. Roland Films (n.d.).

Digging Up the Past. 20 min. B/w. Time-Life Films, Inc. (1969).

Dr. Leakey and the Dawn of Man. 27 min. Color. Films, Inc. (1966).

Evolution and the Origin of Life. 33 min. Color. CRM Educational Films (1972).

Figures in Clay. 9 min. Color. Macmillan Films, Inc. (1972).

How Old Is Old? 30 min. Color. Time-Life Films, Inc. (1971).

Lascaux: Cradle of Man's Art. 18 min. Color. (For Film-library holders from whom this can be leased see *Educational Film Locator*) (1950).

Opportunity Land. 20 min. Color. Modern Talking Picture Service (1966).

The Origins of Art in France (Neolithic-400 A.D.). 40 min. B/w. Time-Life Films, Inc. (1970).

Prehistoric Images: The First Art of Man. 17 min. Color. Macmillan Films, Inc. (1955).

Story of the Earth. 20 min. B/w. Time-Life Films, Inc. (1969).

Tassili N'Ajjer. 16 min. Color. Roland Films (1970).

Water and Life. 20 min. B/w. Time-Life Films, Inc. (1969).

MULTIPLE CHOICE
Choose the best response.

1.   Which of the following statements is incorrect?

   (a)   Pharaohs were offspring of the sun god.

   (b)   Pharaohs had to marry within the family in order to keep the divine blood
         line uncontaminated.

   (c)   All political and religious power was united in the divine personality of
         the pharaoh.

  *(d)   Considered from the earliest periods of Egyptian history to be a divinity,
         the pharaoh exercised unlimited power.

   (e)   During later phases of Egyptian history, women as well as men could
         become rulers of Egypt.

2.   The imminent cause of the Old Kingdom's collapse was

   (a)   the exhaustion of governmental revenues in costly projects having no
         practical value, such as the building of the pyramids.

   (b)   the rebellion of slaves who were forced to build the pyramids.

   (c)   universal poverty and demoralization among pharaoh's subjects.

   (d)   attack by foreign tribes against whom local militias were powerless.

  *(e)   internecine wars between the civil governors of local areas, against whom
         the pharaohs were powerless.

3.   One of the following does *not* correctly represent the civilization of the
     Middle Kingdom.

   (a)   Unbridled ambitions of the nobles were successfully checked by the
         emergence of a new class of merchants, artisans, and farmers during the
         Twelfth Dynasty.

(b) Extensive drainage and irrigation projects, as well as commercial activities and trade contacts, greatly increased the material well-being of the entire population.

(c) Rulers were committed to benevolence and justice for the good of their subjects in this life.

*(d) Slaves could gain their freedom and thus become equal members of the society.

(e) According to contemporary interpretations, the gods were understood to extend to all righteous mortals a hope for salvation in the afterlife.

4. The end of the Middle Kingdom was brought about by all of the following except

*(a) attempts of regional governors to reintroduce slavery.

(b) an uprising of the nobles who hoped to regain the local authority and privileges they had enjoyed formerly.

(c) the inability of the pharaoh to maintain control over vast areas of Egypt.

(d) an unexpected invasion by the Hyksos.

(e) the inability of the pharaoh's infantry to defeat the swift-moving cavalry and chariot-borne military units of the Hyksos.

5. The Hyksos' domination was a challenge to the Egyptians, one that stimulated Egypt to actions that laid a foundation for a new era of achievement. Which of the following statements can best support the adversity and challenge theory of Arnold J. Toynbee?

(a) Local loyalties abated in the face of foreign tyranny, and Egyptians of all classes were willing to unite in a common cause of liberation.

(b) In spite of local differences, the leadership of one person was acceptable to all.

(c) New methods of warfare, the use of cavalry and chariot tactics were successfully employed against the oppressor.

(d) The Egyptian victory helped its leader to consolidate his power and determine future policy for his successors

*(e) All of the above.

6. The Empire's eventual decline was hastened by

(a) Egypt's conquest of vast territories which could not be managed properly and consequently were left in the control of professional military forces.

(b) an influx of slaves and wealth from conquered territories, resulting in a more relaxed, less resolute, and luxury-seeking life style of Egyptians.

(c)   a new nobility composed of officials, priests, and professional military leaders who were interested primarily in furthering their own careers at the court of the pharaoh.

(d)   the extension of state control over all facets of economic life, with the goal of increasing production in order to obtain the revenues needed to maintain the state's vast military machine.

*(e)   all of the above.

7.   According to institutionalized solar worship during the Old Kingdom, the god Re

*(a)   gave immortality to the state and its people.

(b)   guaranteed the individual's welfare and eternal happiness.

(c)   enforced his rule through the actions of his representatives, the priests.

(d)   did not grant blessings and material rewards to people according to individual merit.

(e)   provided justice, truth, and righteousness to all people as individuals.

8.   The worship of Osiris during the Middle Kingdom

(a)   was primarily a nature religion worshiping the forces of new life, which were later ascribed to the life-giving waters of the Nile.

(b)   motivated the average Egyptian to reinterpret life's meaning according to the legend connected with the god's career.

(c)   stimulated thought and reflection about the ultimate ascendancy of good over evil.

(d)   gave hope to all people by encouraging them to prepare for an everlasting, happy afterlife wherein the righteous will be rewarded while the unjust will be utterly destroyed.

*(e)   all of the above.

9.   After the chaos of the First Intermediate Age, the Theban dynasty unified the northern and southern areas of Egypt politically as well as religiously. Among the results of this fusion, which of the following did *not* contribute to the rise of Egyptian institutionalized religion to its highest perfection?

(a)   The two cults of Amon and Re merged.

(b)   Expectations of rewards in a happy and everlasting afterlife were widely professed.

(c)   New, centrally financed building projects such as the temple at Karnak satisfied peoples' material and spiritual needs.

(d) In a period of good will, peace, and nonaggression, ethical and political philosophers could advocate generally acceptable ethical and moral norms.

*(e) Willingness to proselytize non-Egyptian subject peoples brought many new concepts into the Egyptian mode of religious thought.

10. What is the best possible explanation for religion's deterioration during the Empire:

(a) the insecurity of daily life caused by the constant demand for additional military levies required to control the conquered peoples of the vast Egyptian Empire.

(b) the inability of the pharaoh to supply leadership for the unification of Egypt's diverse population, which was split into seven factions during the Empire.

*(c) the prevalence of irrational attitudes fostered by the widespread use of magical charms and formulas believed to secure passage to a blessed everlasting life after death.

(d) the overwhelming haughtiness of the professional military and courtiers of the royal household, an attitude which evoked spite and hatred of these groups in the rest of the population.

(e) the preoccupation of the pharaohs and their associates in the upper social classes with technical, mathematical, and health-related interests to the neglect of ethical philosophy.

11. Which of the following statements best represents Ikhnaton's qualified monotheism?

(a) After driving the priests from the temples and erasing the gods' names from all inscriptions, Ikhnaton established by decree a new, universal god called Aton.

*(b) As the names imply, only the pharaoh and the queen worshiped Aton while their subjects were to worship Ikhnaton, a living deity, heir, and co-regent of Aton.

(c) Ikhnaton's actions changed the polytheistic Amon-Re and Osiris worship into the first monotheistic religion known in history.

(d) The new god Aton was a benevolent father figure for all, the author and upholder of moral order, the rewarder of mankind for integrity and purity of heart.

(e) By encouraging naturalistic-realistic representations of the new god, Ikhnaton brought the masses closer to the idea of one universal god.

12. Which of the following statements concerning Egyptian arts is the least satisfactory?

(a) Egyptian art expresses aspirations to a collectivized, national life in which society is exalted above the individual.

(b) Architecture was preferred to sculpture and painting in glorifying the rulers and testifying to the might of the Egyptian state during the Old Kingdom.

(c) Temples represented the Middle Kingdom's need to express its attitude toward benevolent divinities and the people's hope for personal salvation.

(d) Statues of pharaohs symbolized their power and the timelessness and stability of their rule.

*(e) The introduction of the naturalistic style by Ikhnaton was completely in accord with the collective aesthetic preferences of the Egyptians.

13. Women in Egyptian society

(a) carried a social stigma if they lived in concubinage.

(b) were entirely subordinated to men in monogamous marriages.

(c) could not own nor inherit property.

*(d) could conduct various business transactions.

(e) could never become rulers of Egypt.

14. Which of the following statements is least applicable to the achievements of Egyptian science?

(a) The purpose of all scientific research was practical.

(b) Through astronomical observations Egyptian scientists could predict the annual floods of the Nile and could compile a calendar which marked the dates of religious feasts.

*(c) In the technique of metallurgy and in the refinement of glass manufacture Egypt surpassed all other civilizations in the Near East.

(d) Extraordinary knowledge of physics made possible the building of the pyramids and the monumental temples of Karnak and Luxor.

(e) By 1700 B.C. Egyptian medical science had developed into a fairly adequate system of diagnosis and treatment.

15. There are a number of parallels between the civilizations of the Old Kingdom and the Empire. Which of the following is the least valid parallel?

(a) The government is best described as the pharaohs' control over loosely connected areas governed by civil officials in the Old Kingdom and by various governors during the Empire.

(b) Although the pharaohs were surrounded by nobles and priests in both the Old Kingdom and the Empire, the nobility of the Empire included officials and professional soldiers.

(c) Industrial pursuits were characteristic of both societies.

*(d) A policy of peace and nonaggression directed international relations of both the Old Kingdom and the Empire.

(e) Local deities were united into one superior divinity—Re in the Old Kingdom and Aton in the Empire.

IDENTIFICATIONS

Theocracy
Ahmose
2050-1786 B.C.
1750 B.C.
Book of Proverbs
Plea of the Eloquent Peasant
Book of the Dead

Sphinx
Temple of Karnak
Hieroglyphics
El-Amarna
Hyksos
Ramses III
Aton
Amon-Re

TRUE OR FALSE

T 1. In the late Neolithic Age the inhabitants of the Nile river valley made extensive use of copper and developed irrigation and drainage systems.

T 2. The pharaoh, as son of the sun god, was the head of the state religion and its chief priest.

T 3. The peak of the Middle Kingdom's achievements was reached during the Twelfth Dynasty.

F 4. Control of Egyptian nobles was not a major problem during the first two thousand years of Egyptian history.

F 5. Pacifism and isolationism were the basic principles of the Empire.

T 6. Egyptian rings of copper and gold can be considered the oldest currency in the world.

F 7. Because of abundant agricultural resources, the Egyptians were disinterested in manufacture and trade.

F 8. The symbol of zero was invented by the Egyptians.

T 9. By carefully observing the star Sirium, Egyptian scientists could predict with great certainty the annual flooding of the Nile valley.

T 10. The pyramids were built during the Old Kingdom.

DISCUSSION AND/OR ESSAY QUESTIONS

1. "The religion of the ancient Egyptians went through various stages: from simple polytheism to the earliest known expression of monotheism, and then back to polytheism" (p. 30). Discuss this process with particular references to Re, Amon-Re and Osiris, Aton, and the return to the worship of Amon. In what way was the fusion of various divinities politically expedient to the pharaohs?

2. What were the essential contributions of ancient Egypt to Western civilization?

3. In early Egyptian history a major role was played by the nobles. Many problems of the Old and Middle Kingdoms were initiated by them, and the Empire's late problems can be ascribed to them. What were these problems? When did they occur? How were they solved, or what were the results?

4. Why do we speak of the highest ethical and moral qualities in the religion of the Middle Kingdom? Why did these qualities fundamentally influence society?

5. In what way did Egyptian art represent the power of the state and the divinity of the pharaoh?

SUGGESTED FILMS

Ancient Egypt. 51 min. Color. Time-Life Films, Inc. (1971).

Ancient Egypt. 11 min. B/w; c. Coronet Instructional Films (1952).

The Ancient Egyptian. 27 min. Color. International Film Foundation (1963).

Ancient Egyptian Images. 13 min. B/w. Macmillan Films, Inc.

The Ancient World—Egypt. 2 parts, each. 33 min. Color. New York University Film Library (1955).

Egypt—the Gift of the Nile. 29 min. Color. Centron Educational Films (1977).

In Search of the Mummy's Curse. 29 min. Color. Pyramid Films (1976).

Mysteries of the Great Pyramid. 50 min. Color. Wolper Productions (1977).

Nubia 64 (Saving the Temples of Ancient Egypt). 40 min. Color. Roland Films (1970).

Submerged Glory—a Study in Stone. 28 min. B/w. McGraw-Hill Films (1963).

Tut, the Boy King. 2 parts, each. 26 min. Color. National Broadcasting Co., TV (1977).

Outline

MULTIPLE CHOICE
Choose the best response.

1. Mesopotamian civilizations

    (a)   originated in the upper Tigris valley.

    (b)   with the exception of that of the Persians, flourished among tribes of
          Semitic origin.

    (c)   inherited the foundations of their culture from the earliest civilizations
          of India.

    *(d) were profoundly influenced by the Sumerians.

    (e)   carried on the traditions of their ancestral land in the general area of the
          Central Asiatic Plateau.

2. Which of the following statements is least applicable to early Sumerian civiliza-
    tion in Mesopotamia? Sumerian society was a

    (a)   loose confederation of independent city-states primarily concerned with
          agriculture and commerce.

    (b)   tribal organization of Semitic and non-Semitic peoples which was ruled
          by the king of Ur.

    (c)   collectivistic state in which the temple appeared to have a great share in
          land and business operations.

    (d)   civilization with its own law system which had syncretized various law
          systems from neighboring Semitic tribes.

15

*(e) civilization with an institutionalized religion that viewed all gods as capable of both good and evil.

3. Which of the following statements best illustrates the character of Sumerian civilization?

(a) Faith was institutionalized in a polytheistic, anthropomorphic, monistic religion.

(b) Gods did not provide blessings or spiritual solace, only material gains.

(c) The transitional location of afterlife was believed to be a depressing and wholly undesirable place from which, after a time, the deceased disappeared forever.

(d) Inability to cope with a sense of dependence on powers outside human limits imprinted its mark of desperation on all members of society.

*(e) All of the above.

4. With the *exception* of one statement, Sumerian intellectual achievements include the following:

(a) a method of writing that became the standard in commercial communication for approximately 2500 years throughout the Mediterranean area.

(b) scientific discoveries that surpassed those of the Egyptians.

(c) remarkable artistic and technical skills to which their imaginative metalwork, carved gems, and sculptures bore witness.

(d) generous employment of vaults, domes, arches, and columns in their architecture.

*(e) medical discoveries, as seen in herbal catalogues and diagnostic writings.

5. Which statement best explains the Amorites' success in consolidating their power in Mesopotamia?

(a) By combining their forces with the remnants of the Akkadians they reconquered Ur shortly after 2200 B.C.

*(b) The acceptance and expansion of the Sumerian legal and political model strengthened the Amorite position in Mesopotamia and created a viable social structure.

(c) They selected the Sumerian city Babylon as their capital.

(d) The Assyrians helped the Amorites extend their power throughout Mesopotamia.

(e) Hammurabi's indomitable will in the face of Kassite aggression was the primary reason for the emergence of an Amorite Empire.

6. In the reorganization of Mesopotamia under the Amorites, Sumerian influence can be least noticed in

   (a) criminal law that was applied to local conditions and was characterized by severe penalties.

   (b) expanded business and trade, and the elaborate laws that regulated such activity.

   *(c) supremacy of the king, who claimed divine origin, a contention that enabled him to consolidate his domain through military power, enforced taxation, and compulsory military duty.

   (d) adaptation of a religion replete with basically monistic and materialistic concepts and devoid of hopes for a blissful afterlife.

   (e) acceptance and total absorption of foreign myths and legends.

7. What is the best reason for the downfall of the Assyrians' civilization:

   (a) continuous conquest and aggression which extended the limits of the Empire beyond manageable boundaries.

   (b) the hostility and hatred of Assyria by subjugated nations, necessitating the maintenance of an elaborate Assyrian military machine.

   (c) a neglect of manufacture and trade that resulted in complete depletion of energies and resources.

   (d) the insurmountable chasm within society caused by social and economic stratification of the lower and upper classes, as well as a tenacious segregation of Assyrians and foreigners.

   *(e) all of the above.

8. One of the following is *not* representative of Assyrian culture:

   (a) a magnificent, new capital, Nineveh, built of stone instead of the customary mud brick used in earlier times.

   (b) use of arches and domes, as well as the occasional column, in erecting huge, but artistically unimpressive palaces and temples.

   (c) the highly developed technique of sculpture in low relief representing nature and vivid movements.

   *(d) a completely new literary genre, heroic literature, intended to foster and encourage military virtues.

   (e) major advances in geography, astronomy, and medicine, offering solutions to practical problems.

9. The Chaldean obsession with astral religion resulted in

   (a) a fatalistic resignation to human powerlessness in the face of the eternal gods.

(b) development of a personal approach to the gods through prayer, usually asking for material abundance and physical pleasure.

(c) a belief in the sinfulness of creatures, who are thus not worthy to approach the gods.

(d) increased efforts in astronomical research to divine in the movements of the heavenly bodies the will of the gods and to anticipate the future.

*(e) all of the above.

10. The emergence of the Persians as a major power in the Near East can be best explained by

(a) eager help from a fifth column of captives, priests, and nobles in countries invaded by the Persians, who saw in them the expected liberators.

(b) the inability of opposing forces to cope with new military tactics and weapons of the Persians.

*(c) the prophecy of Delphi, as seen in the writings of Herodotus, which seriously impeded the last rally of will among fatalistic Chaldeans to resist the Persians.

(d) unlimited resources of the former Assyrian and Chaldean Empires.

(e) a tolerant and protective attitude toward subject peoples' institutions.

11. The lasting success of the Persian Empire was insured by all of the following conditions *except*

(a) division of the Empire into satrapies with their local governmental systems and local governors.

(b) building and continuous maintenance of communication routes between major cities of the Empire allowing for the easy, swift transit of troops and commerce from one area to the others.

(c) a belief in the coming victory of Ahura-Mazda, savior of all mankind, which motivated kings and commoners alike to be tolerant of and act benignly toward all conquered peoples.

(d) the cooperation of most peoples, whose local customs, religions, and laws were both protected and fostered under Persian rule.

*(e) arrest and, when necessary, elimination of resisters and troublemakers in accordance with the proven methods of the Assyrians.

12. Which of the following statements is *not* true of Zoroastrianism?

(a) Traces of Zoroastrianism are noticeable back as far as the fifteenth century B.C., although its founder lived around 600 B.C.

(b) It was a reaction against the traditional religious concepts of Mesopotamia.

*(c)   Essentially monistic in character, the new faith proclaimed the existence of one God, in whom eternal good will eventually prevail in the continuous battle against evil.

(d)   Zoroastrianism promised eternal life with appropriate rewards for the just and punishment of the wicked.

(e)   It contained some ritualistic and dogmatic elements that were eventually adopted by Christianity.

13.   Which of the following religions, cults, or political-philosophical systems was least influenced by Zoroastrianism:

(a)   mystical gnosticism.

(b)   Manichean dualism.

(c)   Mithraism and institutionalized Christianity.

*(d)   orthodox Judaism.

(e)   divine-right despotism of the Hellenistic kings and the later Roman emperors.

14.   The philosophy and ethical concepts of Christianity were most profoundly influenced by

(a)   the dualism of a constant struggle depicted between the god of eternal good and the king of evil, identified by Zoroaster as Mani and indirectly implied in the tenets of Mithras.

(b)   the ethical concepts of Zoroastrianism and later Judaism as seen in their interpretations of a universal, eternal, and benevolent God.

(c)   the sufferings, sacrifices, and miracles of Mithras, which appealed forcefully to the soldiers, foreigners, and lower classes of the Roman Empire.

(d)   the rituals of Mithraism, especially those conducted on Sundays and on December 25, the day of the winter solstice.

*(e)   the exclusively powerful, sacred, dogmatic traditions of Judaism.

15.   Which of the following circumstances determined the peculiarly pessimistic character of Mesopotamian existence?

(a)   Open border areas permitted the infiltration into Mesopotamia of new peoples who could interrupt and destroy the bases of Mesopotamian civilization with relative impunity.

(b)   Irregularity of floods, in contrast to the predictable Egyptian pattern along the Nile, forced Mesopotamians to accept a more realistic, warlike, and fatalistic view of life.

(c) A great part of the daily struggle for existence was taken up by fear of unsympathetic gods upon whom Mesopotamians depended for the natural means of acquiring essential material goods.

(d) Present existence became more important than any concern with some dismal and uncertain future existence.

*(e) All of the above.

IDENTIFICATIONS

Kassites
Nabopolassar
Nebuchadnezzar
Patesi
Anthropomorphic religion
Sheol
Lex talionis
Cuneiform

Sennacherib
Arameans
Scythians
Ziggurat
Persepolis
Zoroastrian dualism
Sumerian monism

TRUE OR FALSE

F 1. The Assyrian capital, Nineveh, is on the banks of the Euphrates River.

F 2. The ancient law of *lex talionis* and the system of graded penalties were adopted by the Assyrians from Hammurabi's Code.

F 3. The Sumerians were the first Semitic tribe to settle in Mesopotamia.

T 4. The Persians were of Indo-European origin.

T 5. The influence of Zoroastrianism was enormous in the six centuries following the breakup of Alexander's empire.

T 6. The water clock and lunar calendar were invented by the Sumerians.

T 7. Slavery was an important institution in all Mesopotamian civilizations.

F 8. Women enjoyed equal rights and privileges in Assyrian society.

F 9. Emphasis of ethical values was negligible in Mesopotamian literature.

F 10. Sargon of Akkad initiated the law system that was subsequently expanded into Hammurabi's Code.

DISCUSSION AND/OR ESSAY QUESTIONS

1. "If a son strike his father, they shall cut off his fingers.

> If a man destroy the eye of another man,
>> they shall destroy his eye.
> If one break a man's bone, they shall break his bone.
> If one destroy the eye of a freeman or break the
>> bone of a freeman, he shall pay one mina of silver.
> If one destroy the eye of a man's slave or break
>> a bone of a man's slave he shall pay one-half
>> his price."

—The Code of Hammurabi, lines 195-199

Discuss Mesopotamian society during the Sumerian and Amorite periods in light of this legal code.

2. Discuss in detail how the Sumerian system of law became the basis of Babylonian, Assyrian, Chaldean, and Hebrew laws.

3. Zoroastrianism exercised a major influence over cults and religions as well as political and ethical philosophy for nearly one thousand years after 600 B.C. Describe this extensive and prolonged influence on subsequent major cults. Describe also the attitudes that prevailed among Persian and Hellenistic kings and Roman emperors regarding cult beliefs.

4. "When the gods created man, they let death be his share, and life they kept in their own hands" (p. 54). To what degree does this quotation from the *Gilgamesh* epic represent a hopeless resignation which was embodied in fatalistic, monistic, and apersonal god beliefs by the Sumerians and the Amorites? Does this citation have a meaning for the modern age?

5. Compare and contrast the differences and similarities in the civilizations of Mesopotamia and Egypt due to the geographic peculiarities of these two men.

SUGGESTED FILMS

Alphabet. 30 min. B/w. National Educational TV, Inc. (1957).

The Alphabet—Mark of Man. 20 min. Color. McGraw-Hill Films (1962).

Ancient Cities of the East. 20 min. Color. Gene Blakely Productions (1961).

Ancient Mesopotamia. 10 min. Color. Coronet Instructional Films (1953).

Ancient Persia. 11 min. B/w; c. Coronet Instructional Films (1964).

Digging for the History of Man. 55 min. Color. Roland Films (n.d.).

From Ur to Nineveh. 18 min. Color. Radim Films, Inc. (1966).

Iran—Landmarks in the Desert. 27 min. Color. Compton Film Distributors, Ltd. (1977).

Irqa—Stairway to the Gods. 27 min. Color. Compton Film Distributors, Ltd. (1977).

Rivers of Time. 26 min. Color. McGraw-Hill Films (1962).

Turkey — Crossroads of the Ancient World. 27 min. Color. Compton Film Distributors, Ltd. (1977).

Outline

MULTIPLE CHOICE
Choose the best response.

1. According to various theories and interpretations concerning their origin, the
    Hebrews appear to be

    (a) a Near Eastern Semitic tribe, possibly from the Arabian Desert, indis-
         tinguishable in physical characteristics, language, and animistic cult
         practices from their neighbors.

    (b) an obscure Amorite tribal group that settled in northwest Mesopotamia
         under the leadership of Abraham and later migrated to the northern parts
         of Palestine.

    (c) a fusion of Mesopotamian and other Hebrew tribes who followed a patri-
         archal, anthropomorphic religion and, under the leadership of Jacob,
         became the nation of Israel.

    (d) a loose confederation of various tribes united by Moses on the Sinai
         peninsula.

    *(e) a people whose civilization contains elements of each of the above.

2. Which of the following statements best reflects Near Eastern conditions at the
    time of the Hebrew conquest of Palestine?

    (a) Palestine had been the homeland for some Hebrews since the time of
         Abraham, and so other Hebrews felt justified in an attempt to reconquer
         it after their release from Egyptian captivity.

    (b) With Mesopotamia politically disorganized around 1200 B.C., the Canaan-
         ites could expect no assistance from their allies in resisting the Hebrew
         invasion.

    *(c) The waning strength of the Egyptian Empire and the lack of a strong
         Mesopotamian power greatly enhanced national aspirations among small
         and relatively insignificant tribal units in Palestine to create their own
         territorial states.

    (d)   Fierce Philistine attacks had forced the Hebrews to reorganize their entire tribal system along monarchical lines.

    (e)   The final settlement of the twelve independent Hebrew tribes was a long and arduous affair spanning several centuries.

3.   The development of the Hebrew monarchy was

    *(a)   a response to the adversity of defeat and challenge in the face of Philistine conquests.

    (b)   an attempt to mold from twelve tribes a strong confederation under one ruler.

    (c)   a finalization of Hebrew territorial limits in an area inhabited by hostile neighbors.

    (d)   a result of the monolatrous faith in Yahweh, the powerful upholder of Hebrew territorial integrity.

    (e)   the first step on the path of success in a series of wars against enemies.

4.   Kings of the united Hebrew monarchy

    (a)   wished to build a magnificent Hebrew monarchy by imitating the practices of other Near Eastern monarchs.

    (b)   secured and increased the territory of the Hebrews through military achievements.

    *(c)   eliminated or overcame tribal dissensions and united the twelve tribes into a consolidated state.

    (d)   emphasized the manufacture of goods and trade with neighboring countries.

    (e)   were benevolent and just to all people under their rule.

5.   The kings' mismanagement, extravagance, and oppressive policies during the tenth century B.C. resulted in all of the following *except*

    (a)   discontent, revolution, and the dissolution of the united Hebrew monarchy.

    (b)   a lack of the co-operation necessary to resist Assyrian attack and prevent the eventual destruction of Jerusalem by the Chaldeans.

    (c)   the emergence of the great prophets who reinterpreted the ancient religion along rudimentary monotheistic lines.

    *(d)   the introduction of the concept of an omnipotent Yahweh and eternal bliss for the just in an afterlife.

    (e)   the eradication of many forms of social and political oppression.

6. Which of the following statements is incorrect? During the era of national monolatry Yahweh

    (a) became a national god, whose power was limited to the territory occupied by the Hebrews.

    (b) was perceived as being monistic in character and capable of both benevolence and evil judgment.

    *(c) admitted into His presence and eternal bliss exclusively those Hebrews who had led a righteous life.

    (d) was interested in ceremonies—which often included fetishism, magic, and superstitious rituals—as well as the righteous conduct of his worshipers.

    (e) offered material rather than spiritual rewards in this life to his monolatrous worshipers.

7. Which of the following was not a contributing factor to the prophetic revolution:

    *(a) reunification of the Kingdom of Judah with the Ten Lost Tribes of Israel.

    (b) theological interpretations of a transcendental God who could be explained and understood in abstract terms.

    (c) concepts of humanity's potential to alter nature that were not yet clearly defined.

    (d) the need to purge the older religion of foreign corruptions which had entered into its practice.

    (e) lingering social and political problems not consistent with the Hebrew view of righteous conduct.

8. The prophetic revolution

    (a) partially repudiated the tenets of the older religion and purified it of corrupt practices.

    (b) introduced Yahweh as the ruler of the universe, and rejected all other gods as false.

    (c) reinterpreted Yahweh as a righteous, partially omnipotent God, whose limitations were demarcated by goodness and justice.

    (d) succeeded in stamping out social abuses by insistence upon justice and goodness as foundations of righteous interpersonal contacts.

    *(e) all of the above.

9. In the post-Exilic period

    (a) monistic concepts of faith were upheld and monism was ascribed to Yahweh, the God of the universe.

*(b)   the institutionalization of Hebrew religion was finalized with the development of notions of Satan, eschatology, salvation, and revelation.

(c)   Satan, as the Great Adversary, came to be considered co-equal with Yahweh, the God of the Hebrews.

(d)   Zoroastrianic ideas were completely accepted by the Jews.

(e)   organization of the Old Testament books was finalized by Hellenized Hebrew scholars in the Diaspora.

10.   The Deuteronomic Code

(a)   is an original work of Moses later incorporated into the Old Testament during the prophetic revolution.

*(b)   is a response to the Hebrews' need for religious, social, and political reforms.

(c)   is based on an older code of the Canaanites and Old Babylonians.

(d)   is now proven to be an expansion of the Code of Hammurabi and the earlier Sumerian code.

(e)   indicates Ikhnaton's and the Aton worship's influence on Moses' thought.

11.   The Deuteronomic Code did *not* encourage

(a)   hospitality and kindness to the poor and strangers.

*(b)   the abolition of the institution of slavery.

(c)   the elections of various officials by the people.

(d)   the raising of interest and lasting liability for obligations.

(e)   the transfer of parental guilt from generation to generation.

12.   Which of the following statements is *incorrect*?

*(a)   Most Hebrew writings have high literary merit.

(b)   The books of the Old Testament, as we know them today, were collected and re-edited through centuries of scholarly work.

(c)   The Song of Deborah in Judges is one of the oldest books of the Old Testament.

(d)   Greco-Oriental influence inspired the Book of Enoch and the Wisdom of Solomon.

(e)   Solomon's Song of Songs is probably derived from a Canaanite hymn to Shulamith, the goddess of fertility.

13. Hebrew philosophers

    (a) with the exception of the Greeks, surpassed those of every other people, including the Egyptians.

    (b) paid little attention to the concept of others' rights in the Books of Proverbs and Ecclesiastes.

    (c) although not pure philosophers, did concern themselves with problems of human existence.

    (d) used Egyptian sources from as early as 1000 B.C.

    *(e) all of the above.

14. Which of the following statements does *not* accurately characterize the Essenes?

    (a) They were lower-class Hebrews who demonstrated their disdain of wealth and luxuries with a deliberate ascetic life style.

    (b) They rejected the concept of ownership and led a monastic, communal life.

    *(c) They advocated resistance against governmental control in expectation of a political messiah.

    (d) They greatly influenced the development of Christianity.

    (e) They advocated the immortality of the soul and preparedness for the coming end of the world.

15. Hebrew culture did *not*

    (a) create the foundations for positive morality, charity, and social justice, while similar to other Near Eastern peoples in its negative approach to ethics.

    *(b) contribute the basic elements in earliest Christian art.

    (c) influence religious and ethical formations of Western culture.

    (d) prepare the way for constitutional democracy by emphasizing the sovereignty of law and the work of the individual.

    (e) develop a sustained monotheistic faith and thus become the principal source of institutionalized Christianity.

IDENTIFICATIONS

Apocrypha	Amos, Isaiah, Micah
Diaspora	Sadducees
Animism	Lost Ten Tribes of Israel
Monolatry	"Transcendent" view of God

1025 B.C.	Book of Ecclesiastes
922 B.C.	Rehoboam
Revealed religion	Philistines

TRUE OR FALSE

T   1.   Philistine success was due primarily to the use of iron weapons agains the defender's bronze implements.

T   2.   Until the end of the eleventh century the twelve tribes of the Hebrews were ruled by "judges."

F   3.   The worship of Yahweh was a monotheistic faith of the Hebrews since the time of Jacob.

F   4.   The Psalms of the Old Testament were composed in their entirety by King David.

T   5.   The Code of the Covenant is derived from Canaanite and Old Babylonian sources.

F   6.   Hebrew artisans during the reign of King Solomon were conscripted to build the Temple at Jerusalem.

F   7.   The prophets realized that religious reform could succeed only if the old religion was rejected and if concern for the afterlife superseded efforts to establish social justice here and now.

T   8.   Most authorities consider the Book of Isaiah the work of three authors.

F   9.   Divination, witchcraft, and necromancy were tolerated by the Code of Deuteronomy.

T   10.   The Dead Sea Scrolls depict the life and philosophy of the Essenes.

DISCUSSION AND/OR ESSAY QUESTIONS

1. In the search for a good, omnipotent, universal god, what are the points of similarity in the development of Mesopotamian and Hebrew religions?

2. "Humans must take comfort in the philosophic reflection that the universe is greater than themselves, and that God in the pursuit of His sublime purposes cannot be really limited by human standards of equity and goodness" (p. 83). How does this quotation reflect the Hebrew view of life as seen in the Book of Job?

3. Describe the fundamental characteristics of the four stages of Hebrew religion.

4. What aspects of modern life best reflect Hebrew conceptions of morality and political theory?

5.   "Located as they were after their conquest of Canaan on the highroad between Egypt and the major civilizations of Asia, they [the Hebrews] were bound to be affected by an extraordinary variety of influences" (p. 76). Trace these influences and their impact on developing Hebrew law, philosophy, and literature.

SUGGESTED FILMS

Bring Forth My People—Moses and the Exodus 3,200 Years Later. 52 min. Color. Cameras International Productions (1967).

Christ Is Born. 54 min. Color. Learnex Corporation of Florida (1966).

Dead Sea Scrolls. 15 min. Color. Family Films (1960).

The Holy Land: Background for History and Religion. 11 min. Color. Coronet Instructional Films (1954).

Jerusalem—Center of Many Worlds. 29 min. Color. Atlantis Productions, Inc. (1969).

Masters of the Desert. 20 min. B/w. National Education TV, Inc. (1967).

Outline

MULTIPLE CHOICE
Choose the best response.

1. The Hittites' culture

    (a) probably originated in Turkestan or among the Greeks before their arrival in Europe.

    *(b) is known to us exclusively from archeological evidence that consists of clay tablets, daily utensils, weapons, a few monuments, and architectural remains.

    (c) greatly resembles that of Old Babylonia, as seen in the numerous translations of Hittite writings.

    (d) is clearly Egyptian, as indicated in Hittite philosophical and legal literature.

    (e) was the result of a fusion of all Near Eastern cultures, since the territory occupied by the Hittites was the natural link between East and West in all commercial and military activities.

2. The Hittites' civilization is characterized by

    (a) successful exploitation of material resources, which enabled the Hittites to surpass the civilizations of Egypt and Mesopotamia.

    (b) relatively equal status of women in contrast to Mesopotamia.

    (c) the allowance of tax incentives and concessions to individuals engaged in commerce and business.

    *(d) governmental control of all facets of economic and social life, including ownership, care, and transfer of businesses and property.

    (e) monolatrous worship of one universal sun god.

3. The rapid development of the Minoan civilization was due primarily to

    (a) the initial settlers of Crete—the Hittites.

    *(b) good climate, fertile soil, and ease of access to surrounding land areas.

(c)   confidence in life and hope in the future under the absolute rule of kings.

(d)   a lack of notable inequities in status or wealth between the ruled and the rulers, women and men, free persons and slaves.

(e)   basic engineering skills by which the Cretans developed the island's resources to their best advantage.

4.   Which of the following factors turned Cretan society into the "freest and most progressive [one] in all of early history":

    (a)   confidence and determination of its rulers and subjects alike to create and maintain better living conditions for all despite frequent natural disasters.

    (b)   a benevolent government dedicated to the general welfare of the people.

    (c)   prosperity due to commercial activity and trade of exquisite, locally manufactured goods.

    (d)   nonaggression and peaceful intent demonstrated in all contacts with various peoples throughout the Mediterranean.

  *(e)   all of the above.

5.   What was the most salient stimulus for human creativity within Cretan culture?

    (a)   An aim for excellence in painting, ceramic, and gem-carving arts.

    (b)   In contrast to Near Eastern modes of massive sculpture, the attempt to create delicate sculptures in miniature.

    (c)   A deliberate search for utility and comfort in living and working quarters, dissimilar to the emphasis on grandiose forms and external beauty in Mesopotamian architecture.

  *(d)   Acceptance of the principle of free and peaceful existence as a right, with opportunity granted to all peoples.

    (e)   Emphasis on the values of the individual and not upon values of the powerful few or the tenets of institutionalized religion.

6.   Which of the following statements is *incorrect*? The Greeks

    (a)   were Indo-European invaders who entered Greece around 1900 B.C.

    (b)   were greatly influenced by the culture of Minoan Crete.

  *(c)   constituted a semibarbarous colony under Cretan domination until the eventual destruction of Knossos.

    (d)   are normally called the Mycenaeans, after the name of their leading city, Mycenae.

    (e)   had established their rule over the Aegean and Crete around 1500 B.C.

7. Clay tablets written in Linear B and found on Crete and the Greek mainland

    (a) offer important archeological evidence for the only form of writing in the Minoan and Mycenaean world.

    (b) provide literary evidence for natural disasters and catastrophies that weakened the Cretans' resolve to persist as an organized society.

    (c) contain an account of Greek cosmogony and a chronicle of the Trojan War.

    *(d) indicate that Greeks dominated Crete for about one century in the late Minoan period.

    (e) report minute details of the political and social activism of Cretan kings' subjects.

8. Which of the following statements does *not* represent an aspect of Cretan religion?

    (a) The chief Cretan deity was a monistic goddess who ruled the universe.

    (b) Ceremonies and rituals were administered or presided over by priestesses rather than priests.

    (c) The Mycenaeans were influenced by Cretan religion to a modest extent.

    *(d) Indirect evidence shows that Minoan faith was essentially ethical in its purpose.

    (e) Most of the religious frescoes represented sacred rituals symbols such as the double-axe and the pillars, and featured sacred animals such as the bull, the snake, and the dove.

9. Which of the following *cannot* be considered a feature of *both* Minoan and Mycenaean civilizations?

    (a) Under the supervision of a bureaucratic monarch—the ruler of the largest city—all cities appear to be centers of civilization.

    *(b) As a defensive measure, large armies had to be maintained.

    (c) The economy was substantially trade-oriented.

    (4) Religion was essentially polytheistic, with some local variations.

    (e) Near Eastern civilizations exercised considerable influence on both societies.

10. Which of the following statements best indicates the measure and nature of Mycenaean influence on European civilizations?

    (a) Mycenaean influence is of no importance, since the Mycenaeans' cultural ancestors, the Minoans, were destroyed and the later group itself disappeared more or less without a trace.

*(b)   Influenced by the Minoans, the Mycenaeans acknowledged certain values in art and outlook which reappeared as features of subsequent European civilizations.

(c)   The institutionalized Greek pantheon of gods is derived from the Mycenaeans' religion.

(d)   The Mycenaeans passed on to the Dorians rudimentary elements of social organization which the conquerers accepted, expanded, and transferred to later generations.

(e)   The Greeks' love of athletics and their system of weights and measures is clearly Mycenaean in origin.

11.   The Phoenicians' greatest contribution was

(a)   the discovery of various navigational aids for ocean travel.

(b)   the development of new techniques of glass manufacture and processes in the metal and clothing industries.

*(c)   the refinement of an alphabet based upon principles discovered by the Egyptians and its dissemination among all European peoples.

(d)   the colonization of numerous areas around the Mediterranean Sea.

(e)   the introduction of a new coinage-based banking system in international business transactions.

12.   Which of the following statements concerning the Lydians is accurate?

(a)   Successor to the Hittites and satellite to the Assyrians, Lydia was instrumental in transferring Greek culture to the Fertile Crescent.

(b)   Croesus, the great Lydian king, rebelled against his master, Cyrus the Great, with disastrous results.

*(c)   The Lydians were the first to use coins in their transactions.

(d)   Linguistically they were related to the Semitic peoples of Mesopotamia.

(e)   Their fabulous riches were derived from agriculture.

13.   In the Hittite, Minoan, Mycenaean, Lydian, and Phoenecian civilizations

(a)   economic progress depended on large numbers of slaves in the work force.

(b)   women were occasionally given equal, and—at times—higher, status than were women in Mesopotamia and Egypt.

(c)   people neglected agriculture and were exclusively engaged in manufacture and trade.

*(d)   the favorable geographic location of each people provided the means for material growth and the development of civilized life.

(e)   strong kings, or centralized governments, regulated and managed national wealth for the betterment of all subjects' lives.

14.   Hittite, Minoan, Mycenaean, Lydian, and Phoenician cultural development was due primarily to

(a)   geological and geographic features of their territories which provided means for strong institutional growth.

(b)   specific ethnic attributes of these peoples which were suitable for trade and commerce.

(c)   easy communication routes which readily provided for economic or cultural contacts with neighbors.

*(d)   a lack of Mesopotamian or Egyptian political control in the areas in question which permitted the development of small independent nations.

(e)   absorption of the best features of neighboring cultures.

15.   Which of the following events is not indicated by recent archeological and/or ancient literary evidence to have occurred within the last centuries of the Bronze Age:

(a)   Mycenaean domination of Crete, ca. 1500 B.C.; the destruction of Knossos and other parts of Crete around 1400 B.C.

(b)   a major war later attested to by Homer, fought in Asia Minor between the Mycenaeans and the Trojans, and the contemporaneous Hittite war against the Egyptians.

*(c)   the zenith of Hittite imperialism with a victory over the Egyptians.

(d)   appearance of the Assyrians in lower Mesopotamia and the first attempts of the Hebrews to establish a foothold in Palestine.

(e)   invasion of the Dorians about the time of the Phoenicians' emergence in Palestine and the disappearance of the Mycenaeans.

IDENTIFICATIONS

Hattusas
Carchemish
Bedrich Hrozny
Heinrich Schliemann
Sir Arthur Evans
Bureaucratic monarchy
Matriarchal religion
Michael Ventris

Wanax
Electrum
Dorians
Sardis
Kato Zakros
Halys River
Tyre and Sidon

TRUE OR FALSE

T   1.   Archeological evidence indicates that Hittite influence extended over most of Asia Minor, the Tigris and Euphrates valley, and Palestine.

T   2.   European history began over one thousand years before the Golden Age of Greece.

F   3.   The king of the city of Mycenae had unlimited power over all other cities during the age of Mycenaean civilization.

F   4.   All the Near Eastern civilizations discussed in this chapter—the Hittites, Minoans, Mycenaeans, Lydians, and Phoenicians—were of Indo-European origin.

F   5.   The original settlers of Crete around 3000 B.C. were Semites from Asia Minor.

T   6.   The wealth of the Hittite and Lydian civilizations was primarily due to their metal-mining operations.

T   7.   The Hittites were eventually overcome by the Assyrians, Lydians, and Phrygians.

F   8.   Witchcraft, arson, and theft were punishable only by a fine according to Hittite law.

T   9.   The *Iliad*, the combined work of several scholars, came down to readers centuries later under the name of one author: Homer.

F   10.   The invasion of the Dorians assured the continuity of Mycenaean civilization.

DISCUSSION AND/OR ESSAY QUESTIONS

1.   Discuss the geographic and topographic unity of the Agean Sea, its islands, and the surrounding land masses. What did geography or international political conditions have to do with the sudden emergence of the Hittites, Minoans, Mycenaeans, and Phoenicians between 1500 and 1100 B.C.?

2.   Compare the Hittite law system with the Hammurabi and the Deuteronomic codes.

3.   As the first and earliest civilizations in Europe, the Minoans and the Mycenaeans projected certain "European values and accomplishments," along with a "worldly and progressive outlook" on life, stressing "free and peaceful existence . . . comfort, opulence, love of amusement, zest for life, and courage of experimentation." Present appropriate evidence to defend this statement.

4.   Specify the economic bases of each society—Hittite, Minoan, Mycenaean, Lydian, and Phoenecian—and explain the operation of economic pursuits in the course of its empire building.

5. Argue the validity of this statement: "It seems possible to trace nearly all of the woes of the Near-Eastern nations to wars of aggression and imperialist greed" (p. 102).

SUGGESTED FILMS

The Aegean Age. 14 min. B/w; c. Coronet Instructional Films (1965).

Age of Minos. 36 min. B/w. Time-Life Films, Inc. (1969).

Ancient Phoenicia and Her Contributions. 14 min. Color. Atlantis Productions, Inc. (1968).

A Prince in Crete. 15 min. Color. Ziller (Robert) (1968).

The Search for Ulysses. 53 min. Color. Carousel Films, Inc. (1965).

Outline

MULTIPLE CHOICE
Choose the best response.

1. Which statement is correct?

    (a) The first highly advanced civilizations of India developed toward the end of the Neolithic Age in the fertile river valleys of the Ganges and the Brahmaputra.

    (b) Engaged in extensive trade with Sumeria, the Indus valley civilization imported Mesopotamian standards of weight and measurement and a system of writing in the form of pictographic signs.

    *(c) The civilization of Mohenjo-Daro and Harappa is comparable in level of achievement to that of Mesopotamia, Egypt, and Crete of the same epoch.

    (d) The earliest settlers in the river valleys of India, the Proto-Dravidians, were of Indo-Aryan origin.

    (e) As seen in the small objects and sculpture unearthed by archaeologists at Mohenjo-Daro, the worship of the fertility goddess at Harappa was similar to that of the Minoans' snake goddess.

2. The history of ancient Indian civilization is best characterized by

    *(a) assimilation occurring over the course of centuries of various races, cultures, and languages into a complex, yet distinctive, Indian society, culture, and religion.

    (b) the spread of the Indo-Aryan culture, whose language is dominant in India today.

    (c) the development of a philosophy that stressed the importance of timeless qualities and the insignificance of temporal events and conditions.

    (d) the absence of conflict, turmoil, and upheaval, a peaceful existence due mostly to a geography that discouraged invasion.

    (e) political unity under the domination of Mohenjo-Daro's rulers.

3. Sources for the history of Proto-Dravidian and Early Indo-Aryan civilization are provided by

   (a) factual chronicles collected in the excavations at Mohenjo-Daro, Harappa, and Pataliputra.

   (b) scientific studies by archaeologists of the remains of these ancient civilizations unearthed since the late nineteenth century.

   *(c) a literary tradition dating from as early as 3,000 B.C.; it was passed on orally for at least a thousand years until these peoples devised a system of writing that enabled them to record it.

   (d) a lively oral tradition, still transmitted from one generation to the next in India and adjacent lands.

   (c) Sanskrit epics that describe the turbulent wars which eventually led to India's unification.

4. Early Indo-Aryan society was all the following, *except*

   (a) tribal in character, most often ruled by a *raja*, whose hereditary power was apparently limited by a tribal assembly.

   (b) occasionally organized as an aristocratic republic in which power rested with clan chiefs or with an elected *raja.*

   *(c) concentrated in large urban centers which became the focus of a sophisticated mercantile economy.

   (d) probably divided into four castes out of which the four great castes of the later Hindu system and its many subdivisions would develop.

   (e) carefree, boisterous, and optimistic in its view of life on earth and its expectations for the time after death.

5. Among the major sources of information regarding early Indo-Aryan civilization are the *Vedas*, which include

   *(a) litanies, catalogues of spells and charms, folklore, and insights into philosophical or religious truth.

   (b) prose commentaries for the instruction and assistance of priests.

   (c) prosaic treatises and poems that deal with the nature of being, man, and the universe.

   (d) descriptions of bloody conflicts and amazing exploits in the context of a historic battle fought around 1400 B.C.

   (e) a highly artificial and fantastic narrative epic, which indicates Aryan influence had spread to the Deccan and Ceylon before 400 B.C.

6. Reread the completion alternatives in question 5. Determine the literary work each represents, and indicate which grouping below is the correct order of their presentation.

(a)   *Vedas; Baghavad-Gita; Upanishads; Mahabharata; Ramayana.*

*(b)   *Vedas; Brahmana; Upanishads; Mahabharata; Ramayana.*

(c)   *Upanishads; Bhagavad-Gita; Ramayana; Vedas; Vedanta.*

(d)   *Mahabharata; Brahmana; Ramayana; Vedas; Upanishads.*

(e)   *Ramayana; Upanishads; Vedas; Bhagavad-Gita; Mahabharata.*

7.   Religion in the Vedic Age is best described as

(a)   a belief in the essential benevolence of the gods, who rewarded devout human beings with eternal life.

(b)   the worship of thousands of divine and semi-divine beings endowed with human attributes.

(c)   submission to Aryan deities, who seem to have either completely over-shadowed pre-Aryan Indian deities, or else absorbed the earlier gods into a newer pantheon.

*(d)   a comprehensive polytheism, which at that time had little ethical signifi-cance, and was based on the forces of nature or personifications of these forces.

(e)   a Brahman dogmatism foisted upon the congregation of the faithful.

8.   Which of the following statements best represents the goal set up for human beings in the *Upanishads*, namely, mastery of self and of the cosmos?

(a)   Life after death can be reached only through patient denial of the enjoyments afforded by material existence.

(b)   Good works, worship, pure devotion, and daily meditation will be rewarded by the "World Soul" with an ability to free the spirit from earthly cares.

(c)   Actions, thoughts, and motives will be rewarded or punished in the life of the spirit after death.

*(d)   By disinterestedness and complete detachment from the expectation of reward for personal merit, one can liberate the soul, enabling it to unite with the Universal Soul or eternal Absolute Being.

(e)   The state of *nirvana* can be reached only through unfailing and punctilious observance of the holy rites.

9.   The Brahmans were all the following, *except*

(a)   holders of an exclusive right to study and to interpret the sacred Vedic texts.

(b)   priests who enjoyed great social prestige by virtue of their position as mediators between gods and human beings.

(c)   an example of social and religious authority intertwined, yet not part of a theocracy.

*(d)   primitive medicine men who asserted that by magic and animistic rituals they could compel the gods to conform to their wills.

(e)   priests who were basically interested in maintaining sacred traditions through emphasis upon mechanistic ceremonies.

10.   Which of the following statements is *not* derived from the *Bhagavad-Gita*?

(a)   Knowledge is better than works of diligence prescribed by reason.

(b)   One should act without thought of material or spiritual reward.

(c)   The faithful performance of *dharma* is a form of moral uprightness and the conscientious discharge of one's duties.

(d)   Worship, or pure devotion and meditation, are beyond the obfuscations of "priestly lore."

*(e)   Discussion and the power of personal example that demonstrate kindness and patience are the only means to establish truth.

11.   The conceptual foundations of Hinduism include all the following, *except*

(a)   mystic contemplation, through which one may attain the soul's union with Brahma, a personification of the Absolute Being.

(b)   the belief that a person's good *karma* will carry him upward on the ladder of social pre-eminence in another earthly existence, a reward for meritorious behavior.

(c)   the people's identification with and worship of personal gods, rather than emphasis upon knowledge of abstractions as a means to power, suggested in the *Upanishads.*

(d)   a particularly celebrated triumvirate of divinities among thousands of such divine and semidivine beings of the Indian pantheon.

*(e)   change, i.e., growth and decay, seen as the only fixed, universal principle, and which constitute the Absolute Being.

12.   The two major reform movements of the sixth century B.C.

(a)   advocated strengthening the caste system, since it was a part of nature's order and of human societies from their very beginnings.

(b)   successfully recombined Hindu traditions of philosophy and religion into new and distinct religions.

*(c)   were started by two leaders of the *kshatriya* caste as protest movements that resisted increased authority of the priests, while, in general, remaining faithful to Hindu philosophic tradition.

(d) originated with a movement led by devout Brahmans who wished to liberalize the mechanistic aspects of Hinduism.

(e) emphasized scientific inquiry in medicine, astronomy, and mathematics.

13. Among the lasting social effects of Hinduism upon Indian society, the most pervasive has been

(a) the emergence of a privileged class of Brahmans, which attempted to dominate all other groups, at the top of a carefully defined social pyramid.

(b) the fact that society became rigidly stratified and characterized by pessimistic resignation to life's apparent injustices.

(c) the development of the caste system, which deprecates the position of women, and treats the lowest groups on the scale inhumanely.

*(d) a social system that, the negative aspects notwithstanding, can give the Indian people a sense of identity and individuals a feeling of security as it fosters mutual assistance among peer caste members.

(e) the political influence exercised by the priests as advisors or tutors to the rulers and governments.

14. Choose the sentence completion that most fully describes the assimilation of the caste structure into Indian religion. The caste system

(a) is supported by the Hindu religion as well as by all later reformist movements.

(b) developed out of the traditions of Early Vedic Age Indo-Aryan society.

*(c) came to be recognized as a social arrangement consistent with the natural order, and was sanctioned by popularly-maintained religious beliefs and observances.

(d) defined patterns of everyday social intercourse and elementary measures of hygiene.

(e) fostered the virtues of patience, diligence, and conformity, since these were logical conclusions of the concepts of *dharma* and *karma*.

15. Gautama Buddha's teachings include all the following, *except*

(a) Nothing exists except matter.

(b) The source of human anxiety is the individual's attempt to attain the unattainable.

(c) Matter is in a constant state of flux; thus, all things are impermanent.

*(d) It is possible for a diligent individual to attain *nirvana* in three lifetimes.

(e) The ultimate purpose of existence is the extinction of *karma* through selflessness, so that the cycle of birth, work, and tragedy will be no more.

IDENTIFICATIONS

Ahimsa	*Maya*
Mahavira	Sanskrit
Hinayana	*Soma*
Council of Patna	*Deva*
Mahayana	Dravidian
Jat	Andaman Islands
Shiva	Brahma
Vishnu	

TRUE OR FALSE

F   1.   The so-called Epic Age and the emergence of Hinduism does not overlap the so-called Vedic Age.

T   2.   Polyandry might have been an accepted institution in the pre-Dravidian period.

T   3.   Caste was unknown to the Indo-Aryan society of the early Vedic age.

F   4.   Darius I of Persia turned Hindustan and the Deccan into a single satrapy of the Persian empire.

T   5.   Chandragupta established the Maurya dynasty after the death of Alexander the Great.

F   6.   King Asoka reigned as a true theocrat according to the principles of Hinduism.

F   7.   Buddhist monks take vows of poverty, chastity, and obedience just as Christian monks do.

F   8.   Hinduism is a religious complex with a unified creed, set of dogmas, and established church under the control of the Brahmans.

T   9.   The *karma* of an individual depends on the nature of personal conduct and will result in good or evil, according to the choices made.

T   10.   The *Mahabharata* is more than seven times the length of the *Iliad* and the *Odyssey* combined.

DISCUSSION AND/OR ESSAY QUESTIONS

1.   Why does available evidence suggest "the normal amount of conflict, turmoil, and upheaval" during the Early Indo-Aryan period?

2.   Discuss Indo-Aryan political and legal institutions and compare them with those of the Sumerians, the Amorites, and the Hittites.

3. Explain, and illustrate with appropriate examples, the proverb: "If it is not in the *Mahabharata*, it is not in India."

4. "Hinduism does not distinguish ideas of God as true and false, adopting one particular idea as the standard for the whole human race. It accepts the obvious fact that mankind seeks its goal of God at various levels and in various directions, and feels sympathy with every stage of the search."

(in "The Hindu View of Life")

Analyze this statement of S. Radhakarishnan. Which contentions are supported by Hindu concepts or institutions? Include speculation on the evolution of Hinduism prior to its taking shape as a social-religious complex, i.e., before the caste system became rigid.

5. Contrast the abstract idealism found in the *Upanishads*, and its translation to daily life as Hindu ritualism with the reformist philosophies of Mahavira and Buddha. Discuss the common ground these systems share.

SUGGESTED FILMS

Buddhism. 16 min. B/w. McGraw-Hill Textfilms (1962).

A Century of Indian Archaeology. 17 min. B/w. Indian Government Films Division, Ministry of Information and Broadcasting (1961).

Discovery—A Visual Impression of India. 30 min. Color. Time-Life Films, Inc. (n.d.).

Four Religions: Part I—Hinduism and Buddhism. 30 min. B/w. McGraw-Hill Textfilms (1961).

Glimpses of India—Central Region. 11 min. Color. National Education and Information Films, Ltd. (Bombay) (n.d.).

Glimpses of India—Southern Region. 15 min. Color. National Education and Information Films, Ltd. (Bombay) (n.d.).

Immortal Stupa. 13 min. B/w. National Education and Information Films, Ltd. (Bombay) (n.d.).

India—The Land. 9 min. Color. Alpha Film Productions. (1968).

India's History—Early Civilization. 11 min. B/w; c. Coronet Instructional Films (1956).

Jainism. 16 min. Color. Doubleday Multi-Media (1968).

Nagarjunakonda. 17 min. B/w. Indian Government Films Division, Ministry of Information and Broadcasting (1958).

Sun Temple. 10 min. Color. Amin Chaudhri (New York) (1972).

Outline

MULTIPLE CHOICE
Choose the best response.

1. With *one exception*, the following statements are correct in saying that Shang
    society
    (a)   was inaugurated by military conquest among the Neolithic farming com-
          munities on the plain surrounding the middle Yellow River valley.

    (b)   represents the earliest genuine civilization of Eastern Asia, and laid the
          foundations for a distinctive and lasting Chinese cultural pattern.

    *(c) developed as an independent and durable culture, contemporary to that
          of Sumeria and the Old Kingdom.

    (d)   did not engage in conquest, but exercised commercial and cultural influ-
          ence over a wide area, including the Yangtze valley.

    (e)   probably ended as the result of an internal power struggle, and not by
          conquest.

2. Which statement describes Chinese agricultural practice most accurately?

    (a)   Experience had taught the Chinese to adapt themselves to the potentiali-
          ties of the environment, and foresight enabled them to do so to their
          advantage at various points in their history.

    (b)   Nearly every piece of arable land was tilled by hand in ancient China
          in order to produce the greatest yield possible.

    *(c) The use of draft animals was restricted in early Chinese farming because
          human labor could be utilized more cheaply and efficiently on small
          plots of land.

    (d)   Agricultural techniques changed constantly in response to technological
          advances and thus caused productivity to rise steadily.

    (e)   The use of an extensive method of agriculture made possible the growth
          of a large population.

3. The essential reason for a continuity of cultural development in ancient China,
    and the eventual emergence of the pattern of Chinese civilization, is the fact that

    (a)   the Yellow and Wei River valleys were especially suitable for the develop-
          ment of a unified cultural and political system.

*(b)   the new Chou rulers did not break with the civilized traditions of the Shang peoples, but, instead, attempted to fit their government into accepted social and political conventions.

(c)   the Chou people possessed a culture similar to that of the Shang, with whom they had shared a common frontier—the Chou to the east of Shang territory—and had had considerable contact prior to the Shang demise.

(d)   the new Chou dynasty claimed—probably for propaganda purposes—that they were legitimate successors to the house of Shang.

(e)   the Chou rulers attempted to convince the people that the new dynasty had a commission from Heaven to remove the incompetent and debauched Shang ruler.

4.   The economies of the Shang and Chou societies principally rested on

(a)   manufacturing and trade, which originated in large towns, and was financed by an ambitious merchant class.

(b)   the conquests of frontier principalities rich in natural resources.

*(c)   agriculture, which from time immemorial was the all-important Chinese enterprise.

(d)   improved handicraft techniques that increased industrial production by rendering human labor more efficient.

(e)   the special ability of the Chinese people to adapt to the natural resources they discovered in their land, and to respond to traditional objectives of their societies.

5.   Although a form of feudalism existed during the time of the Shang and Chou dynasties, a full-blown feudal regime was prevented *mainly* by

(a)   Chinese society's primary investment in agriculture, which could be best carried on under the jurisdiction of one ruler, especially since the arable valleys were sufficiently proximate to form an "agricultural kingdom."

*(b)   the growth of towns and trade, and the increasing economic importance of the merchant classes, which included a part of the aristocracy.

(c)   the administrative system's granting of broad military and judicial powers to certain hereditary princes or royal appointees in the territories, without requiring these territorial lords to reciprocate with services to the king.

(d)   programs of centralization in the larger states that generated localized systems of taxation based on trade and administrative bureaucracies.

(e)   a well-educated and affluent lesser aristocracy that could not fit comfortably into a proto-feudal society.

6. A feudal system in China, quite similar to the one in Europe some 2000 years later, originated with

   *(a) early Western Chou's institution of indirect rule over conquered territories through appointed officials.

   (b) successful overthrow of King Yu by an alliance of barbarian tribes and one disgruntled Chou noble.

   (c) disunity and internal strife among hereditary princes, against whom the king, not in command of a large standing army, was powerless.

   (d) the installation of a weak king, who had little jurisdiction over the nobles, who themselves had unrestricted authority over Chou territories.

   (e) frequent wars from Shang times onward with marauding frontier tribes, against whom regional defensive measures had to be taken.

7. Which statement is accurate?

   (a) The aristocracy of ancient China remained a solidly united order, able to feign inherent superiority over the lower classes.

   (b) Women, subordinate to men within the patriarchal family system, were not allowed any rights or privileges.

   (c) Slavery was restricted to prisoners captured during the continuous defensive wars against barbaric tribes surrounding ancient Chinese lands.

   *(d) The only two clearly distinguishable classes in the Chou period were the great landowners and the peasants.

   (e) The polygamous family appears to have been the basic unit of Chinese society in ancient times.

8. Which feature of family life *best* accounts for cohesion in early Chinese society?

   (a) In a basically agrarian economy, work on the family plot was not considered to be women's normal daily chore.

   *(b) The family was the basic unit of Chinese society: its members included several generations of the living; it defended them and promoted their welfare; it respected its leaders and venerated its ancestors.

   (c) Authority over every other member of the family was vested in the father, or grandfather, and filial piety and loyalty were supreme moral principles.

   (d) The heads of Chinese families were indispensable religious functionaries in the veneration of ancestral spirits.

   (e) While polygamy might have existed in the royal families or among the greater aristocrats, the monogamous family seems to have been the usual practice in Chinese society.

9. Which of the following correctly describes an aspect of Chinese religion?

   (a) Human sacrifice on a large scale was exercised throughout the Shang and Chou periods.

  *(b) Polytheistic in their religious outlook, the Chinese worshipped a formidable array of spirits, ranging from those of one's ancestors to the great divinities Shang-Ti and T'ien.

   (c) The *Tao-Teh-Ching*, probably written around the third century B.C., became the sacred book of dogmas, rituals, and priestly laws for one of the organized Chinese religions.

   (d) An educated class, priests were prominent figures in the development of a formal religious system that eventually professed a fixed creed based on the "Mandate of Heaven."

   (e) As in Mesopotamia and Egypt, the king, as "Son of Heaven," was considered to be divine.

10. Which of the following statements is correct?

   (a) The "Book of History" is an indispensable chronicle of the Shang and Chou dynasties.

  *(b) Advanced pictographs and ideographs of the Shang period, in conjunction with phonetic principles, supplied the foundations for the Chinese literary language.

   (c) Widespread literacy during the Shang period greatly contributed to the development of a superior Chinese ethical system.

   (d) The "Book of Changes" describes the war waged by the Ch'in province that ended the Eastern Chou dominion of the Middle Kingdom.

   (e) The Shang system of writing was only used for keeping official documents, proclamations, and speeches during the Chou period.

11. According to the philosophy of Mencius, the government

   (a) is an immutable institution created by divine ordinance.

   (b) is a natural institution devoted both to the promotion of the general welfare and to the growth of individual personalities.

  *(c) can possess the "Mandate of Heaven" only if it is benevolent and enjoys the tacit consent of the people.

   (d) is the source of all iniquity in human life.

   (e) has only one legitimate purpose: to promote human happiness.

12. Which statement best describes the standards of legitimacy for the "ruler" as understood by ancient Chinese philosophy?

(a) It is the duty of the ruler to carry out the will of Heaven, which is the promotion of the common welfare.

(b) A ruler is a benevolent father of his people, who not only commands, but sets an example for his people to follow.

(c) A leader has to set an example to develop the inherent goodness of his people, lessen inequalities, and raise living standards.

(d) An authoritarian sovereign will be able to control people's behavior through rewards and punishments carefully chosen and administered.

*(e) A ruler exercises authority only by the sufferance of the governed, and rules rightly only so long as he conforms to the "Mandate of Heaven."

13. Lao-Tzu's thoughts on human nature are consistent with which proposition?

(a) Since man is by nature selfish and incorrigible, people must be controlled by fundamentally punitive laws.

*(b) Nature is perfect, and people are best off when allowed to follow their intuitive desire to live in harmony with nature.

(c) Human nature is inherently evil and can be improved only by coercive discipline.

(d) Human nature is essentially good, but it needs to be guided by education, the cultivation of manners, and the observance of ceremonial forms.

(e) Universal and impartial love of mankind will diminish the selfishness of human nature and is a goal within reach of the conscientious.

14. Reread the five statements in question 13. Determine what thinker or philosophy each represents and indicate which series below is the correct order of their presentation.

(a) Lao-Tzu; Taoist; Legalist; Confucius; Mohist.

(b) Hsün-Tzu; Mencius; Lao-Tzu; Legalist; Taoist.

*(c) Mencius; Legalist; Confucius; Mohist; Lao-Tzu.

(d) Legalist; Taoist; Hsün-Tzu; Confucius; Mohist.

(e) Confucius; Lao-Tzu; Mohist; Taoist; Hsün-Tzu.

15. Which statement is in conformity with Confucius's ethical principles?

(a) With self-discipline and high-mindedness, distinction between "self" and "other" can be transcended and a satisfactory community of peoples can be established.

*(b) The cultivation of sympathy and cooperation with fellow human beings should begin with the family and radiate into ever larger areas of associa-

tion creating a series of loyalties that starts at home and extends to the world community.

(c) If people were left to follow their own intuitions, they would live in harmony.

(d) Love in human relations, non-retaliation for injury, and equal distribution of material goods will promote human happiness.

(e) Unquestioning submission to the laws of an authoritarian ruler will help overcome selfish and incorrigible traits of human nature.

IDENTIFICATIONS

Shang-Ti	Middle Kingdom
T'ieu	Vegetable civilization
"Mandate of Heaven"	*Wang*
"Son of Heaven"	"First Noble"
"Book of Changes"	The Period of the Warring States
"Book of Poetry"	Oracle bones
"Chariot Sacrifice"	Loess
Utilitarianism	

TRUE OR FALSE

F   1. During the Chou era, princes were regularly given instruction in history, apparently with better results than those that have attended modern efforts of this sort.

F   2. A large majority of ancient Chinese nobility and merchants, as well as the priests, was literate.

T   3. The Tao-Teh-Ching often exalts nature in the sense of an impersonal Cosmic Force, and calls it the "Boundless," or the "Absolute."

T   4. The Shang bow and arrow was of the composite or reflex type, and is said to have been almost twice as powerful as the English longbow.

T   5. The technique employed in the making of early Chinese bronzes was superior to that used at the height of the Italian Renaissance.

F   6. Pictographic Shang writing evolved into classical Chinese writing during the Chou period, when the addition of ideographs and phonetic symbols simplified Chinese grammar.

T   7. Cowrie shells were used for jewelry and probably served as money in Shang society.

T   8. The first stage of the Great Wall of China was an earthen mound erected to protect Chinese lands from Mongolian invasions. It was constructed south and north of the Yellow River after Eastern Chou had expanded to Southern Manchuria.

F   9.   The ascendancy of the Chou dynasty marks the onset of the Iron Age in China.

F   10.   Chinese methods of agriculture radically changed when the ox-drawn plow was introduced around the sixth century B.C.

DISCUSSION AND/OR ESSAY QUESTIONS

1.   "The concept of governmental power as a commission from Heaven rather than an absolute and inalienable right . . . was to become a persistent element in Chinese political history."

Use themes from Chou political history and philosophy to support this statement. Among other topics, include ample discussion of 1) the teachings of the four major schools of ancient Chinese philosophy regarding the role of governors and citizens; 2) the importance of these to the forms and transformations of feudalism during the Chou; 3) the transitions from Shang to Chou and Western to Eastern Chou dynasties, focusing on the reformist attitudes possibly underlying these changes.

2.   What were the main features of Shang culture? Identify and analyze the level of civilization as characterized by material culture: art, writing, lifestyle, political organization, and religious practices.

3.   What are the reasons culture could develop in China in such a way as to create a civilization independent in character, as well as origin, from those elsewhere in Asia and the Middle East, and one apparently unmatched in durability?

4.   What area of life is referred to when the term "laissez-faire" is used in connection with Taoism? Is the Taoist ideal, in effect, anarchism?

5.   Discuss the similarities between Mohist and Christian ethics.

SUGGESTED FILMS

The Ancient Orient—The Far East. 14 min. B/w; c. Coronet Instructional Films (1959).

Outline

MULTIPLE CHOICE
Choose the best response.

1. The Greeks' view of ethics and morality is best represented in which of the
    following statements?

    (a)   Knowledge and acceptance of eternal ideas of goodness and justice, and
           a proper balance of physical and mental conditions will enable a person
           to exercise reasoning that can achieve the highest good.

    *(b)   As seen in Greek art, the ethical and aesthetic—good and beautiful—were
           identical in the consciousness of the Greeks; for them true morality meant
           rational living and avoidance of the offensive.

    (c)   Through the speculative life, and without interference from the gods, some
           Greeks searched for the abstract meanings of truth, seeking to distinguish
           between good and evil, spirit and matter.

    (d)   The relative values of "good" and "justice," "right" and "wrong" were
           preached by some using the slogan "Man is the measure of all things."

    (e)   Soldierly virtues—bravery, self-control, patriotism, wisdom, love of friends,
           and hate of foes—were supposed to make a Greek a better person.

2. Throughout history the Greeks experimented with a variety of political systems
    and political philosophies. Which of the following statements might illustrate the
    the practical political reality of Hellenism?

    (a)   A progressive and practical approach to problems, emphasis on individual rights and values, and the rejection of absolutes in matters of ethics and morals will spontaneously generate the conditions necessary for a stable and humane government.

    (b)   Democracy is the weakest form of government; rule by an intellectual elite and/or the philosopher king is the best solution possible for the efficient conduct of government.

    (c)   Neither oligarchy nor democracy is the answer; perfect government has to utilize the best elements and methods of each.

    (d)   Pride in the city-state and consciousness of national unity can be best promoted and declared by masterpieces of art and architecture.

   *(e)   Distrust, antagonism, and hatred between states will foster chauvinism, militarism, and, ultimately, overt aggression.

3.   All but one of the following are applicable to the history of Greece for the three centuries following its Mycenaean Age.

    (a)   The collapse of Mycenae and the invasion of the Dorians introduced a period that most historians call the Dark Ages.

    (b)   Most Greeks settled in widely scattered rural communities within geographically defined tribal, or clan, areas.

    (c)   Civilization retrogressed to less advanced levels in which agriculture rather than commerce prevailed.

    (d)   Governmental functions were exercised by tribal rulers whose privileges barely exceeded those of the individual members of their communities.

   *(e)   In the harsh struggle for daily existence, writing, literature, and basic cultural achievements were, by necessity, neglected throughout the Greek world.

4.   The government in a Dark Ages society

    (a)   imitated Mycenaean traditions in art, religion, and social functions.

    (b)   provided justice according to a uniform code of laws which included the right of appeal.

    (c)   granted unprecedented equality to men and women and eliminated the burden of slavery.

    (d)   offered tax incentives to specialists and professionals, such as artists, scribes, and tradesmen.

   *(e)   was in the hands of rulers who commanded the army in time of war and sacrificed to the gods on behalf of the community.

5. Dark Ages religion is

   *(a) characterized by the Greeks' individualistic, relaxed attitude toward their gods whom they were free to approach or disregard without fear of divine punishment.

   (b) a less than adequately institutionalized cult wherein oblation was made with as much expectation of material gain or physical benefit as with a sense of atonement or repentance for sins committed.

   (c) a belief in gods and goddesses whose attributes were similar to those of mortals, whom the gods rewarded for good deeds and punished for sin.

   (d) an insufficiently structured, vague belief in an anthropomorphic concourse of gods and goddesses totally disinterested in human affairs and worshipers' destinies.

   (e) built upon the expectation of a happy afterlife in Hades, the Elysian Plain or the region of Tartarus, a precept that inevitably strengthened ethical and moral principles of goodness and righteousness.

6. The Archaic Age is *not* characterized by

   (a) development of urban centers within tribal territories; these centers absorbed excess population and provided institutionalized governments for defensive, commercial, and cultural purposes.

   (b) the appearance of landed aristocrats who expelled the kings and established oligarchic forms of government.

   *(c) unification of large territories under a tyrant or a timocracy.

   (d) economic changes due to population increase, vigorous trade contacts, and colonization.

   (e) discontent and resultant political changes which eventuated the establishment of democratic governments.

7. Sparta's peculiar conservatism is *best* explained by

   (a) a fear of helot uprisings, especially after the Messenian wars, which hardened Spartan resolve to avoid any change whatever and especially froze its aggressive foreign policy.

   (b) prohibition of trade and travel, intended to eliminate the infiltration of subversive influences from outside Sparta.

   (c) concern with and a genuine fear of the growing importance of Athenian democracy.

   (d) rules, regulations, and limitations which totally regimented all facets of life.

   *(e) a system of education based on military training, iron discipline, and unquestioning obedience.

8. Which of the following statements is the *least* satisfactory? Spartan society

   (a) was ruled by a minority, since citizens represented only approximately 20 percent of the population.

   (b) allowed the *perioeci* a relative degree of freedom to engage in manufacture and trade.

   *(c) was communistic in character, since helots and the land were owned by the community.

   (d) can claim the dubious honor of having established the first secret-police organization to control politically subversive elements.

   (e) was militaristic and totalitarian.

9. The Spartan constitution can be called an oligarchy because

   *(a) the five ephors, as chief executives of the state, held veto power over legislation.

   (b) the assembly, composed of all adult male citizens, could vote on proposals and elect officials.

   (c) twenty-eight elderly nobles were appointed as a deliberative body functioning within the assembly.

   (d) two kings commanded armies and functioned as chief priests.

   (e) a council of thirty prepared legislation and served as the high court for criminal trials.

10. Direct democracy in Athens is best represented by the

   *(a) assembly, which could initiate legislation and ratify or reject proposals forwarded by the council.

   (b) ten generals, who were the chief legislative and executive officials.

   (c) elected council with its supreme control over executives and administrators.

   (d) people's right to ostracize citizens who were looked upon as dangerous to democracy.

   (e) supreme court of six thousand citizens selected by lot from among members of the assembly and against whose decision no appeal was possible.

11. By comparison to a modern democratic system, Athenian democracy was distinct in

   (a) its excessive reliance on the political capacity and wisdom of every citizen.

   (b) the limits it placed on elected officials' terms, allowing only one year in office.

    (c)   its system of election by lot, which risked putting unsuitable executives at the head of the state.

    (d)   granting franchise to a small minority of the population and in excluding women from political activity.

   *(e)   all of the above.

12.   Fifth-century-BC Athenian society is characterized by

    (a)   lack of distinction between citizens and noncitizens, free men and slaves.

   *(b)   imperialistic and aggressive attitudes toward those states that could not appreciate the finer points of Athenian direct democracy.

    (c)   a simple life style with relative equality in distribution of wealth and provision for all individuals to enjoy certain basic luxuries which were imported from the Near East.

    (d)   an exemplary and elevated status of women.

    (e)   tolerant and just attitudes toward those espousing different, even if challenging or potentially destructive, opinions or plans.

13.   The causes of the Peloponnesian War were *not* aggravated by

    (a)   the jealousy, distrust, and fear persisting between Sparta and Athens.

    (b)   Athenian mismanagement of the Delian League, and aggressive, imperialistic tactics of the Athenians.

    (c)   hostility of the Spartan ephors, who suspected that Athenian agents were instrumental in financing and inciting helot rebellions in Messenia.

    (d)   aggressive Athenian trade activities in the Corinthian Gulf which proved detrimental to Corinthian commerce.

   *(e)   Melian attack on Athenian shipping that operated within international waters.

14.   The high point of Athenian democracy between the Persian and Peloponnesian Wars was accompanied by an intellectual revolution of the Sophists. Which one of the statements below is *incorrect*? The Sophist's philosophy

    (a)   reflects contemporary conditions in a society preoccupied with individualism and the political power of the citizen.

   *(b)   by condemning the enforcement of a second-class status and dispelling claims of differences actually caused by superficial traditions, elevates the status of women to complete equality with men.

    (c)   denies absolutes in human values and advocates the consideration of ethical and moral standards as relativities without limits that might be understood and dogmatically decreed.

(d)   motivates subsequent philosophical inquiry into the essence of absolutes.

(e)   by championing the rights of the individual and rejecting human folly and cruelty, liberates society from one strident and tradition-laden way of looking at life.

15.   The matrix of Greek religious beliefs did *not* include

(a)   a primitive polytheism and anthropomorphism in which humans could bargain with gods on an equal footing for expected material benefits.

(b)   a worldly, mechanical faith without concepts of sin or salvation, and with the practical aim of serving humanity.

*(c)   faith and hope in eternal afterlife, where conscious earthly effort to find truth, beauty, and virtue will be rewarded.

(d)   philosophical monotheism, as well as philosophical atheism.

(e)   glorification of the gods in art, in order to glorify and ennoble the individual.

IDENTIFICATIONS

Basileus	Elegy
Archaic Age	Liturgies
Tyrants	Perioeci
Timocracy	Areopagus
Oligarchy	Delian League
Strategus	Milesian school
Sophrosyne	Atomists
Polity	

TRUE OR FALSE

T   1.   Although the Homeric epics describe the Trojan War, they provide also information about Greek customs prevalent in the Dark Ages.

F   2.   Messenia and Lacedaemonia are districts of Attica.

F   3.   Having no antecedents, philosophy originated abruptly with the Greeks in Miletus.

T   4.   Aristotle's teleological interpretations imagined a conception of and a purpose to the universe.

F   5.   Euclid discovered that the square of the hypotenuse of any right-angled triangle is equal to the sum of the squares on the other two sides.

T   6.   The dictum of Hippocrates of Cos, "Every disease has a natural cause and without natural causes nothing ever happens," is a widely accepted principle of modern medicine.

F   7.   Lyric poetry was usually recited with musical accompaniment.

T   8.   The mystery cults satisfied the human need for personal union with the divine, and reiterated promises of salvation and immortality.

F   9.   Priests of the Greek gods defined dogmas and directed intellectual inquiry into the questions of eternal truth and moral absolutes.

T   10.   Urban centers within geographically limited areas became established around market places and fortifications to facilitate trade and insure defense; these centers later became the seats of governments within the city-states.

DISCUSSION AND/OR ESSAY QUESTIONS

1. The Spartan system is described as one that more closely resembles fascism than communism. Offer evidence in support of this contention.

2. Discuss in detail the theories of the Athenian Sophists. Can you see any modern parallels to their practical and progressive interpretation of relativism, skepticism, and individualism?

3. Discuss the elements of Athenian ethical and moral thought in Greek tragedy and comedy.

4. "There Lawfulness dwells and her sisters,
   Safe foundation of cities,
   Justice and Peace, who was bred with her,
   Dispensers of wealth to men
   Golden daughters of wise-counseling Right."
            —Pindar, on the city of Corinth, *Olympian Ode XIII*

   "Now, what is characteristic of any nature is that which is
   best for it and gives most joy. Such to man is the life according
   to reason, since it is this that makes him man."
            —Aristotle, *Nichomachean Ethics* (pg. 109)

   Illustrate with examples how lawfulness and reason did and/or did not become guiding principles of the Greeks during the Hellenic Age. Do these principles have an appeal to the Modern Age?

5. Discuss the basic elements of Athenian direct democracy. What are the benefits and what are the pitfalls in such a system? Finally, compare the Athenians' system with that of the United States.

SUGGESTED FILMS

The Acropolis of Athens. 30 min. Color. McGraw-Hill Films (1964).

Age of Sophocles. 30 min. Color. Encyclopaedia Britannica Educational Corp./ Films (1959).

Ancient Grecian Images. 10 min. B/w. CCM Films, Inc.: cf. Macmillan Films (1953).

Ancient Greece. 11 min. Color. Coronet Instructional Films (1952).

The Ancient World—Greece. 2 parts, each 33 min. Color. New York University Film Library (1955).

Aristotle's Ethics—the Theory of Happiness. 30 min. Color. (From Humanities: Philosophy and Political Thought series.) Encyclopaedia Britannica Educational Corp./Films (1962).

Civilization: The Frozen World. 2 parts, each 26 min. Color. Time-Life Films, Inc. (1970).

Death of Socrates. 45 min. B/w. Time-Life Films, Inc. (1969).

Edith Hamilton (Per Greek civilization). 30 min. B/w. Films, Inc. (1960).

From Doric to Gothic. 20 min. B/w. Macmillan Films, Inc. (1952).

Greek Pottery (1500-400 B.C.). 19 min. Color. Time-Life Films, Inc. (1970).

Man and the State: The Trial of Socrates. 29 min. Color. Bernard Wilets (1972).

Plato's Apology—the Life and Teachings of Socrates. 30 min. Color. (From Humanities: Philosophy and Political Thought series.) Encyclopaedia Britannica Educational Corp./Films (1962). (Revised.)

Plato's Drinking Party. 40 min. B/w. Time-Life Films, Inc. (1969).

Outline

MULTIPLE CHOICE
Choose the best response.

1. Hellenic continuity in Hellenistic civilization is described most accurately by which of the following statements?

    (a)   Faithful to Plato's and Aristotle's political theories, Alexander and his generals succeeded in creating ideal states under philosopher kings' rule.

    (b)   Despite increased profits and revenues, trade continued to be administered justly and principally for the benefit of the people governed.

    (c)   Emphasis on realism and/or emotionalism in art during the fourth and third centuries B.C. was a logical and necessary progression from the simplicity and restraint predominant in the Hellenic Age.

    (d)   With the opening of trade routes to India, previously established business contacts and trade activities were augmented and now enjoyed the assistance and security of insurance and banking firms.

    *(e)   Greek became the language of all cultured classes; as a result scientific achievement and philosophical inquiry emanated from and retained patterns set in the fifth century B.C.

2. Which of the following did *not* occur within the Hellenistic economy?

    (a)   In order to feed large populations, Alexander's successors confiscated occupied lands and either doled these out to political favorites and/or leased them to tenant farmers.

    (b)   To increase productivity, governmental policy was responsive to the needs of the laboring classes and was manifested in the high wages paid to industrial and transportaion workers.

    (c)   World markets were manipulated through governmental price fixing with the result that the highest financial benefits were reaped by the ruling and merchant classes.

(d)   After Alexander's conquest of vast territories, industry and trade became main sources of governmental revenue; production and trade were bolstered by investment houses and banking institutions whose purpose was to insure their stability in an international money economy.

(e)   To further increase profits and revenue, the government regulated industry and commercial activity in ways typical of the Near Eastern economic world.

3.   Politics in the territorially vast Hellenistic states

    (a)   was based on the despotic, authoritarian rule of kings, who imitated Near Eastern monarchical systems and adhered to Alexander's militarism.

    (b)   was overseen by shrewd military leaders turned despots, who attempted to represent themselves as divinities and whose impostures met with various degrees of success.

    (c)   meant that its leaders, preoccupied with regional events and local needs, were unable to gain a foothold in Greece, so that Greece itself remained largely independent until it passed under Roman rule.

    (d)   benefited greatly from the popularity of Stoic philosophy, since this system advocated participation in public affairs as an indispensable part of human living and a duty for all citizens of sound mind.

  *(e)   all of the above.

4.   After the death of Alexander, several Greek states

    (a)   succeeded in a revolt against Macedonian rule and preserved their independence until the Roman conquest in 146 B.C.

  *(b)   organized defensive alliances, or confederate leagues; these efforts constitute the nearest approach in Greek histroy, save in modern times, to a voluntary national union.

    (c)   refused to accept the Near Eastern concept of semidivine rulers and carried on Hellenic traditions of individuality and classical democracy.

    (d)   established federal councils with comprehensive powers of government.

    (e)   limited the power of elected officials to a one-year term and eligibility for reelection to alternate years.

5.   Among the carefully drawn-up stipulations of the Hellenistic Greek alliances, one of the following statements *incorrectly* implies that in the Achaean and Aetolian leagues

    (a)   a federal council, consisting of representatives from the several states, held the power to enact laws.

    (b)   the central authority was dependent on revenue and militia that only governments of the member states could provide.

(c)   the central government's power was limited to questions of war and peace, issuing common coinage, and regulating weights and measures.

*(d)   independent action of member states could be limited according to the more inclusive needs of the confederation.

(e)   an assembly composed of all citizens could decide matters of peace and war and could elect officials.

6.   New trends in religion during the Hellenistic Age are reflected *most* accurately in which one of the following statements?

(a)   Some intellectuals accepted the theories of philosophers who claimed that divine beings consist of matter.

*(b)   Philosophy, worship of fortune, or faith in emotional religions supplanted the civic religion of the Hellenic Age.

(c)   A majority of the people of the Hellenistic world believed in the divinity of their various rulers.

(d)   The common people were inclined to follow mystic and other Near Eastern religions with their ethically significant mythologies and doctrine of redemption through a personal savior.

(e)   The Jewish experience of political defeat and dispersion from a Palestinian homeland actually strengthened their belief in an unknowable, transcendent God far removed from the material world and human affairs.

7.   The rapid economic development of the Hellenistic states did *not* result in

(a)   concentration of wealth in the hands of the rulers, the upper class, and the merchants.

(b)   a decline of slavery, since Stoic ethical teachings were gradually popularized and free laborers were readily available for low-wage hire.

(c)   growth and multiplication of cities to house-expanding industry, governmental centers, and the necessary labor force.

*(d)   the stability of cost and standard of living; the increased manufacture of goods and unlimited economic opportunities afforded the average Hellenist comparative economic security.

(e)   development of large food-producing estates with which small, independent farmers could not compete.

8.   Which of the following statements is incorrect? Both Stoicism and Epicureanism

(a)   saw reason as the key to solutions for human problems.

(b)   concerned themselves with the ultimate good of the individual.

(c)   were thoroughly materialistic and therefore mechanistic in their approach to the world, denied afterlife, and suggested tranquility and serenity of mind as the only feasible goals for an individual.

*(d)   urged their followers to refrain from participation in politics and to endeavor instead to reach equanimity of mind.

(e)   which were universal and equalitarian in thought, implied that people and human action are the same the world over.

9.   Stoic philosophy

(a)   emphasized serenity of mind that might be achieved through exercise of the Stoic cardinal virtues—duty and self-discipline.

(b)   upheld principles of equalitarianism, pacifism, and humanism against the harshness of the Hellenistic Age.

(c)   encouraged people to submit—fatalistically, yet without bitterness or protest—to the cosmic order of the universe.

(d)   pointed out that violence and war cannot insure beneficial social changes; further, Stoics urged people to tolerate and forgive one another since evil is an unavoidable aspect of human existence.

*(e)   all of the above.

10.   Which of the following statements is *incorrect*? The Skeptics

(a)   followed the typical Hellenistic resolution to escape from a harsh world that can be neither undertsood nor reformed by human imagination and energy.

(b)   taught that equanimity can be reached only by abandoning fruitless searches for absolute truth and worries over good and evil.

(c)   expanded the Sophist teaching that all knowledge is the union of sense perceptions and, as such, is relative, not universal.

*(d)   expressed grave concern over contemporary political and social problems in their search for happiness.

(e)   suspended judgment on the supernatural.

11.   Scientific achievements of the Hellenistic Age were made possible in large part by

*(a)   generous support for research by Alexander and his successors.

(b)   financial incentives which the wealthy offered for inventions that could increase their luxuries and comfort.

(c)   demands of industry and trade for better machinery and labor-saving devices.

(d)   the encouragement offered by philosophers whose teachings also addressed problems of a disorganized and often unsatisfactory earthly life.

(e)   all of the above.

12.   With one exception, the following represent some of the greatest scientific achievements in the Hellenistic Age:

*(a)   Theophrastus's work in biology and chemistry was especially important since these fields of endeavor were of practical value to Hellenistic industry and trade.

(b)   Discoveries by Hipparchus and Eratosthenes greatly facilitated the work of navigators traveling great distances on land and sea.

(c)   The ingenious labor-saving inventions of Hero of Alexandria might have been a boast of their age, but these did not become popular in Hellenistic industrial circles because human labor was then abundant and cheap.

(d)   Erasistratus was the first to reject Hippocrates' humoral theory of disease and excessive bloodletting as a treatment.

(e)   Herophilus of Chalcedon is antiquity's greatest anatomist whose discoveries concerning the heart and arteries laid a basis for understanding the human circulatory system.

13.   Hellenistic literature is *most* notable in

(a)   producing a new type of poetry that the works of Theocritus exemplify.

(b)   Menander's comedy—a naturalistic rather than satirical comedy, free from consciously political and intellectual pursuits.

*(c)   utopias, which described, wishfully, ideal states wherein all are equal and free from greed, want, and oppression.

(d)   histories, which deal with social and economic issues as well as politics and wars.

(e)   extremely popular, somewhat gossipy biographies of noted contemporary personalities.

14.   Which of these aspects of Hellenistic civilization *least* reflects the "spirit of the modern age":

(a)   a variety of governments with inclination toward authoritarianism and militarism.

(b)   emphasis on international trade between developed and less developed nations, and the growth of profits.

(c)   disproportionate increase of urban populations alongside less than adequate housing and job opportunities in the cities.

    (d)   specialization in learning; mediocrity in art and literature; and a note-worthy popularity of mysticism, skepticism, and unbelief.

  *(e)   international cosmopolitanism without a marked sense of national patriotism.

15.   Which statement is incorrect?

    (a)   Christianity and Western civilization were influenced by the Stoic concepts of pacifism, equalitarianism, and humanitarianism.

    (b)   The central authority of the American states, as seen in their Articles of Confederation, is strikingly similar to that of the Achaean and Aetolian leagues as regards member states and jurisdiction.

    (c)   The followers of Zoroastrianism and Gnosticism, but more than any others, the Hellenistic Jews, were responsible for the spread of Christianity outside of Palestine.

  *(d)   Modern artists follow Hellenistic examples of monumentalism and violently naturalistic and emotional realism..

    (e)   Human dissection and vivisection—essential elements of medical research—were first practiced by Hellenistic scientists.

IDENTIFICATIONS

Ptolemy	Polybius
Ipsus	Galen
Pastoral poetry	Alexandria
Seleucus	Cassander
Lysimachus	Diogenes
Zeno	Carneades
Neo-Pythagoreanism	*Aphrodite of Melos*
Philo Judaeus	

TRUE OR FALSE

F   1.   The two major trends in Hellenistic philosophy rejected reason as the key to the solution of human problems.

F   2.   The Skeptics ceaselessly searched for an "honest" man.

T   3.   Epicurus modified the absolute, mechanistic interpretation of Democritus's atomic theory in order to reject fatalistic philosophical theories.

T   4.   Repudiating everything traditional and artificial, the Cynics urged adoption of a "natural" life based on self-sufficiency.

T   5.   Utopias constitute a specific genre of prose literature in the Hellenistic Age.

F   6.   Ptolemy's *Almagest* was based on the theories of Aristarchus of Samos.

T   7.   Much of Euclid's *Elements of Geometry* was a synthesis of previous discoveries and concepts.

F   8.   Hellenistic literary figures did not become famous chiefly because their works were not read much beyond their lifetime.

F   9.   Those who ruled Macedonia after Alexander believed themselves to be divinities according to the Near Eastern tradition of rulers as manifest gods.

T   10.   Traders of the Hellenistic Age established contact with China and India.

DISCUSSION AND/OR ESSAY QUESTIONS

1. What are the differences between Hellenic and Hellenistic art and literature?

2. Compare the government of the American states under the Articles of Confederation to that of the Greek states under the Achaean and Aetolian leagues.

3. Philosophies of the Hellenistic Age attempt to find a way of salvation from the evils of human existence by advocating various means to reach earthly happiness. How are these ways represented by the Cynics, the Stoics, the Epicureans, and the Skeptics?

4. Why were intellectuals of the Hellenistic Age attracted to Stoicism and Epicureanism in particular?

5. Why did the common people tend to embrace the mystery cults and more emotional religions?

SUGGESTED FILMS

Alexander the Great and the Hellenistic Age. 14 min. B/w; c. Coronet Instructional Films (1964).

Coins of the World—History in Metal. 18 min. Color. Centron Corporation (1976).

Zoroastrianism and the Parsis. 7 min. Color. Doubleday Multimedia, a Division of Doubleday and Co., Inc. (1976).

Outline

MULTIPLE CHOICE
Choose the best response.

1.   Which of the following statements explains that peculiar course of cultural development which aided Rome in building a historical bridge between Greek and Roman traditions?

    (a)   Geographic characteristics of the Italian peninsula invited the influx of peoples from Central Europe and from across the seas whose cultural characteristics were absorbed by the Romans.

    (b)   Military conquests brought new institutions and new ideas to Rome.

    *(c)   A tension between two different cultural outlooks present in the Roman character was successfully resolved by a synthesis of basic conservative Roman traditionalism and urbanized Greek intellectualism.

    (d)   Extensive trade with other areas provided a necessary stimulus for intellectual development.

    (e)   As colonizers of the entire Mediterranean region who wished to maintain the *Pax Romana*, the Romans fostered and supported local traditions.

2.   The founders of Rome were

    (a)   various Mediterranean tribes who had entered Italy in the Neolithic Age from Africa, Spain, and Gaul.

(b) Indo-European immigrants from north of the Alps who were probably related to the Hellenic invaders of Greece.

*(c) Italic peoples who lived in the area south of the Tiber River.

(d) Greek colonists from the area of Taranto and Naples in southern Italy.

(e) the Etruscans, whose kings, the Tarquins, founded the Roman monarchy.

3. One of the following statements *incorrectly* implies that the Etruscans

(a) had great artistic talents in metalworking and architecture.

*(b) —according to the evidence of their written language—were Indo-European immigrants.

(c) showed comparatively great respect toward women; Etruscan wives ate with their husbands and, in some instances, ancestors were listed through the maternal line.

(d) engaged in flourishing trade with the East.

(e) passed on to the Romans their love of gladiatorial combats and the practice of foretelling the future by various means of divination.

4. With the exception of one condition below, the Roman state

(a) was essentially an extension of the patriarchal family in which authority and stability prevailed.

(b) remained basically despotic even after the plebian victories, for ultimate authority of the state over citizens was never really challenged.

(c) was understood to be protected from its enemies by the gods, who bestowed material blessings upon the state and augmented its prosperity and power.

*(d) was subordinated to the personal interests of loyal and patriotic citizens.

(e) was governed by members of the upper classes because the Romans "never abandoned the principle that the people were not to govern but to be governed."

5. The political system of the early Republic included all the following *except*

*(a) unlimited power vested in the Senate in matters legislative, priestly, military, and judicial.

(b) annually elected officials who did not rule jointly, but cooperated with the Senate and held executive and judicial authority.

(c) tribunes whose veto power over unlawful acts of the magistrates generally protected all citizens.

    (d)   in cases of military or civil emergency a dictator held sole power.

    (e)   none of the above.

6.   The political and constitutional changes during the Republic were greatly influenced by a

    (a)   continuous struggle of the plebeians to reach full equality with their patrician overlords.

    (b)   lasting conviction among Romans that kingship was evil.

    (c)   tradition-bound conservatism of the upper classes which precluded political accommodations with the plebeians.

    (d)   policy of violence and repression as the best possible means to resolve political or social differences.

    *(e)   all of the above.

7.   With the exception of one observation below, the Roman assembly

    (a)   was a body that could ratify proposals submitted by the consuls but that did not have the right to initiate legislation.

    *(b)   was composed of all adult males of military age regardless of citizenship.

    (c)   did have the right to enact measures that became binding upon the state without the Senate's approval.

    (d)   was frequently exploited by ambitious politicians during the last two centuries of the Republic.

    (e)   gained power practially equal to that of the Senate during the second cenutry B.C.

8.   The immediate results of the Second Punic War can be seen in the following changes within Roman society *except*

    (a)   the initiation of the policies of westward expansion and conquest of the Hellenistic East.

    (b)   the growth of a monied middle class with a resultant cleavage between the wealthy and the poor.

    (c)   a marked increase in slavery for use in productive labor and the resultant increase in jobless city dwellers.

    (d)   replacing the old-fashioned ideals of duty and sacrifice to the state with an indulgent, pleasure-seeking, individualistic life style.

    *(e)   the political compromise between the senatorial aristocracy and an emerging class of equestrians, the effect of which was to establish military dictators as heads of state.

9. What was the main result of Roman expansion upon the Romans themselves and upon the conquered peoples of the Hellenistic world?

   (a) The use of the Greek language became fashionable among Roman upper classes and led to Latin imitations of the more popular forms of Greek literature and translations of Greek works.

   (b) Stoicism became popular within the leading circles of Rome because it emphasized the same qualities that were considered the ancient virtues of the Romans.

   (c) Substantial economic and social differences among the various classes of Romans and conquered peoples were clearly used by politicians ambitious for supreme power.

   (d) The mystical yearnings of most people for an all-powerful Providence were satisfied by the teachings of the various salvation-oriented mystery religions.

   *(e) All of the above.

10. Which statement correctly reflects the constitutional basis of Augustus's power?

   (a) As a republican at heart, he disdained the unconstitutional tactics of the Gracchi and those of the military leaders following them.

   (b) As the sole, adopted heir of Julius Caesar, Octavian automatically became Caesar's successor upon his death.

   *(c) As a princeps, with permanent authority of a tribune and a proconsul, Augustus could rule within the frame of the Republican constitution.

   (d) To eliminate civil wars, Octavian accepted the full authority of Augustus and emperor with the consent of the Senate and the army.

   (e) None of the above.

11. Hellenistic influence is *least* noticeable in Roman

   (a) revival and expansion of the Stoic and Epicurean concepts of peace, serenity, and tranquility of mind, by which generations of Roman thinkers hoped to find the path to good living.

   (b) literary masterpieces in which ancient traditions were idealized and society criticized according to individualistic tendencies of the Roman age.

   (c) monumental architectural and engineering achievements that were essential to the adminsitration of a vast empire.

   (d) development of its law system's three branches, especially that of natural law.

   *(e) treatment of women, whose position became equal to men's in all facets of Roman life except politics.

12. What was the main cause for continuous change in the religious practices and faith of the Romans?

    (a) Their belief in animistic spirits whose functions were similar to those of the Greek and Etruscan divinities.

   *(b) The exclusively political orientation of their religion, which neither attempted to establish a mutually satisfactory relationship between humans and the gods nor promised an afterlife.

    (e) The acceptance of new philosophical interpretations of the Stoics, Epicureans, and Neoplatonists, which satisfied the needs of intellectually inclined men and women who wished to come to grips with questions of the divine and afterlife.

    (d) The sudden popularity of the new and occasionally orgiastic cults of Serapis, Great Mother, and Mithraism among the less intellectually inclined segments of the popularion.

    (e) The emergence of the salvationist faiths, which elevated humanity from the depths of savage immorality to new levels of human decency by a promise for eternal life that can be gained through faith and good deeds.

13. In the age of the so-called *Pax Romana* the Romans enjoyed all *except*

    (a) peaceful co-operation with the various nations under beneficient Roman rule throughout the Empire.

    (b) profitable trade connections from the British Isles to China.

    (c) gory gladiatorial plays for the amusement of the urban masses.

   *(d) total equality and freedom of women, who were always considered to be the upholders of traditional Roman values.

    (e) deeper and more personal understanding of duty, self-discipline, and the natural order of things, as well as the hope offered by the new salvation cults.

14. Wracked by internal and external difficulties, the half century between A.D. 235-284 was an age of

    (a) civil wars fought by ambitious military commanders who sought to seize power.

    (b) economic chaos due to constant civil wars.

    (c) defeats in Rome's attempts to fight off its external enemies.

    (d) anxiety, characterized by the extreme interpretation of Platonic spiritualism.

   *(e) all of the above.

15. The most important contribution of Rome to future civilizations was the transmission of

   *(a) Greek concepts of urbanization and intellectualism to the anchor lands of Western civilization.

   (b) architectural forms and statuary that survive to the present age.

   (c) legal maxims and the legal systems that exist to the present day in most European countries.

   (d) literature that inspired the revival of learning in Europe.

   (e) ritual and organizational systems of the Catholic Church.

IDENTIFICATIONS

Equestrians
Praetors
Emanationism
Pontiffs
Cato the Elder
Julian calendar
On the Nature of Things
"The father of Roman eloquence"

"Enriching the soldiers and scorning the rest"
Asceticism
Aeneid
Law of the Twelve Tablets
Spartacus
Tacitus
31 B.C., most significant event

TRUE OR FALSE

F   1. The Italian peninsula, surrounded by water and capped by the Alps, was not exposed to constant invasions by external forces.

T   2. Rome's strategic location was a determining factor in the early struggles for its control and Rome's eventual suzerainty over the surrounding territories.

F   3. The Neoplatonic theory of mysticism accepted the complete union of the mystical and the soul with matter and advocated uniting both soul and body with the divine.

F   4. The plebeians' successful struggle for a larger share of political power soon resulted in complete plebeian domination of the government.

T   5. The battles of Pharsalus and Actium were turning points in Roman history. The outcomes of these Roman power plays guaranteed continuity in the consolidation of Greek ideals in Rome and the eventual transfer of these ideals to a future Western Europe.

T   6. The clients were plebeians who were obliged to render various services to patricians in return for protection.

F   7.   Lucretius attempted to remove human fears of the supernatural by denying the existence of the gods.

F   8.   Unlike other intellectuals of his time, Marcus Aurelius did not reject the Stoic concept of an ordered universe, but, rather, fervently believed in a blessed immortality.

T   9.   Roman art and architecture sought to symbolize the grandeur of the state rather than the simplicity, harmony, and beauty of life.

T   10. The law of peoples was held to be the customs common to all people under Roman rule regardless of nationality.

DISCUSSION AND/OR ESSAY QUESTIONS

1.   What were the causes of the Gracchan revolt? In what way did this revolt affect the outcomes of social struggles in the late Republic?

2.   The text specifies that "Octavian was determined to preserve the form, if not the substance, of the constitutional government." In what manner is Octavian's government different from both the government of the Republic and that of the Late Empire, A.D. 180-284?

3.   Traditional Roman ideals included the virtues: bravery, honor, self-discipline, reverence of gods and ancestors, and duty to country and family. To what degree were these concepts strengthened by Roman Stoic philosophers?

4.   Roman law is generally considered to be one of the noblest achievements of Roman civilization. Explain.

5.   What were the causes of the decline of characteristically Roman civilization?

SUGGESTED FILMS

Ancient Rome. 11 min. Color. Coronet Instructional Films (1969).

Assassination of Julius Caesar. 27 min. B/w. Columbia Broadcasting System (CBSTV) (1965).

Christ and Disorder. 38 min. B/w. Time-Life Films, Inc. (1970).

The Christians: A Peculiar People (27 B.C.-300 A.D.). 39 min. Color. McGraw-Hill Films (1979).

Decline of the Roman Empire. 14 min. Color. Coronet Instructional Films (1959).

The Etruscans. 16 min. Color. Vedo Films (1972).

Etruscan Tombs of Volterra (300-100 B.C.). 11 min. Color. Time-Life Films, Inc. (1970).

Julius Caesar—the Rise of the Roman Empire. 22 min. Color. Encylopaedia Britannica Educational Corp./Films (1964).

Legacy of Rome. 2 parts, each 25 min. Color. American Broadcasting Co., TV (1966).

Pompeii—City of Painting (200 B.C.-79 A.D.). 12 min. Color. Time-Life Films, Inc. (1970).

Pompeii—Once There Was a City. 25 min. Color. Learnex Corporation of Florida (1969).

Pompeii—the Death of a City. 14 min. Color. McGraw-Hill Films (1966).

Roman Britain—Fortifications. 14 min. Color. Hugh Braddeley Productions (1974).

Roman Britain—Towns. 15 min. Color. Brigham Young University (1974).

Splendor in the Sand (Leptis Magna, ca. 300 A.D.). 15 min. Color. McGraw-Hill Films, (1967).

Outline

MULTIPLE CHOICE
Choose the best response.

1. Learning in late antiquity

    *(a)   was based on a continuation of classical concepts and modes of expression
           within the framework of Christian thought.

    (b)   originated in the monasteries of Western Europe under the influence of a
           monastic thinker named Cassiodorus.

    (c)   would have been impossible had monks not transcribed classical Latin
           literature, including such "licentious" writings as the poems of Catullus
           and Ovid.

    (d)   is best reflected in St. Augustine's works wherein his demonstrated
           scholarship in subjects necessary to the intellectual growth of a free
           people successfully combined the secular with the otherworldly.

    (e)   was systematized through the efforts of Boethius, whose foremost
           concern was the preservation of as much ancient scholarship as possible,
           especially by his translations of, and commentaries on, Aristotle's logical
           treatises.

2. Which of the following statements is correct?

    (a)   The empress Theodora demanded and gained full equality for women in
           her fight against the male supremacists of the ancient world.

    (b)   According to St. Paul (Galatians 3:28), spiritual equalitarianism guaranteed
           equal roles for women in everyday life.

    (c)   According to the Neoplatonic concepts of Plotinus, women were more
           "fleshly" than men and, therefore, should be subject to men within
           marriage just as flesh is subject to spirit.

*(d)   Unlike other religions, Christianity did accord women some rights of participation in worship and equal hope with men for otherworldly salvation.

(e)   Christianity rejected the ancient view that women's major earthly role was to serve as a mother.

3.   Which of the statements below is *incorrect*? The fourth-century Roman emperors

(a)   —with the support of an imperial bureaucracy—reestablished dynastic monarchy, a system that Rome and discarded eight hundred years earlier.

(b)   concerned themselves with reuniting the eastern and western parts of the Empire.

*(c)   controlled the growth of the Church from Constantinople, and all but eliminated the surging alienation between East and West that had plagued the third-century Roman rulers.

(d)   by adopting the title *dominus* and introducing oriental ceremony in their courts, ruled as eastern potentates and behaved as if they were gods.

(e)   hoped that Christianity could bring a lasting spiritual and political unity to the Empire. Thus, they did not hesitate to interfere in the affairs of the Church with the aim of counteracting regionalism and squelching doctrinal dissent.

4.   One of the following aspects of developing Christian philosophy is not derived, directly or indirectly, from classical philosophy.

(a)   Since life in the material world is merely an illusion, only an emphasis on the primacy of spiritual forces and expectations for otherworldly salvation can have meaning within mortal life.

*(b)   God's gift of grace will help some humans, but not others, in their quest for salvation.

(c)   The cardinal virtues of duty and self-discipline and the principles of equalitarianism, pacifism, and humanism should be centered in reverence of, and search for, God.

(d)   Human sinfulness can be ameliorated by doing good, by avoiding cupidity, and by loving the one, omnipotent God as well as one's neighbor.

(e)   Happiness is to be found in the highest good which is God, and not in worldly fame and riches.

5.   Which of the following statements incorrectly illustrates the roles Christianity played as one of the greatest shaping forces of Western political development?

(a)   Christianity's rejection of the material world and its insistence on the dominance of spiritual and otherworldly elements in human thought contributed to theological advances and to political decline.

(b) Christianity's social dimensions and organizational framework lent themselves, even in the early centuries, to development of a rationalized administrative structure for the Church in the secular world.

*(c) The Christian charge to do good and love one's neighbor with the purpose of worshiping the one, omnipotent God made it imperative for people and their secular governments to tolerate doctrinal differences.

(d) In matters of morality, secular power was sometimes subordinated to the dictates of Christian moral theology, as in the case of Theodosius's chastisement.

(e) Western Christian thinkers of late antiquity determined the direction of political thought in the West for eight hundred years after the sixth century.

6. Which statement is *incorrect*? The Germans

(a) were loosely connected tribes of Indo-European origin, related to the Greeks and Latins and, by the fourth century, had come under the lasting influence, if not rule, of Roman civilization.

*(b) rose up in protest agianst Roman officials who mistreated them because they were Arians.

(c) ended the Western Roman Empire, according to conventional historiography, by deposing the emperor Augustulus in 476.

(d) —without serious interruption or displacement of Roman settlement patterns or administrative apparatus—had created several tribal states in in the West by the late fifth century.

(e) did not succeed in establishing lasting Continental kingdoms, save that ruled by Clovis, the Frank.

7. The appeal of Christianity in late antiquity might be explained by all the following *except*

(a) Christianity's unique response to the problems of humanity in the "age of anxiety," including its acceptable explanation for evil in the world and promises that the lowly of the earth will be exalted.

(b) the exclusive belief that Christianity is the carrier of absolute truth concerning God and evil, and its demand that believers espouse this one religion only.

(c) its offer of security within the Christian community in a secular age of fear, and its promises of eternal bliss as reward to the faithful and eternal punishment as retribution against nonbelievers—a comprehensive salvationist doctrine in contrast to that of rival cults.

(d) its admission of all classes to worship, including women, and especially the lower and middle classes.

*(e)   continuous persecutions of Christians that bred dissentience among the Romans and resulted in the mass conversion of Romans from the time of the emperor Nero forward.

8. Which was *not* a major change in organized Christianity after it became dominant in the Roman Empire?

    (a)   To resolve tensions between intellectual and emotional tendencies within the religion and to eliminate doctrinal disputes, uniform theological doctrines were promulgated.

    (b)   Since Christian unity was viewed as essential to the preservation of political unity, some emperors—especially in the East—interfered in religious matters and occasionally assumed religious control and carried out programs of persecutions against doctrinal dissenters.

    (c)   After Paul's time, a new hierarchical organization crystallized within the Church and later established clear lines of authority which were to become particularly influential in preserving governmental functions in the West.

    *(d)   Ruthless persecution of heretics and pagans increased considerably the number of intellectuals who "converted" to the new religion.

    (e)   Emerging secularism within the priestly ranks was countered by the spread of monasticism—a lay movement at the outset—in both East and the West.

9. Which of the following statements correctly describes various ecclesiastical activities after the time of Constantine?

    (a)   The early popes convened the first eight general Church councils, held between 325 and 869.

    (b)   As a response to political turbulence, economic hardship, and existential hopelessness in an "age of anxiety," many individuals became monks to pursue communal asceticism within monastic orders and—in the hope of salvation—underwent forms of inhumane and humiliating excesses of self-mortification.

    (c)   The Council of Nicea defined the difference between laity and clergy and settled the issue of priests' supernatural powers.

    *(d)   Western monasteries exercised tremendous influence upon Western civilization in religious practices and in the conservation, transmission and development of culture, agriculture, and industry.

    (e)   St. Basil and St. Benedict both emphasized poverty, labor, and religious devotion as basic elements of democratically run monastic communities.

10. Within the developing Church

    (a)   women were excluded from the priesthood and its administration of the

Church's sacraments, but, as nuns, they could participate equally with men in ceremonial practices during formal worship.

*(b)   the supernatural powers that were alloted to priests and resulted in a clear separation of clergy and laity, though sometimes controversial, were the means that helped Christianity grow and flourish.

(c)   the supreme authority of the Bishop of Rome was unquestioningly accepted by all Christian congregations.

(d)   the episcopal administrative structure in the West was not recognized by the popes until the theory of the Mass was formally promulgated in 1215.

(e)   priests were not allowed to marry, a customary restriction since the time of the Apostles.

11. Which one of St. Augustine's theological theorizations went unquestioned throughout the Middle Ages as a reasonable interpretation of history?

(a)   All humans possess the power to choose good over evil.

(b)   People are powerless against God's predestination, which eternally determines an otherworldly fate of heaven or hell for individuals.

(c)   By living "according to God" and doing good, one can still only hope to be among the chosen few.

*(d)   The human race was and will continue to be composed of two warring factions: one will be damned to the "City of Earth," while the other will be elevated to immortality within the "City of God."

(e)   A certain amount of education in the "liberal arts," a knowledge of the Bible, and personal piety will grant mortals true wisdom.

12. Which of the following statements is *incorrect*? Justinian's *Corpus Juris Civilis*

(a)   was compiled by a commission under Tribonian and consists of four books of laws, legislation, responses by earlier jurists, and legal principles.

(b)   is the basis of all European states' law and jurisprudence, excluding that of England, and of the Napoleonic Code which influenced law in the Latin American as well as European countries.

(c)   granted absolute power to the sovereign under the maxim "What pleases the prince has the force of law."

(d)   influenced late Middle Ages and modern views of the state by insisting that the state is a public and secular entity.

*(e)   denied that a sovereign's power is derived from the people and maintained that it is obtained directly from God.

13. The Apostle Paul laid the basis for a religion of personal salvation when he taught each of the following steps toward salvation *except*

(a)   rejection of ritualistic legalism as a worthy means to procure salvation.

(b)   faith and God's grace "through the redemption that is Jesus Christ."

(c)   contempt for luxury and ceremony.

(d)   denunciation of greed and licentious living, accompanied by examples of personal humility and self-denial.

*(e)   assent to the Church's organizational framework that emphasized separation of clergy and laity and exalted priestly functions.

14.   The doctrinal disputes that resulted in dogmatic uniformity of faith were evoked principally by

(a)   secularization of the Church in the West, since its smoothly functioning administrative organization made possible intervention and influence in governmental affairs.

*(b)   a general tension between intellectual and emotional tendencies within the newly victorious faith, as well as regional differences within the Roman Empire.

(c)   military pressures from the Germans whose Arian faith and practices endangered political unity in the Empire.

(d)   the rigorously ascetic life and disdain toward women as advocated by St. Jerome.

(e)   the Pauline concept of truth being extended to various aspects of an absolute and exclusive religion.

15.   In his successful reorganization of the Empire at the end of the third century, Diocletian did all the following *except*

(a)   separating military administration from civilian administration in order to check the then oppressive dominance of the military in deciding affairs of state.

(b)   underscoring an ongoing shift of power to the East in the Roman Empire when he divided the Empire into four administrative districts with emphasis on the Eastern sectors.

*(c)   encouraging Arianist expansion and the conversion of the Germans to Arianism when he persecuted St. Athanasius.

(d)   diminishing already dwindling supplies of manpower and wealth by creating a new bureaucracy on which the Empire came to depend.

(e)   ruling as an oriental potentate who forced agricultural workers and townspeople to stay in their places of work in order to secure an even flow of goods in all areas of the Empire.

80

IDENTIFICATIONS

Dynastic monarchy
Edict of 380
Athanasians
Petrine succession
Ascetic hysteria
Vulgate
On the Duties of Ministers
Confessions

The Consolation of Philosophy
Arians
Lombards
Belisarius
St. Benedict
Alaric
Theodoric

TRUE OR FALSE

F   1.   Christianity was declared the sole religion of the Roman Empire in 311 by an edict of Galerius.

F   2.   Mithraism was one of the few cults of antiquity that guaranteed salvation for women as well as men.

T   3.   For centuries after the execution of Boethius all Western European writers known to have existed were priests or monks.

F   4.   Lieutenants of the co-emperors, called "caesars," were introduced into the Roman administrative system by Constantine.

T   5.   The architectural plan of Diocletian's palace at Split (Yugoslavia) clearly shows how he favored regimentation in all things.

F   6.   The radical teachings of Jesus were actually more compatible with the Essenes' hopes for Jewish overthrow of Roman rule through armed rebellion than with the salvationist hopes of other cults.

T   7.   After 476, the rulers of Constantinople, as Roman emperors, maintained some claim of authority in the West.

F   8.   At Adrianople the Germans fought one of the few pitched battles in the history of their advance into Roman territories.

T   9.   St. Augustine's theology is based on the principles of divine omnipotence and the sinfulness of humans.

F   10.   The dogmas of the Catholic faith were fixed at the Council of Nicea.

DISCUSSION AND/OR ESSAY QUESTIONS

1. Why was the Roman Empire a fertile breeding ground for a new religion of other-worldly salvation during the time from 284 to 395?

2. Discuss the general trends and particular events that either caused or reinforced a steady shift in the weight of Roman civilization from west to east.

3. Discuss those aspects of Neoplatonic philosophy which could have influenced the development of Christian attitudes toward sexual abstinence, celibacy, women, and marriage. What were these atittudes in late antiquity and the early Middle Ages, and how might these attitudes seem to have changed or remained the same today?

4. What are the greatest contributions of monasticism to the development of Western civilization?

5. What are the basic principles in St. Augustine's doctrine of predestination? How does St. Augustine explain the early pilgrimage of humans, and how does he see predestination as playing a role in the history of the human race?

SUGGESTED FILMS

Christiantiy in World History—to 1000 A.D. 14 min. Color. Coronet Instructional Films.(1963).

The Christians: The Christian Empire (312 A.D.-800). 39 min. Color. McGraw-Hill Films (1979).

Decline of the Roman Empire. 14 min. Color. Coronet Instructional Films (1959).

Legacy of Rome. 2 parts, each. 25 min. Color. American Broadcasting Co., TV (1966).

Outline

MULTIPLE CHOICE
Choose the best response.

1. For several centuries after the overthrow of the Mauryans, Indian civilization
    flourished in the Deccan despite political contention. This was possible, in part,
    because

    (a) the cultured Indo-Aryans came to the Deccan in large numbers, seeking
         refuge from the onslaught of barbaric tribes in the North.

    *(b) the major states of the Deccan, free from invasion from the north and
         from serious challenges from foreign powers, were carrying on vigorous
         commercial and missionary activities with both neighboring and distant
         lands.

    (c) Indian states were able to unite and repel assaults by foreign powers from
         Southeast Asia and the Malay Archipelago.

    (d) the Dravidian view of life was easily reconcilable with the doctrines of
         Buddhism.

    (e) continuous economic, military, and administrative aid was provided to
         this area by the rulers of the Gupta Dynasty, whose capital was in
         Hindustan.

2. The Gupta Dynasty gained a firm foothold because its founders

    (a) energetically resisted the attacks of nomadic tribes from Turkestan.

    *(b) revived the principles of King Asoka and used their authority for the
         promotion of public welfare, including the support and maintenance
         of public hospitals, rest houses, and other charitable institutions.

    (c) revoked temperance, vegetarianism, and other policies inconsistent with
         the ethical mandates of several contemporary philosophies.

    (d) as generous patrons of art, literature, and religion, brought Hindu civiliza-
         tion to full maturity through rational government.

(e)   re-established a stable economy, lowered taxes, and encouraged the development of industry and commerce with the Near East and the Roman West.

3.   One of the following *cannot* be considered a hallmark of Gupta civilization:

(a)   vigorous development of agriculture, commerce, and civic systems, such as rudimentary urban centers and extensive road networks, made possible in part by an amenable geography.

(b)   leadership in maritime trade and control of an intercontinental market.

*(c)   governmental restraints against foreign influence, designed to maintain cultural homogeneity and the loyalty of special interest groups, such as the merchants of India.

(d)   governmental support of scholarly activities and long-term endowment of libraries and universities, which were under the administration either of the Brahmans or Buddhist monks.

(e)   the universality of the ancient sacred writings, which had already been translated into Sanskrit, and were accepted both in Hindustan and the Deccan by Gupta times.

4.   Asian civilizations' impact on the West is recognizable in all the following, *except*

(a)   Indian and Chinese maritime trade that provided, among other things, jewels, ivory, tortoise shells, spices, silk, textiles, and porcelain to the Hellenistic and Roman West, especially during the first two centuries A.D.

(b)   medical and scientific knowledge that, due to circumstances of trade, came to Europe by way of Arab intermediaries.

(c)   the widespread adaptation of Indian ("Arabic") numerals, completed in Europe in the Middle Ages, which apparently began in North Africa much earlier; Alexandria may have been familiar with these by the second century A.D.

*(d)   the Sanskrit drama in its highest form, combining song, dance, and gesture with narrative and dialogue, which resembles Western cantata and opera.

(e)   the growth of Christian monasticism among the hermit monks of Syria and Egypt, very likely influenced by Hindu and Buddhist elements of asceticism and mystic exaltation.

5.   Which of the following facts about Indian art and architecture points out an artistic form that may have developed through the influence of Western art?

(a)   The treatment of the human form was idealistic and spiritual, rather than realistic, and trends like the incorporation of things from the natural world, and emphasis upon a sense of tranquility, allowed art to convey peculiarly Indian ideals.

*(b) The figure of Gautama was first delineated in northwestern India in a realistic style that evolved into the conventional, cross-legged posture of repose.

(c) A curvilinear tower with vertical ribs in a characteristic feature of one of two major types of freestanding Hindu temple.

(d) Inspired by religion, wall paintings within ancient Hindu temples proclaim spontaneously, and with depth of feeling, an appreciation of physical beauty and the attainment of spiritual insight.

(e) Though there are many examples of realistic reliefs in Indian places of worship, scenes that portray India's historic and legendary past go beyond mere anthropomorphism and tend to depict gods in ways that reflect the Hindu tradition of spiritual abstraction.

6. Reread the statements immediately above, and identify the prominent Indian architectural style or site to which each refers. Below, mark the list that corresponds to their order of presentation in question 5.

   (a) Ellora, Hindu; Indo-Aryan; Ajanta; Gupta; Greco-Buddhist.

   *(b) Gupta; Greco-Buddhist; Indo-Aryan; Ajanta; Ellora, Hindu.

   (c) Ajanta; Hindu, Jain; Ellora; Greco-Buddhist; Gupta.

   (d) Greco-Buddhist; Ajanta; Hindu, Jain; Ellora, Hindu; Indo-Aryan.

   (e) Indo-Aryan; Gupta; Greco-Buddhist; Hindu, Jain; Ajanta.

7. The Ch'in Dynasty's rule was characterized by

   (a) its rejection of superstition and faith in the magic-working formulas of Taoist writings.

   (b) the opening of philosophic schools and the encouragement of free and open discussion of everything from religion to politics.

   *(c) the systematic application of calculated, cynical Legalist doctrines of coercion, punishment, and fear in the course of government.

   (d) a lack of respect for China among foreign powers.

   (e) a social and economic policy designed to promote commerce and manufacturing at the expense of agriculture.

8. The Chinese form of government developed within the Han Dynasty remained largely unchanged until the present century. Its characteristic features include all the following, *except*

   (a) the expansion of frontiers and their protection against neighboring tribal states, many of which eventually acknowledged Han suzerainty or were annexed outright.

    (b)   an administrative bureaucracy centralized under a king, with officeholders selected for their abilities, irrespective of birth.

  *(c)   a deeply entrenched hereditary aristocracy, whose prestige lay in royal favor rather than in imperial grants of land.

    (d)   the prominence of scholars in the administration, and the revival of philosophy; reinstitution of the imperial policy of toleration benefited Confucianism, which had, along with Mohism, been diminished by the Ch'in persecutions.

    (e)   concern for general prosperity, the minimizing of internal strife, and the preservation of China's reputation in foreign territories through trade, diplomacy, or the force of arms.

9.   Which statement describes the most important and enduring development in Chinese society during the period of political disunity that followed the overthrow of the Han Dynasty?

    (a)   For about 250 years, the Wei and Yellow River valleys, as well as other North China territories, were ruled by dynasties of nomadic Hunnish, Turkish, and Mongol tribes from Central Asia, who, to the advantage of later Chinese dynasties, tended to uphold the indigenous culture.

    (b)   The Chinese people showed they could respond to the challenge of adversity by persevering in the fundamental principles of their civilization, regardless of political or other controversies.

    (c)   The overwhelmingly strong and cosmopolitan Chinese civilization quickly absorbed the non-Chinese rulers and their nomadic peoples.

    (d)   The subsequent T'ang rulers' expansion through Central Asia would have been impossible without the alliance of non-Chinese tribes that inhabited China's frontier territories.

  *(e)   Buddhism took hold in the period of upheaval and gradually permeated Chinese institutions, so that by about 500 A.D. China was recognizable as a Buddhist society.

10.   Which statement most accurately reflects the nature of the social organization of Chinese society during the Han and T'ang periods?

    (a)   Although imperial policy meant to encourage agriculture, the reality was that a rigid five-class system existed and the peasantry were overburdened by the demands of state support, which exacted payment in produce or drafted citizens into military and civil labor.

    (b)   By outlawing the remnants of feudal structures and by distributing land among the poor, dynasties after the Ch'in contributed to the gradual disappearance of farmers' indebtedness, serfdom, and slavery in China.

(c)   Titles, distinctions, and advancement in official positions were granted as rewards for valorous military service, and government service jobs, when not dependent upon patronage, were open to anyone of any class who demonstrated superior abilities through competitive exams.

*(d)   Chinese society came to accord highest recognition to intellectual ability, while violent and nonproductive occupations were held in low esteem.

(e)   The merchant classes shared with farmers an honored position on the social scale, and pro-merchant imperial policy helped make China the world's leading urban and commercial country by early T'ang times.

11.   Cultural and economic changes during the ten centuries between the Ch'in Dynasty and the decline of the T'ang were due to

(a)   Indian, Near Eastern, and Hellenic economic and cultural interchange.

(b)   the flourishing of Buddhism after the Han, and Taoism's attainment of status as an otherworldly religion, which stimulated the development of a distinctive style of sculpture and architecture, painting, and a variety of literary forms.

(c)   ingenious technical and scientific discoveries, often far in advance of similar progress in the West, e.g., the means to smelt iron (c. 300 A.D.), a crude seismograph (132 A.D.), and the magnetic compass (c. 500 A.D.).

(d)   intellectual vitality, enhanced by a uniform writing style and script, which the first Ch'in emperor had instituted, the invention of paper about 100 A.D., and printing from blocks, invented about 500 A.D., plus the heritage of scholarship which these engendered.

*(e)   all of the above.

12.   Which of the following was *not* a feature of early Japanese society?

(a)   Clans—groups of families related by blood, who worshipped a deity unique to their clan, and who recognized the leadership of one family whose head served both as warrior chief and priest—retained importance.

(b)   Women and early matriarchal family units were prominent, although a transition to the patriarchal system may have occurred in ancient times.

(c)   Hereditary privileges and traditional local power of pre-eminent aristocrats could not be eliminated by the Taika Reform Edict, and, instead, became the basis of later public administration.

*(d)   It was characterized by a pantheistic religion based on fear of the supernatural and characterized by a primitive ethical system.

(e)   Claims of divine ancestry were made by all important families, along with the construction of myths to justify the political aims of particular clans.

13. The Japanese imperial system rested on

  (a) the genius of the Taika Reform Edict, which reconstituted the government according to China's T'ang, and earned popular support by establishing a surprisingly efficient bureaucracy and professing allegiance to the principles of Buddhism.

  (b) the successful adoption of the Chinese system of centralized paternalism, which undermined local or feudal powers, and the promotion of community welfare.

  *(c) the illusion of imperial sanctity supported by a family or interest group which exercised real political power with little interference from the emperor.

  (d) effective imperial control of agricultural lands, even in remote areas, through prudent land-reform measures that included the redistribution of farmland among its peasant cultivators.

  (e) perpetual rule by one family, a line "unbroken for ages eternal," whose head was commonly considered a divine descendant of the Sun Goddess, with coercive powers over the people.

14. Which of the following statements is *incorrect* in describing the impact of Chinese civilization upon Japan?

  (a) Japanese painters and sculptors achieved a degree of technical proficiency in following Chinese models, and were able to express themselves with originality and creative vigor that went beyond imitation.

  (b) Untrammelled by education in Chinese literature and the timely custom of imitating it, women of the nobility and the court used their native language to create the first great prose literature of Japan.

  (c) Since Chinese had long been the language of formal education in Asia, the Japanese scholars and *literati* of ancient times wrote in Chinese, but seldom did they learn to speak it.

  *(d) In planning the first imperial headquarters near the present town of Nara, the Yamato rulers insisted upon a unique Japanese style of urban planning, which departed from Chinese customs of broad streets and public squares.

  (e) As Japanese cultural institutions evolved, the practical applications made of Chinese concepts were very different from the original Chinese practices that inspired them.

15. The advance of indigenous civilization in sub-Saharan Africa after 900 A.D. was primarily due to

  *(a) the discovery and application of iron-smelting techniques by the Bantu and by North Africans settled in the West, which, together with the introduction of new crops to Africa, triggered an agriculture revolution.

(b) land-based trade with Northern and Northeastern Africa across the Sahara via camel caravan, and maritime contact with the Near and Far East.

(c) tribal characteristics of the Bantu and Berber tribes, which migrated throughout Africa sharing culture with the regions they visited.

(d) the practically unlimited natural resources and European markets eager to receive them.

(e) Roman and later Muslim influence in East Africa, which made apparent the need to centralize political authority among groups engaged in mining and marketing activities.

IDENTIFICATIONS

Ainu	"First Emperor"
Kami	Wang Mang
Soga	Sanskrit Drama
"Tale of Genji"	Stupa of Sanchi
Ch'ang-an	Ellora
Haya	Srivijaya
Borobudur	Bantu
Angkor Wat	

TRUE OR FALSE

F   1. In the time of King Asoka the sacred texts of Buddhism were written in the Sanskrit dialect.

F   2. The greatest examples of Hindu architecture and sculpture were created during the centuries when Hinayana Buddhism was dominant in India.

T   3. The cliff excavations at Ajanta and Ellora are located in the principality of Hyderabad in Northern India; works at Ajanta date between the second century B.C. and the fifth A.D., while those of the more elaborate Ellora span about nine centuries from 300 to 1200 A.D.

T   4. The turbulence and disunity that began in the Late Han period and continued for four centuries ended when the brief Sui Dynasty reunited China and, subsequently, when the T'angs extended its borders and cultural influence.

T   5. The rise of Tibetan power in the late eighth century was checked by a treaty of alliance between Harun-al-Raschid, the caliph of Baghdad and the T'ang court, which was still recovering from territorial losses to the Arabs.

F   6. The many varieties of Chinese Buddhism are mainly offshoots of the Hinayana School.

T   7. Looking at Japanese cultural achievements, Ellsworth Huntington's climatic hypothesis might be best illustrated by the variability of temperature, the occasional cyclonic storms, and the severity of the winter in Japan.

T   8. Indian as well as Chinese sculpture was influenced by Greek or Hellenistic and Persian art.

F   9. The Ch'in Dynasty accepted astrology and the concept of a seven-day week from the Nestorian Christians of Syria, who had settled in Southern India.

T   10. Indian Ocean trade, like that of the Sahara, acted as a powerful catalyst for the development of centralized authority in various regions of Africa.

DISCUSSION AND/OR ESSAY QUESTIONS

1. What were the reasons for the relatively slow development of sub-Saharan Africa? What were the reasons for a lack of early development in Japan? Compare and contrast early sub-Saharan Africa with primitive Japan. Discuss the circumstances that dramatically increased the pace of economic, social, and cultural development, and the long-term effects of trade, travel, and communication upon political systems in these regions.

2. What were the reasons for the remarkable vigor, as well as artistic and intellectual creativity, of Indian culture during the first seven or eight centuries of the Christian era? By what routes did culture travel from Indian civilizations to Europe and the small Asian principalities?

3. "The typical dynastic cycle of China illustrates not only the rise and fall of successive ruling families but also the close relationship between the condition of society and the durability of a political regime."

   Illustrate the above quotation with appropriate examples from the 1000 years of Chinese history between the rise of the Ch'in and the fall of the T'ang dynasties.

4. Why could a typical Chinese be a Confucianist, but at the same time a Taoist, a Buddhist, or a combination of both?

5. "Indirect government, sometimes removed by several stages from the nominal sovereign, has been the rule rather than the exception in Japan ever since her attempt to incorporate the Chinese political machinery."

   What is "indirect government"? How did it function under the Yamato administration? What does it suggest about Japan's tendency to modify principles it borrowed from Chinese political ideology?

SUGGESTED FILMS

INDIA

Cave Temples of India—Buddhist. 10 min. B/w. Information Service of India (Consulate General, San Francisco) (n.d.).

Cave Temples of India—Hindu. 11 min. B/w. National Education and Information Films, Ltd. (Bombay) (n.d.).

Ganges—Sacred River. 27 min. B/w; c. National Broadcasting Co. (1965).

Malwa. 17 min. B/w. Indian Government Films Division, Ministry of Information and Broadcasting (1963).

Madurai of the Naiks. 17 min. B/w. Indian Government Films Division, Ministry of Information and Broadcasting (1956).

Khajuraho. 20 min. B/w. Indian Government Films Division, Ministry of Information and Broadcasting (1956).

The Pink City. (Jaipur). 30 min. Color. Time-Life Films, Inc. (1969).

CHINA

Chinese Journey. 25 min. Color. Peter H. Robeck and Co., Inc. Time-Life Films, Inc., distributor (1967).

The Ancient Chinese. 24 min. Color. International Film Foundation (1974).

Flowing with the Tao. 14 min. Color. Hartley Productions (1973).

The Imperial City. 9 min. B/w. Fitzpatrick Pictures (1930).

JAPAN

The Ancient Orient—The Far East. 14 min. B/w; c. Coronet Instructional Films (1959).

Japan—Land of the Kami. 29 min. Color. Sterling Educational Films (1963).

AFRICA

The Ancient Africans. 27 min. Color. International Film Foundation (1970).

Continent of Africa—Lands Below the Sahara. 22 min. B/w; c. Encyclopedia Britannica Educational Corporation (1963).

Niger—Iron-Making, the Old Way. 18 min. Color. Texture Films, Inc. (1970).

Niger—Water on the Savanna. 20 min. Color. Texture Films, Inc. (1970).

People of the Chad. 13 min. B/w. *Les Actualites Francaises* (1948).

CHAPTER 13.   ROME'S THREE HEIRS: THE BYZANTINE,
ISLAMIC, AND EARLY-MEDIEVAL
WESTERN WORLDS   357

Outline

MULTIPLE CHOICE

Choose the best response.

1.   With one exception, the doctrines of Islam specify that

    (a)   mortals must surrender themselves completely to Almighty God the
Omnipotent Creator.

    (b)   those who make a fundamental choice to lead a life of divine service will
be granted eternal life in a paradise of delights; those who refuse to
submit to God will become irredeemably wicked and will be sent to
eternal fire and torture.

    (c)   a faithful believer will be guided to blessedness by following the revealed
directives of the Koran, the ultimate source of religious authority.

    (d)   rectitude, compassion toward others, and observance of religious rules
satisfy the Prophet's requirements.

    *(e)   the divinity of Jesus is clearly attested to by the Old and New Testament
books, all of which were divinely inspired.

2.   Arab expansion and conquests, especially those of the seventh and eighth
centuries, can be *best* explained by

    (a)   religious fanaticism that motivated the Muslims to conquer Byzantium,
Persia, and a great part of the Old Roman world in less than a century.

    (b)   the attitude of Christians and Jews under oppressive Byzantine rule that
led them to receive the Arabs with open arms and to eagerly convert to
the faith of the Prophet.

    (c)   the success of the Shiite faction in extending its authority over most new
converts after 750.

    *(d)   the excitement of finding richer territories, expectations of booty, and
weakness of enemy empires.

(e)   the reticence of Charlemagne, who had recently established diplomatic relations with Harun al-Rashid.

3.   The dyanmism and cosmopolitanism of Islamic culture is *least* represented by

    (a)   equalitarianism and tolerance which permitted most Muslims opportunities for social mobility.

    (b)   the ready acceptance of sophisticated Byzantine and Persian ideals of urban culture.

  *(c)   the rights newly granted to women after exposure to the more liberal Christian and Byzantine traditions.

    (d)   a prosperous town life greatly enhanced by the emphasis Arabs placed on trade between the Far East and the West.

    (e)   a corresponding development of industry throughout the Islamic territories; in its variety of manufactures and craftsmen's practical arts the Muslim world outstripped the Christian West until the twelfth century.

4.   Which of the following statements describes the work of Islamic philosphers during the early Middle Ages in particular?

    (a)   Averroës of Cordova succeeded in reconciling extreme Greek rationalism with the Islamic belief in the immortality of the individual soul.

  *(b)   Arab *faylasufs* taught that the universe is rational and that a philosophical approach to life is the highest god-given calling.

    (c)   Relying heavily on Hellenistic precedents, the scientific work undertaken by the *faylasufs* as their wage-earning work did not manage to go beyond the achievements of the Greeks in astrology, medicine, alchemy, and mathematics.

    (d)   Islamic philosophy was rooted in the sociopolitical regulations of the Koran, and so it did not look to other civilizations for inspiration of its philosophical systems.

    (e)   None of the above.

5.   Muslim influence upon the West was *not* significant in

    (a)   spurring the imagination of Westerners, who, while looking down on the Byzantine Greeks, both respected and feared the less comprehensible and so more mysterious Muslims.

    (b)   providing for the eventual translation of Greek works into Latin during the early Middle Ages by creating repositories of Arabic translations of the original Greek.

    (c)   the adoption of most Greek philosophical and scientific works, which were preserved and further interpreted by Muslim scholars throughout the Islamic world and early Middle Ages.

*(d)   the evolution of a stylistically anticlassical and nearly surrealistic technique
        of manuscript illumination among the Irish monks.

(e)   economic and scientific accomplishments that were absorbed by the West,
        as seen in the technical vocabulary—of Arabic or Persian origin—common
        to most European languages.

6.   Which of the following is the least satisfactory explanation for traditional hatred
     between Byzantine and Western Christians?

(a)   Charlemagne's coronation as "Emperor"—considered a declaration of
        independence from the East—was resented in Constantinople, whose
        rulers actually laid claim to being the heirs of Augustus.

(b)   Religious differences caused by the Iconoclastic Controversy forced the
        popes to turn away from Constantinople and seek support from the
        Frankish kings.

(c)   The schism of 1054, the uncivilized behavior of crusaders within Byzantine
        territories, and the eventual rapine of Constantinople in 1204 irreparably
        damaged East-West relations.

*(d)   Unduly attentive to the later superiority of Western civilization, Western
        historians until recently denigrated Byzantine civilization and tended to
        identify Constantinople as the incubator for all problems arising between
        East and West.

(e)   Eastern cultural superiority went unchallenged by the West even during
        the ninth and tenth centuries. This was due to an absence of the disruptive
        invasions which limited Western economic growth.

7.   Which of the following statements is applicable to religion in the later Byzantine
     Empire?

(a)   Byzantine preoccupation with religion is a characteristic result of the
        freedom of thought granted by the government in theological disputes.

(b)   The belief in a ruler's divine appointment made it possible to keep religious
        peace throughout the history of Byzantium.

(c)   The Iconoclastic Controversy was motivated exclusively by theological
        considerations.

*(d)   As a result of Iconoclasm's defeat, contemplative piety and faith steeped
        in traditionalism became the hallmark of Byzantine religiosity.

(e)   The interpretations Byzantine theologians forwarded concerning sin and
        salvation were readily accepted in the West.

8.   Byzantium's survival and longevity as an empire was facilitated by

(a)   the conversion of Slavs to Eastern Christianity, especially the conversion
        of Russians who became more thoroughly Byzantine in their attitudes and
        loyalties than the Byzantines themselves.

*(b) the laity's access to education, which enabled the establishment of an efficient, literate bureaucracy capable of running the empire during times of upheaval.

(c) the dedicated support of a core of Byzantine free peasants and women who enjoyed unprecedented equality in all facets of society.

(d) the religious fervor and emotional belief in the role of Byzantium as the uninterrupted successor of the Roman state.

(e) the assistance of the Italian cities of Genoa and Venice, which took over the management of commerce during the last two centuries of Byzantine history.

9. Which of the following is an aspect of Byzantine cultural achievements?

(a) Based on Hellenistic concepts, Byzantine architecture is a powerful expression of belief in the spiritual qualities of the individual.

*(b) Cultivation of the classics by educated men and women was essential to the preservation of the bulk of Greek literature for later ages.

(c) The structural design of Santa Sophia in Istanbul closely follows that of the much-admired Roman Colosseum.

(d) The destruction of a large amount of religious art by the orders of Emperors Leo and Constantine V resulted in the development of a completely new, more vigorous art form in the East.

(e) Byzantine mosaics depicted human figures in a realistic, naturalistic way in order to mirror the actual piety and majesty of their subjects.

10. With one exception, the following common denominators in Byzantine, Islamic, and Western cultures during the early Middle Ages fundamentally contributed to the development of Western culture:

(a) the preservation and transfer of classical literature and philosophy for later ages.

(b) alterations of the Classical style in art and architecture and departure from these styles, leading to the creation of new ones.

*(c) achievement of a uniformity in culture around the Mediterranean, resulting in a single "language" of culture being generally accepted throughout the area.

(d) acceptance and expansion of human values that had endured from classical philosophy, and the attempts to apply these values to conditions of contemporary societies.

(e) the worship of a universal, omnipotent God, and the belief in a dualistic afterlife of eternal bliss for the good and punishment for the wicked.

11. The independence of the Western Church was achieved through all the following events *except*

(a)   the theological teachings of the "Latin fathers," which resulted in new aspects of a Christian credo and which were applied as dogmas exclusively among the faithful in the Western Church.

(b)   a simplified version of Latin prose as the language of state and diplomacy in the West and a uniform system of plainsong adopted as an integral part of the Western, Roman Catholic, ritual.

*(c) agreement among the kings of England, France, and Germany that the pope—bishop of Rome—had the sole right to determine national boundaries in the best interests of peace.

(d)   the reassertion of earlier claims of papal primacy and the cooperation of Church officials with emerging Western governments.

(e)   the need of Western rulers for nearly indispensable services rendered by Benedictine monks as missionaries and literate supporters of various secular administrations, especially in rulers' bids for more mainland European territories.

12.   The various rulers of western Europe and during the early Middle Ages

(a)   recognized that political and/or social cooperation with the papacy was impossible because of the Church's uncompromising attitude toward subjects' religious allegiance.

*(b) succeeded in establishing western Europe as a separate cultural entity, independent from the East and having a distinct, although not mutually exclusive, historical destiny.

(c)   forced the pope to separate the Western Church from Constantinople.

(d)   were the initial organizers of the Crusades and contributed money and manpower to the ruthless sack of Constantinople in 1204.

(e)   maintained diplomatic contacts with the Muslim court at Baghdad.

13.   In the early Middle Ages the developing Western culture did *not*

*(a) reach the same heights as did Islamic and Byzantine cultural achievements.

(b)   establish schools that taught reading and writing and that stressed practical revival of studies.

(c)   cultivate the writing of history in Latin and the writing of poetry of a rudimentary form in the various vernacular languages.

(d)   produce beautifully illuminated manuscripts which are artistically distinct according to regionally determined stylistic preferences.

(e)   produce a new international style of art later called "Romanesque."

14.   With one exception, the following might be pinpointed as common denominators of Byzantine, Islamic, and western European civilizations:

(a) Organized religion, in close cooperation with the aims of political power, was an extraordinarily important part of human life in the early Middle Ages.

(b) The revealed books of the Old and New Testaments were basic to Islam as well as both versions of Christianity, Eastern and Western.

(c) Military power was essential for defense or expansion of territories.

*(d) The material basis of society was industry and trade in and between large urban centers of these contemporaneous empires.

(e) The eastward cultural orientation of the Abbasid caliphate, the strong Greek background of the Byzantines in Asia Minor, and the contrasting western cultural unity under the Franks seem to have been related and compensatory historical developments.

15. By 1050 western European society was characterized by

(a) strong, centralized governments such as were established in England, France, and Germany.

*(b) the beginnings of future European kingdoms and city-states, which eventually became leading forces in the history of the world.

(c) a unity of purpose that emerged after the reestablishment of the territorial integrity of the old Roman Empire through the coronations of Charlemagne and Otto as emperors.

(d) the integration of the most remarkable elements of Byzantine and Muslim cultural achievement by scholars in monastic centers of learning, a compilation of the best medieval thought that was to provide a firm basis for a new Western culture.

(e) a new urban society and mercantile economy which all but eliminated primitive material conditions that had prevailed since late antiquity.

IDENTIFICATIONS

717, most significant event
Manzikert
Alexius Commenus
Kabah
Hijrah or Hegira
Moses Maimonides (1135-1204)
Sufis
Anna Comnena

Mayors of the palace
Carolingian Renaissance
History of the English Church and People
Beowulf
Book of Kells
Einhard
St. Boniface

TRUE OR FALSE

T 1. Followers of Muhammad's cousin and Muhammad's son-in-law Ali claim that only the descendants of Ali can be caliphs or wield authority within the Muslim comumnity.

F 2. Comprising about one-tenth of the current world-wide population of Islam, the Sunnites—claiming that they are the only true preservers of the faith—rule in Iran today.

T 3. One measure indicating the Abassids' orientation toward the East was their abandonment of Mecca and the building of a new Islamic capital in Iraq.

T 4. Avicenna's *Canon* was accepted in Europe as an authoritative medical textbook until the seventeenth century.

F 5. One of the greatest achievements of Muslim mathematics was the invention of a numerical system, the "Arabic numerals," including the concept of "zero."

T 6. Differential emphasis on performing acts of penance and the concept of purgatory is one of the major dogmatic rifts between the Eastern and Western Churches.

F 7. In general, Byzantine spiritual life stemmed from an understanding of salvation as attainable through doing good works and not through living a solitary contemplative life.

F 8. With the exception of political and imperialistic ideology, Russian art and thought was not as permeated by Byzantine traditions, principles, and ideas as were other eastern European kingdoms.

T 9. Many Christians in Syria, Persia, and Egypt during the time of Islam's rise to imperial prominence in fact looked upon the conquering Arabs as liberators from the tyranny of Byzantine orthodoxy.

T 10. Gregory the Great (Pope Gregory I, reigned 590-604) undertook to convert Anglo-Saxon England to Christianity, a successful project which greatly affected future Frankish-papal relations and Western Christianity in general.

DISCUSSION AND/OR ESSAY QUESTIONS

1. "Unity within multiplicity was an Islamic hallmark which created both a splendid, diverse society and a splendid legacy of original discoveries and achievements." Explain.

2. While literacy in Byzantium was the basis of government there, no literate laity existed in the West between 600 and 1200. How, then, did Frankish and English

kings cope with the problems of governmental administration? What were the benefits and pitfalls of extensive literacy for the Byzantine government?

3. "Muslims were also remarkably tolerant of other religions." What are the reasons for and the results of that attitude of toleration within the Islamic world of the early Middle Ages?

4. What is the significance of the Carolingian Renaissance for the subsequent development of western European culture?

5. How did the Iconoclastic Controversy affect the development of Byzantine Christianity? How did it intensify religious and political alienation of the East from the West?

SUGGESTED FILMS

Ancient Petra. 10 min. Color. Encyclopaedia Britannica Educational Corp./Films (1953).

The Byzantine Empire. 14 min. Color. Coronet Instructional Films (1959).

Christianity in World History—to 1000 A.D. 14 min. Color. Coronet Instructional Films (1963).

The Christians: Faith and Fear. 39 min. Color. McGraw-Hill Films (1979).

The Christians: The Birth of Europe.(410-1084). 39 min. Color. McGraw-Hill Films (1979).

English History: Earliest Times to 1066. 11 min. B/w; c. Coronet Instructional Films (1954).

The Fall of Constantinople. 34 min. Color. Time-Life Films, Inc. (1971).

Invaders and Converts (Persia). 30 min. Color. Time-Life Films, Inc. (1969).

Islam. 19 min. B/w. McGraw-Hill Films (1962).

A series on the Islamic world. Each 30 min. Color. Institutional Cinema, Inc. (1979).
The Inner Life
Knowledge of the World
Man and Nature
Nomad and City
Patterns of Beauty
Unity

The Middle East. 28 min. Color. International Film Foundation (1959).

Sahara—La Caravane du Sel. 52 min. Color. Films, Inc. (1969).

Vanished Vikings. 2 parts, each 15 min. Color. Journal Films, Inc. (1954).

Outline

MULTIPLE CHOICE
Choose the best response.

1.   Which ot the following statements most fully describes city and town society
during the High Middle Ages?

(a)   Although independent of each other, the northern Italian manufacturing
and commercial cities cooperated after the defeat of Frederick I Barbarossa
at Legnano in 1176.

(b)   Contrary to official Church dogma, landed aristocrats and Church officials
openly supported the financial dealings of merchants.

(c)   As a demonstration of enlightened rule and departure from Church control
of the monarchy, heretics and Jews were allowed complete equality within
the professional merchant guilds and craft guilds of France during the
reign of King Louis IX.

*(d)   The guilds were professional associations operating to protect and promote
common interests of members and to serve social functions.

(e)   Regulations that governed guilds have no counterparts in those of modern
trade unions.

2.   Which of the following circumstances might *best* explain the fragmentation or
decentralization of authority in Italy after the death of Frederick II?

(a)   Many Italian cities were organized as republics or "communes," with participation of leading citizens in governmental affairs and, therefore, with
strong local loyalties.

(b)   Interference from Germany all but eliminated former efforts to consolidate
a strong central power in Italy.

*(c)   Because of diverse economic and family interests, as well as continuous
internal strife, political stability and the determination to establish a
unified country were lacking among the governments of Italian cities.

(d) Popes were neither strong nor ambitious enough to provide the leadership necessary to unite Italy into a national state.

(e) Southern Italy and Sicily were not joined closely by trade, language, or tradition to central or northern Italy.

3. What was the main cause of the emergence of western Europe as a great civilization during the High Middle Ages?

(a) Successful resistance against marauding bands of Vikings, Magyars, and Muslims secured the relative stability conducive to a systematic development of economic life.

(b) The rich alluvial plains and a spontaneously improved climate offered optimum advantage to the West for surplus food production and the resultant further consolidation of wealth and additional monies for investment.

(c) The administrative frames of new national states guaranteed appreciable stability of internal and external affairs in that bureaucracies could maintain state functioning despite acts of violence by its neighbors.

(d) Experiments in better means of cultivation resulted in develpoment of more effective tools and methods of farming.

*(e) All of these favorable circumstances in conjunction made possible the high medieval "great leap forward."

4. As a historical approximation, the term *feudalism* corresponds to

*(a) as essentially decentralized political system wherein landlords held all the authentic governmental powers under a king who, though practically a figurehead, was nonetheless recognized as the primary force fostering political cohesion.

(b) an agrarian economic system precisely organized according to the concepts of the large Roman estates.

(c) what became the uniform, dominant form of government throughout western Europe during the High Middle Ages.

(d) a spontaneous and highly flexible form of social organization in which the different obligations between lords and serfs were carefully specified.

(e) a method that offered rulers a carefully ordered means to control independent-minded dukes, counts, and knights, and for the governance of vast territories through these vassals.

5. The agricultural revolution did *not* result in

*(a) the complete freedom of the serfs from previous onerous duties of work without recompense and the payment of humilitaing dues as well as subjugation to a lord's legal jurisdiction.

(b)   considerable improvements in the finances of monarchs and nobles, as well as the rapid growth of the Church.

(c)   stimulation of all aspects of economic life, as well as the burgeoning of schools and centers of intellectual activity.

(d)   a stable food supply and better diet for all, which increased the life expectancy and the birth rate and resulted in a threefold population growth between 1050 and 1300.

(e)   a new European-wide prosperity and subtle changes in Europeans' outlooks. Optimism and a willingness to experiment prevailed in the West during the High Middle Ages.

6.   Only one of the following did *not* occur along with the increase in nobles' wealth:

(a)   the development of the idea of chivalry which revered the virtues of honor, truth, bravery, and kindness and disdained unfair advantage and sordid gain.

(b)   a relatively sophisticated life style mainly reliant on collected rents that allowed the nobles to travel and participate in the Crusades and the affairs of royal courts.

(c)   the utilization of new techniques for construction of housing as well as the adoption of new styles in manners, clothing, and diet, which together set the nobles apart as a class from serfs, newly freed peasants, and urban dwellers.

(d)   a radical change in attitudes toward women within the upper classes, an attitudinal shift expressed in values of a gentler, more respectful culture.

*(e)   the nobility's preoccupation with techniques of business partnerships and international trade.

7.   The Magna Carta

*(a)   was a feudal document in which the king as a feudal lord pledged to respect the traditional rights of his vassals to which he previously agreed.

(b)   defined the duties of the permanent High Courts during session of a grand jury and jury tirals.

(c)   was a legal document closely resembling the Justinian Code and which specified the functions of the Chancery.

(d)   outlined the principles of representative government and defined the role of the "commons."

(e)   greatly expanded the role of clerks of the *Exchequer.*

8. The *main* cause of urban growth during the High Middle Ages was the

   (a) revival of long-distance trade in the Mediterranean "lake" between 750 and 1050.

   *(b) symbiotic relationship between towns and the countryside with towns providing markets for the agricultural products of peasants and the wares of artisans.

   (c) mushrooming agricultural village communities located around central market places.

   (d) opening and rapid expansion of leading universities in ancient Roman urban centers.

   (e) establishment of secure settlements by itinerant merchants eager to protect their mercantile interests, concerns usually at odds with those of feudal vassals of the rural areas.

9. The new cities and towns of the High Middle Ages were *not*

   (a) vital centers of trade and industry that began and sustained thriving systems of commercial capitalism.

   *(b) centers of prosperity, general piety, and civilized living where different classes could live together without intense rivalry and where a variety of faiths was tolerated.

   (c) effective in stimulating the intellectual experimentation of scholars in the more advanced schools.

   (d) instrumental in the development of governments by providing new models for administration and public participation in decision making.

   (e) the hubs of intellectual life in the West, for most new schools and universities were consciously located in urban environments to take advantage of the domestic and legal protection towns and cities could offer.

10. If religion played a pervasive role in all of medieval life, then which of the following statements is *not* correct?

   (a) The Church consistently opposed illicit gain and never abandoned its prohibition of usury.

   *(b) The popes never could gain the support of French kings in papal struggles against the German emperors.

   (c) Before the time of Henry IV, bishops and archbishops had run the German government and served to counterbalance the powers of the dukes in the five large German territories.

   (d) The Church quarreled bitterly with Henry II of England over the exercise of judicial authority over accused clerics.

(e)   In order to repeal Hohenstaufen advances into Italy, the papacy declared crusades against the successors of Frederick II.

11. Which of the following statements cannot be applied to the government of Edward I?

(a)   The independent power that William the Conqueror had vested in barons of his choosing was curtailed by Edward I when he limited baronal rights to hold court and to grant their own lands as fiefs.

(b)   The Parliament—the king's feudal court in its largest gathering—was called together as an advisory and deliberative body, yet existed principally as a means to gain quickly the consent of those present to new taxation and legislation.

(c)   Wales and Scotland were partially united with England by force of arms.

*(d)   The "commons" in the Parliament were representatives of the unfranchised serfs and peasants in the counties and towns.

(e)   For his statute laws which applied to the entire realm and were conceived of as applying indefinitely, Edward I was often called the "English Justinian."

12. Which of the following statements misrepresents the comprehensive development of the English judicial system during the High Middle Ages?

(a)   Unlike rulers on the Continent, William the Conqueror retained his royal prerogative to adjudicate major criminal cases.

(b)   Itinerant circuit judges administered justice in the various parts of the realm as direct representatives of the king.

*(c)   Church courts were brought under royal control in England during the reign of Henry II.

(d)   By involving groups of men familiar with local conditions or knowledge-able regarding the facts of civil cases brought before itinerant judges, England supplied precedents for both the grand jury system and jury trials.

(e)   Control and administration of the legal apparatus of the English realm were centralized under the permanent High Court.

13. The consolidation of royal power in Germany did not succeed because of the

(a)   southward orientation of the Hohenstaufen emperors and their neglect of the powerful dukes and counts in the north who continued to colonize lands east of the Elbe River.

(b)   resistance of Pope Gregory VII and his successors who wished to free the Church from secular control.

(c)   fierce independent-mindedness of the Lombard cities in northern Italy, the area of transit between Germany and Rome.

(d)   the oriental absolutism of Frederick II in southern Italy and his total lack of interest in German lands north of the peninsula.

*(e)   all of the above.

14.   One of the following statements does *not* correctly reflect the effects of feudalism.

*(a)   Since feudalism was a form of decentralization, the progression and final growth of a modern state was not reached in western Europe until strong rulers eliminated the individualistic pettiness of landlords and knights by disfranchising uncooperative vassals.

(b)   Although feudalism was a centrifugal political system, governmental centralization did follow rapidly upon the full establishment of feudal structures.

(c)   The experience of people in government functioning at the local level drew more people into direct contact with the workings of political life and resulted in the development of loyalties that reached beyond the limits of the local feudal unit.

(d)   Local lords could bend to the dictates of local customs and, thus, could establish precedents for building stronger governments.

(e)   By emphasizing the courts, Kings required vassals to appear annually to "pay court" and serve on "courts," thus providing training for vassals in governmental business and politics. Eventually the experienced vassals could be used by rulers of large territories in administrative positions within monarchical states.

15.   The Capetian dynasty's successes *cannot* be explained by

(a)   the longevity of its kinds and male heirs who had achieved adulthood when they succeeded to the throne.

(b)   the growth of agriculture and trade in its territories and the fame of its capital, Paris.

*(c)   substantial material aid and spiritual support from the English kings.

(d)   conquests of new territories that were subsequently incorporated into the royal holdings and administered by loyal officials.

(e)   support of the popes, who allowed Capetian rulers direct control over the local Church.

IDENTIFICATIONS

Villein
Demesne
St. Bonaventure
Second Lateran Council
Kingdom of the Two Sicilies
Clerks of the *Exchequer*
Constitutions of Clarendon
    (1164)

Île de France
Baillis
Las Navas de Tolosa
Canossa (1077)
Three-field system
Holy Roman Empire
Fief
Limited monarchy

TRUE OR FALSE

T   1.   In northwestern Europe, the manorial system—the dominant form of agrarian social and economic organization—emphasized communal enterprise and solidarity.

F   2.   The extremely idealistic and artificial "courtly literature" could not express the true attitude of men toward women during the High Middle Ages.

T   3.   Frederick Barbarossa's policy of focusing imperial attention and resources southward virtually assured the demise of the German Empire as a western power during the Middle Ages.

T   4.   Southern Italy and Sicily became a strong monarchy under Norman-French descendants of the Vikings.

T   5.   Unified Anglo-Saxon England was on the verge of falling apart when William defeated Harold at Hastings.

F   6.   Without too much difficulty, the Capetian dynasty established a strong central power since Charlemagne had united France and curtailed the dukes' and counts' competitive powers.

T   7.   A centrally controlled bureaucratic power superimposed on local governmental practices by Philip Augustus became the basic pattern for French government, maintained even to the present.

F   8.   The role given the Estates General—convened by Philip the Fair—closely paralleled that of English Parliaments.

T   9.   In the eleventh century, medieval people started to concentrate on land transport as well as communication in order to maintain a renascent land-based and sea-borne trade.

T   10.   The liberation of the Mediterranean from Muslim rule between 1050 and 1300 was achieved by the northern Italian city-states, which subsequently granted a trade monopoly to the cities of Genoa, Pisa, and Venice.

DISCUSSION AND/OR ESSAY QUESTIONS

1. "Greek intellectual life [too] was based on thriving cities. Thus it seems that without commerce in goods there can be little exciting commerce in ideas." Explain, offering examples from civilizations that flourished before 1050 and those of the High Middle Ages.

2. Why did the Magna Carta make arbitrary government difficult, while centralized government remained possible under its articles?

3. What geographical and ecological conditions and political and social circumstances prevailed in England and France that profoundly affected the course of monarchical centralization and nation building in these countries? How did various rulers exploit conditions in order to centralize government?

4. Voltaire said that the German "Holy Roman Empire" had become neither holy, nor Roman, nor an empire. On what did Voltaire base his contentions?

5. Admitting that generalization can only approximate, compare, and contrast the life of a common person with that of a noble during the High Middle Ages.

SUGGESTED FILMS

The Crusades (1095-1291). 16 min. Color. Centron Educational Films (1969).

The Holy Roman Empire. 14 min. B/w; c. Coronet Instructional Films (1961).

The Norman Conquest of England. 20 min. Color. Radim Films, Inc. (1971).

Rise of Nations in Europe. 13 min. B/w; c. Coronet Instructional Films (revised edition, 1977).

Outline

MULTIPLE CHOICE
Choose the best response.

1. Which of the following statements is *not* properly applicable to the great religious revival during the High Middle Ages?

    (a) Due in part to the decentralization of political and religious authority after the collapse of the Carolingian Empire, corruption and indifference within the established religion provoked a revival of religious spirit and dedication.

    (b) Because monasteries had developed somewhat more independently of lay control than had the secular clergy or bishopric, these became centers of religious revival.

    (c) Without the enthusiastic interest of Westerners in religion, attempts to reform the Church would not have succeeded.

    (d) Most popes of the High Middle Ages attempted to deprive secular authorities of their powers to appoint Church functionaries and to separate the clerical estate from the secular one.

    *(e) Kings and secular lords bitterly opposed the establishment of revivalist centers and relentlessly fought the revival reformist popes.

2. The Age of Faith can be described by its

    (a) emphasis on activism as the perfect ideal for an "athlete of Christ," working toward reforms and world evangelization.

    (b) growth of morality due to the papal decrees against simony and clerical marriage, as well as the popes' demands for absolute obedience and chastity from the clergy.

    (c) idealistic monastic movements within the Church that succeeded in maintaining religious enthusiasm among the faithful until nearly the end of the thirteenth century.

    (d)   burst of intellectual and artistic achievements, the tangible results of the influence of Christianity on the society of the High Middle Ages.

  *(e)   all of the above.

3.   The vitality of popular religion during the High Middle Ages was evoked by

    (a)   the success of the Crusades in bringing the holiest shrines of Christianity under Christian rule.

  *(b)   Gregory VII and his successors' ability to bring uniformity to religious practices of Christians and generally to protect the defenseless and raise the morals of the clergy.

    (c)   the inability of the emperors and kings to resist strong popes in struggles for supremacy.

    (d)   the spectacular economic development which satisfied the material needs of the faithful and permitted them time to concentrate on spiritual matters.

    (e)   an uncompromising attitude against heretics, whose teaching acted as a centrifugal force on united Church teaching.

4.   Which statement is *incorrect*?

    (a)   The Carthusian and Cistercian orders were centralized congregations free from both local ecclesiastical and secular powers.

    (b)   Enthusiasm inspired increasingly large numbers of laymen to join or patronize monasteries.

    (c)   Heightened religious commitment sustained the need for new monastic orders within which Christians might hope to reach the fullness of monastic ideals of Christian perfection.

    (d)   The new orders of friars vowed to follow a rule that stressed absolute obedience to the pope, poverty, direct ministery to the sick and poor, and preaching and teaching activities.

  *(e)   Most popes of the twelfth and thirteenth centuries were first Dominican or Franciscan friars.

5.   Which of the following statements *best* represents the development of Christian theology during the High Middle Ages?

  *(a)   The veneration of relics was replaced by a renewed emphasis on the sacrament of the Eucharist.

    (b)   Popular veneration of the Virgin Mary helped create a central, enduring, and honored place for women in the Christian religion and its theology.

    (c)   The Sacrament of Penance was declared at the Fourth Lateran Council to be an indispensable means to God's grace and salvation.

(d) Pilgrimages came to be considered excellent means of doing penance.

(e) A dominant motivation for religious fervor was the clerical practice of granting plenary indulgences—promising that a person is free from other-worldly punishment and guaranteeing that the soul will go directly to heaven upon death.

6. The popes' concept of the "right order in the world" is related to *all but one* of the following papal stances. The popes of the High Middle Ages

(a) sought to establish a papal monarchy over all secular princes and have this authority generally recognized, and to assert the right to name candidates for ecclesiastical benefices.

(b) demanded full obedience in secular and religious matters in order to unify all Christendom under papal hegemony.

(c) both advocated and blessed Christian campaigns against Muslims in Spain, Greeks in Italy, and Slavs in the East.

(d) ordered the establishment of cathedral schools whose purpose was to enlarge the number of literate and trained clerics and lay administrators.

*(e) gained the loyalty of all the faithful in Christendom regardless of local or national allegiance.

7. Which of the following statements correctly represents one aspect of the administration of Pope Innocent III?

(a) The kings of Aragon, Sicily, and Hungary succeeded in resisting the establishment of feudal overlordship of the pope in their territories.

(b) Innocent III consolidated his power around Rome and completely dominated all papal lands in Italy.

(c) During the Fourth Crusade, in 1204, Constantinople was destroyed at the direct order of Innocent, whose aim it was to bring the excommunicated Eastern Church under the rule of the papal monarchy.

*(d) During the Fourth Lateran Council, Innocent called a Crusade against the Muslims, and Church doctrines of the Sacraments and the Eucharist were defined.

(e) Dynamic spirituality within the Church was greatly enhanced by papal patronage of all idealistic religious groups.

8. Urban II called a Crusade at the Council of Clermont. His major goal was to

(a) establish unity among the various national states in Europe and to strengthen the Gregorian concept of papal monarchy.

*(b) demonstrate that the pope along—as the spiritual leader of all Christians— could provide the "right order in the world."

(c) cleanse the world of Jews and distribute Jewish property among the poor.

(d) provide new lands to the faithful and, thus, to expand the territorial limits of the papal states.

(e) offer fallen Christians an opportunity to do penance by means of a lengthy and often hazardous pilgrimage to the Holy Land of Christianity.

9. Which of the following statements is *least* representative of the consequences of the Crusades?

(a) The concept of papal monarchy over secular rulers was initially victorious, but misuses and subsequent failures of crusading irreparably damaged the prestige of the papacy.

(b) The early crusading successes evoked a self-confidence and optimism among westerners, and travels to lands other than their homelands broadened the crusaders' limited cultural horizons.

(c) The growth of commercial contacts with the East substantially increased Western prosperity as a whole.

(d) The development of various forms of national taxation was given precedent in the system of taxation established for financing the Crusades.

*(e) Close contacts with Jews and Muslims greatly enhanced westerners' new-found cooperation with the Greek Orthodox Church and led to a lasting peaceful toleration of the Eastern Christians and Muslims as well.

10. With one exception, the following statements explain the decline of papal authority.

(a) Crusades called by the popes against other Christian rulers undermined the popes' temporal authority.

(b) The steady erosion of papal prestige and the simultaneous growth of royal power resulted in Christian loyalties shifting from the pope to the kings.

(c) The decline in the papacy was closely interrelated with clerics' questionable practice of offering plenary indulgences to all participants in the several Crusades and to financial backers of these wars.

(d) In ruling the Papal States and utilizing new means of raising revenues such as clerical taxes Innocent III's successors began to appear much like ordinary acquisitive rulers.

*(e) The charge of heresy against Boniface VIII was proven in ecclesiastical courts by Cistercian and Dominican prosecutors. This prosecution disenchanted many former papal loyalists.

11. One of the following statements is not fully applicable to the development of the European educational system.

(a)   The role that monasteries had assumed before 1179 in educating a few nonreligious individuals was abandoned when the papal monarchy ordered the establishment of cathedral schools.

(b)   A revival of the study of the classics and attempts to imitate them has led scholars to refer to a twelfth-century "renaissance."

(c)   While most cathedral schools remained primarily clerical, alternate schools were established to cater to the needs of lay folks seeking preparation for careers such as law or within the mercantile fields.

(d)   Typical medieval institutions, organized to protect common interests of members, the universities originally were corporations or scholars or students in cities where food was plentiful and peace and stability prevailed.

*(e)   North of the Alps the most prominent university became that of Paris, mainly because of its control by academicians and the continuous financial support provided by successors of Pope Gregory VII.

12.   One of the following statements is not correct. Scholastic philosophers

(a)   gave primacy to the soul over the body, and to the concept of salvation after death, and put extraordinary faith in the powers of human reason.

(b)   Considered Biblical Revelation concerning the mysteries of faith sufficient to demonstrate absolute truth.

*(c)   relied entirely on newly translated Greek and Arabic sources in acquiring their perspective on the knowledge of nature, a means of knowing they claimed to be compatible with teachings imparted by Divine Revelation.

(d)   followed the theories of Peter Abelard, who treated theology as a science and attempted to harmonize religion with rationalism.

(e)   followed St. Thomas Acquinas, whose deep confidence in human experience and reason came extremely close to reconciling Aristotelian philosophy with Christian theology.

13.   Which of the following is true of High Middle Age literature?

(a)   Religious enthusiasm is clearly reflected in literature as its predominant topic.

(b)   With the exception of Dante's *Divine Comedy* and some late thirteenth-century drama, all literature continued to be written in exemplary Latin.

*(c)   The *Divine Comedy* encompasses the best in medieval learning.

(d)   High Middle Age ballads, lyrics, songs, and romances idealized women according to the Dominicans' emphasis on the Virgin Mary.

(e)   Coarseness, anticlericalism, and sexual innuendos found in the various narrative *fabliaux* were directed solely to audiences drawn from the uneducated.

14. With the exception of one innovation listed here, the Gothic form of architecture

  *(a) manifested the glory of God by subordinating all architectural details to a severe, massive construction style, with huge, engaged piers and small windows above round arches.

  (b) utilized the pointed arch, groined and ribbed vaulting, and flying buttresses in order to reflect perfectly the soaring religious enthusiasm of the High Middle Ages.

  (c) provided, through its sculptural representations, medieval knowledge and tradition for those who could not read.

  (d) expressed interest in the human person by including scenes of daily life on the stained-glass windows.

  (e) provided a new style for building cathedrals that became the source of urban pride throughout western Europe.

15. The features and general character of Western music originated in High Middle Age polyphonic music, which

  (a) was an encyclopedic collection of homophonic melodies collected during the time of Pope Gregory VII.

  (b) was a system of musical notation originating with the Greeks, developed by the Romans, and transferred to the peoples of western European national states.

  (c) became popular during pilgrimages and the Crusades as marching songs and hymns for use during liturgical functions.

  (d) was discovered by the troubadours, who accompanied their ribald, secular songs with a form of music later appropriated by the pious followers of St. Francis and St. Dominic, who substituted liturgical texts for the secular ones and began to use these works in Church liturgy.

  *(e) was the instrumental and/or vocal combination of two or more harmonious melodies in "counterpoint."

IDENTIFICATIONS

Simony	Transubstantiation
Concordat of Worms	Goliards
"Sicilian Vespers"	Heroic epics
"Peace of God" and	Courtly romances
"Truce of God"	Inquisition
Primogeniture	Albigensians
Plenary indulgence	Waldensians
Saladin	*Book of Sentences*

TRUE OR FALSE

F   1.   The papal *consistory*, a final court of appeals established in the twelfth century under Church canon law, was composed of the pope, the cardinals, and bishops.

F   2.   During the struggle against erosion of papal power, the assertive Pope Boniface VIII forced his ineffective predecessor to resign and murdered him shortly afterward.

T   3.   The diplomacy of the Hohenstaufen emperor Frederick II restored Jerusalem to the Christians together with a narrow access route to that city. This settlement occurred in 1299 and ended the Sixth Crusade.

F   4.   Tenth-, eleventh-, and twelfth-century Romanesque style—vast in scope, consciously symmetrical, and aiming to manifest the glory of God—is a vivid and fully developed analogue to the *Divine Comedy*.

T   5.   The abbey church of St. Denis in Paris, a Gothic building replacing an earlier church on the same site, is a shrine to France's patron and the burial place of the French kings.

F   6.   Polyphonic music was first performed in 1300 at the order of Pope Boniface VIII during the celebration of the papal jubilee.

T   7.   Pope Innocent III forced King John of England to grant England to the papacy as a fief.

F   8.   The Fourth Crusade, initiated by Pope Innocent III during the Fourth Lateran Council, succeeded at least in forestalling the entrance of Ottoman Turks into eastern Europe.

F   9.   By 1200 most graduates of cathedral schools were lay people who hoped to become lawyers or civilian administrators, or who wished to function as notaries or merchants.

F   10.   The revered Christian saint, Martin, was a professional soldier and chief expositor of codes of conduct that included and justified Christian warfare.

DISCUSSION AND/OR ESSAY QUESTIONS

1.   Provide evidence from literature, art, and philosophy that the twelfth century was as experimental and dynamic as the twentieth is.

2.   Discuss the investiture struggle between the papacy and the European rulers, explaining the participants' ambitious and arguments for exclusive legitimate authority. What compromise was reached, and what were the lasting political and religious results of this struggle?

3. What were the causes of each of the six Crusades? How did the Crusades contribute to the deterioration of the "Papal monarchy"?

4. How did Scholasticism reconcile explanations of knowledge based on sensory evidence, experience, and reason, with acceptance of Divine Revelation as a source of human knowledge?

5. Characterize Dante's *Divine Comedy*, and find within the high medieval Gothic-style architectural equivalents to the work's preoccupations and message.

SUGGESTED FILMS

Art of the Middle Ages. 30 min. Color. Encyclopaedia Britannica Corp./Films (1963).

Cathedral of Chartres. 16 min. Color. Time-Life Films, Inc. (1972).

The Christians: The People of the Book (569-1492). 39 min. Color. McGraw-Hill Films (1979).

Civilization: Romance and Reality. 2 parts, each 26 min. Color. Time-Life Films, Inc. (1970).

Images Medievals. 18 min. Color. Film Images, a Division of Radim Films, Inc. (n.d.).

Romanesque Painters (1000-1200). 11 min. Color. Roland Films (n.d.).

The Year 1200. 19 min. Color. BFA Educational Media, a Division of CBS, Inc. (1970).

Outline

MULTIPLE CHOICE
Choose the best response.

1.   The slowdown during the late Middle Ages of dramatic progress was primarily due to

   (a)   constant warring of the French and English monarchs, which left the agriculturally rich and especially productive French countryside devastated.

   (b)   weak and impious popes, whose primary concern was the strength of the papal state and not the spiritual welfare of the faithful.

   *(c)   "acts of god"—i.e., plagues and diseases—that reduced the population of Europe by an estimated one-half to two-thirds during the late Middle Ages.

   (d)   relentless attacks by the Muslims, who succeeded in gaining a foothold in Europe, thereby, disrupting the social and economic equilibrium in western Europe.

   (e)   late-medieval peoples' preoccupations with inward mysticism, excluding all concern with necessities of the here and now.

2.   With one exception, new economic and social realities in western Europe after 1400 led to

   (a)   specialization in patterns of production with most regions adapting crops or livestock according to soil conditions and climatic variables.

   (b)   a shift in the growth of importance of towns and cities relative to the countryside, with urban centers growing as manufacturing and overland trade centers and maritime cities being established to control long-distance trade across the seas.

   (c)   the development of sophisticated financial institutions and management techniques to cope with rapidly increasing international trade and its attendant business problems.

115

    *(d)   an artificially augmented cash flow, which prompted an inflationary spiraling of prices for staple foods.

    (e)   wealthy merchants gradually admixing with the former feudal aristocracy, a social mobility sometimes brought about by merchants buying feudal lands from the impoverished nobles.

3.   European recovery from the economic depression of the late Middle Ages was marked by all the following *except*

    (a)   the expansion of towns and cities as manufacturing centers of industrial goods in which both manufacturers and workers had a greater hope for a relatively secure existence since they could adjust to market demands, supplying different kinds and amounts of wares as needed.

    (b)   an increased determination of people to reorganize their lives on a sounder footing in the face of challenges posed by the Black Death and economic depression.

    *(c)   the equal determination of all Europeans to resist attempts of the Muslims to encroach upon any European territory.

    (d)   a return of normalcy in agricultural production, the lowering of food prices, and regional specialization in agricultural production according to soil and climatic conditions.

    (e)   the creation of a commercial equilibrum through reciprocal trade of basic commodities and the resultant growth of towns and cities as commercial centers.

4.   Which of the following statements is *not* correct? The humiliation of Pope Boniface VIII by Philip the Fair

    (a)   resulted in a clear victory for the French king that set the stage for the Babylonian captivity of the papacy in France.

    (b)   germinated discontent of European Christians, whose demands that the pope return to Rome resulted in the Great Schism.

    (c)   initiated a series of events that would eventually restrict the popes' secular power to central Italy.

    (d)   stifled the Gregorian concept of papal monarchy and the ieda that a pope could use morally enlightened political power to establish and preserve right order in the world.

    *(e)   eliminated all vestiges of heresy, so apparent during the High Middle Ages, and provided doctrinal uniformity based on the work of the Council of Constance and the Council of Basel.

5.   The Council of Constance

    (a)   reaffirmed the main resolutions of the Council of Pisa of 1409, which had removed the papacy from Avignon, ending the Babylonian captivity.

*(b)   eliminated all claimants to the papacy and returned Pope Martin V, elected by the council in 1417, to Rome, ending the Great Schism.

(c)   granted papal prerogative in controling the conciliar form of government.

(d)   favorably responded to the pleas of John Hus and promulgated his platform of reform for the Church. In its action the council managed to reverse trends of ecclesiastical corruption and to refocus Christians' attention on social justice.

(e)   agreed to tolerate the reform-minded Bohemian Church organization if it would forgo its claim of religious autonomy and operate under the direct control of the pope.

6.   The early English success in the Hundred Years' War was essentially due to the

(a)   internal dissension of France and the divisive attempts of French aristocrats to assert regional autonomy during the reign of inept French kings.

(b)   support of the participants in the "Jacquerie," who regarded the English as their liberators from abject poverty.

*(c)   superior military tactics, tight discipline, and use of the longbow against heavily armored French knights, tactics instrumental in the victories at Crécy, Poitiers, and Agincourt.

(d)   financial contributions and spiritual support of the popes, who saw in the English their only hope of escape from the Babylonian captivity.

(e)   logistical supplies provided by the Flemish burghers, who wished to be free from French rule.

7.   All but one of the following statements represent aspects of political and social development in England during and after the Hundred Years' War.

(a)   Largely a reaction against the French and all things not English, a sense of national identity began to crystallize around 1400.

*(b)   After the defeat at Bordeaux, the Crown succeeded in expanding English territory by annexing Scotland.

(c)   Once concern with France was past, the English were free to concentrate energy and resources on other issues such as overseas expansion.

(d)   Governmental institutions such as the Parliament were strengthened, and their operations became more sophisticated.

(e)   The position of the central government remained strong and grew in importance despite occasionally rebellious aristocrats.

8.   The following statements describe some of the results of the epoch-making technological advances during the late Middle Ages. Which statement is *incorrect*?

(a) Movable print and cheap paper insured that ideas spread quickly, and revolutionary concepts could not be easily suppressed after they were published in hundreds of books.

(b) Efficiency in production as well as human anxiety and tensions grew with the discovery and popularization of clocks.

(c) The term of workers' productive activity was extended by the discovery of the eyeglass, which allowed older people to continue their work, often at the peak of their careers.

(d) The world suddenly became smaller through the discovery and improvement of the magnetic compass and navigational aids.

*(e) The discovery of artillery and musketry enabled small states to resist the imperialistic expansion of the large, national states.

9. The causes of rural and urban insurrections during the fourteenth and fifteenth centuries include all *except*

(a) economic crises caused by the Black Death, extreme taxation of the rural population, or these factors in combination.

(b) internal political instability, which led to revolts, conspiracies, and frequent upheavals in one or another European territory.

(c) the differences between upper and lower classes' standards of living, inflammatory inequities that aristocratic luxury and the proliferation of chivalric orders further aggravated.

*(d) the inability of nobles to cooperate with the merchant classes in agreeing upon equitable systems of taxation.

(e) religious protests against ecclesiastical wealth and the corruption of priests, bishops, and popes.

10. With one exception, the following circumstances might properly explain the lowering of clerical prestige among the laity of the Christian Church.

(a) In view of the ostentatious luxury of the papal court, demands for greater financial contributions were greatly resented by lay people.

(b) Human nature being what it is, priests and bishops often deserted their posts during the plague and, in so doing, helped erode the claim of clerics to moral leadership among the faithful.

(c) Increased lay literacy often challenged the intellectual leadership of priests and bishops.

*(d) The papal withdrawal to Rome after the Council of Constance totally alienated nearly all Christians, who had become tired of the bitter quarreling and inconsistency of institutional Christianity.

(e) Alternate sources of Christian piety were found more satisfactory to many devotees than was the conventional sacramental religion.

11. Most people's hunger for a satisfying relationship with the Divine was fulfilled during the late Middle Ages through each of the following *except*

(a) exaggerated devotional practices carried out in hopes of gaining divine favor in this life and eternal salvation.

*(b) the new monastic orders established expressly to preach to the faithful that salvation is possible only through the Church and its sacraments.

(c) the buying of indulgences in an attempt to secure exemption from after-death punishment in purgatory.

(d) the spread of mystical teachings, which sometimes instructed a total detachment from life in this world and at other times suggested integration of the secular and the sacred.

(e) borderline, or extreme, heretical interpretations of the Bible and earlier theologians' teachings aimed at elimination of worldly excesses of popes, bishops, and priests.

12. The major trend in late medieval literature, naturalism

(a) was a reaction against the medieval explorations of human conduct by Chrétien de Troyes, Wolfram von Eschenbach, and Dante.

*(b) paralleling the emphasis on realism in art, attempted to describe things the way they really were.

(c) provided theological and philosophical arguments in portraying people's true characteristics.

(d) also was a dominant trait of late-medieval art which emphasized abstract designs and ethereal, otherworldly human figures.

(e) none of the above.

13. In late-medieval culture the integration of religious piety and daily human experience is best reflected in

(a) philosophical treatises, which undermined Thomistic confidence in the powers of human reason to comprehend the supernatural.

(b) vernacular literature, which provided eatily readable theological explanations to the steadily increasing numbers of educated lay people.

*(c) paintings, which depicted expressions of religious faith and minute details of human experience side by side.

(d) fully three-dimensional paintings that represented human life more naturally.

(e) the emphasis on all that is human in a robust, witty, and frank way.

14. Human reaction to the disasters of the late Middle Ages varied. Which of the following statements *best* describes the motivating cause for the recovery of Europe from the disasters of the late Middle Ages?

   *(a) Human resolve and a tenacious recuperative ingenuity prevented devastation and consequent suffering from causing the collapse of European civilization.

   (b) Exorbitant luxuriating and revels in crude entertainments provided escape from visions of sudden unavoidable death that were as real to the aristocrat as to the merchant or peasant.

   (c) Most people found hope and solace in exaggerated religious practices or in a mystical emotional union with the Divine.

   (d) A determination to find new territories for a better life led some Europeans to start a successful overseas expansion.

   (e) Convinced by the disasters of the age, some philosophers, in separating the supernatural from earthly things, developed a skepticism about divine intervention in the natural order.

15. In the late Middle Ages governmental centralization and the growth of cultural nationalism was primarily due to

   (a) the commercial equilibrium achieved through reciprocal trade agreements, which provided basic commodities cheaply to all Europeans.

   (b) the concordats between secular rulers and the popes that granted kings and princes much authority over the various local churches.

   *(c) the dissemination of royal decrees and books in a uniform language, which superseded all local dialects.

   (d) the growing importance of towns, which helped create the social and economic equality of all classes.

   (e) the invention of artillery and firearms that introduced new and devastating military tactics against heavily armored mounted knights and fortified stone castles.

IDENTIFICATIONS

Knights of the Garter and Knights of the Golden Fleece	Hubert and Jan van Eyck
	Hanseatic League
Imitation of Christ	Battle of Nancy (1477)
Nominalism	Wars of the Roses
Empiricism	Ciompi
Decameron	Master Eckhart
Tempera	Lollards
Giotto	Wat Tyler

TRUE OR FALSE

T   1. Premodern history tends to show that whenever population becomes excessive, natural controls appear to reduce it to proportions manageable according to the existing economic and social means.

F   2. Avignon was a free city within the territory of the French kings and was garrisoned by French troops.

F   3. The treaty of 1454, which had established a peaceful balance between competitive Italian states, was reaffirmed by France and Spain in 1494.

T   4. By the end of the fifteenth century Austria and Brandenburg emerged as the most powerful princely territories in Germany.

T   5. Various rulers' attempts to consolidate central powers were one of the main causes of political turmoil during the late Middle Ages.

T   6. After the defeat of the English in the Hundred Years' War, Charles VII and his successors strengthened the power of the French monarchy and returned to the high-medieval concept of governance based on local diversity balanced against bureaucratic centralization.

T   7. The continuous spread of education for the laity and the growth of national pride greatly encouraged the use of the vernacular in literature.

F   8. The northern Italian cities of Venice, Milan, and Florence were ruled by merchant oligarchies throughout the late Middle Ages.

F   9. The continuous support aristocrats provided the central government made England one of the most stable national monarchies between 1307 and 1485.

F   10. William of Ockham taught that the existence of God and other theological matters described in the Scriptures can be demonstrated by observation of nature and human experience.

DISCUSSION AND/OR ESSAY QUESTIONS

1. What were the reasons for the prolonged economic depression of the late Middle Ages?

2. "Abject desperation" or "frustrated rising expectations" were the causes of some lower-class rebellions. Explain and illustrate with appropriate examples.

3. What were the main features of late-medieval art and literature.

4. "Late medieval culture often seems to border on the manic-depressive." Explain this statement and describe the various reactions of people trying to cope with their fears during this era.

5. How and why could Europeans be motivated by economic recovery and new technological discoveries "to start to make the whole world their own after 1500"?

SUGGESTED FILMS

Chaucer and the Medieval Period. 14 min. Color. Coronet Instructional Films (1957).

Civilization: The Great Thaw. 2 parts, each 26 min. Color. Time-Life Films, Inc. (1970).

Dijon—the Four Grand Dukes of Burgundy (1300-1500). 15 min. Color. Roland Films (1970).

Joan of Arc—a Profile in Power. 25 min. Color. Learning Corporation of America (1976).

Medieval England—the Peasants Revolt. 31 min. Color. Learnex Corporation of Florida (1969).

Paracelsus. 30 min. B/w. Indiana University Audio-Visual Center (1965).

Outline

MULTIPLE CHOICE
Choose the best response.

1.   The success of the Muslim invasion of India can be best explained by

   *(a)   the political division and lack of solidarity among the inhabitants of
           Hindustan in the period from Harsha's downfall until the Muslim
           conquest.

   (b)   the vigor and energy of the conquerors, inspired by promises of recom-
           pense for carrying on *jihad* against the infidels.

   (c)   the stultifying effects of the caste system with its prescribed activities
           and loyalties, including having one relatively small sub-group assume
           responsibility for defense of the whole kingdom.

   (d)   the "welcome" extended by descendants of the Huns and Mongols in
           Northern India, who after seven centuries of residence were classified
           as "untouchables."

   (e)   the inability of the *Rajput* cavalry to stem the tide of highly-motivated
           Turkish hordes attacking from Afghanistan.

2.   The Muslim administrative system in India is best characterized by

   (a)   a ruthlessly enforced, discriminatory taxation system foisted upon all
           "unbelievers."

   (b)   forced conversion of Hindus to the Muslim religion.

   *(c)   unpredictable administrative practices—enlightened, tyrannical, humane,
           and cruel in erratic sequence—determined by the current ruler's whim.

   (d)   the widespread destruction of Buddhist temples, monasteries, and centers
           of learning.

   (e)   employment of Mongols as mercenaries to control the newly conquered
           Hindu population.

3.   The effects of the Turkish conquests in India include all the following, *except*

(a) almost complete eradication of Buddhism as a viable force in India.

(b) greater subjugation of women, making them a silent, powerless sector of society through customs such as veiling and seclusion.

(c) marked decline in intellectual and artistic endeavors, at least in Hindustan.

(d) the creation of more factions in a society already polarized by the caste system.

*(e) introduction of prostitution in the temples and the compulsory burning of widows.

4. During the Sung, Yüan, and Ming dynasties, the novel and drama developed as major art forms for reasons given in *all but one* of the following statements:

(a) Civil service examinations were suspended and natives were excluded from governmental posts during the Yüan dynasty.

(b) Talented Chinese, unable to find creative outlets in official careers, turned to the medium of popular entertainment during the latter half of the thirteenth century.

*(c) Western literary masterpieces, which came to China by way of Nestorian Christian missionaries, were translated into classical Chinese and achieved popularity as forerunners of the novel and the play.

(d) So sterile was the academic atmosphere under the Mings that men of letters began to experiment with writing adventurous narratives in the plain language of the people, infusing their writings with emotion, and combining the writing of history with social commentary.

(e) Neo-Confucianism taught the metaphysics and ethics of Chu-Hsi and deprecated scholarly speculation, so that by the fifteenth century innovative thinkers were unwelcome in civil service circles.

5. Chinese navigation developed and expanded rapidly during the early years of the Ming dynasty *mainly* because

(a) it became necessary for China to defend its maritime interests against Japanese piracy, which troubled ships in the coastal waters near the Yangtze delta and Hangchow during Ming times.

(b) the Southern Sung rulers were unable to resist Khitan and Juchên encroachment upon northern China and the Central Asian caravan routes, and so shifted emphasis from overland to overseas trade.

*(c) China as a whole reacted to Mongol control of caravan routes across Central Asia by engaging in maritime activities and curtailing overland travel.

(d) the mariner's compass was invented in the eleventh century, and new shipbuilding techniques followed shortly thereafter.

(e) members of the Ming court and nobility craved goods from the East Indies, the Malay Archipelago, India, and the West.

6. The potency and durability of Chinese institutions during Sung, Yüan, and Ming times is manifest in

(a) the ability of China to maintain peaceful contacts with various nations during periods of internal stress and in the face of external threat.

(b) the acceptance of a man of low birth, a former monk turned bandit who led the successful rebellion against Mongol rule, as founder of the long-lasting Ming dynasty.

(c) the Ming revival of the ancient administrative system, its restoration of a civilian bureaucracy—suspended during the Yüan—and its policy of territorial and economic expansion, reminiscent of the T'ang.

(d) the influence of traditional Chinese culture upon those of the semi-nomadic Khitans and the nomadic Mongols, who eagerly embraced it and contributed to its progress during their political ascendancy in northern China.

*(e) all of the above.

7. At one time or another during the Sung, Yüan, and Ming dynasties, government was characterized by all the following, *except*

(a) reformist policies, in accordance with Confucian principles, based on reaffirmation of man's natural capacity for goodness.

(b) a paternalistic state administration, inspired by rational, ethical, and moral codes rooted in the metaphysics of a "Supreme Ultimate."

(c) the imposition of conquerors' civil administration systems, which excluded Chinese from governmental posts while permitting foreigners of various nationalities to serve therein.

(d) a revival of the T'ang system of administration, including the power and duties of a civilian bureaucracy.

*(e) a religio-political system based on an explicit Neo-Confucian creed, which established the equality of all humans.

8. Japanese culture progressed during the Shogunate *mostly* because

(a) a prominent school of Buddhism, whose monks fostered Chinese learning and art, contributed the idea that diligent scholarship and gradual cultural refinement would bring about society's Enlightenment.

*(b) Japanese writers and artists displayed originality and freshness even in their imitations of other peoples' art, and could, for example, adapt Chinese styles to reflect Japanese tastes and conditions.

    (c)   scholarship escalated among the competing religious sects and stimulated individual creativity, both within the religious communities and among the samurai who admired their teachings.

    (d)   Chinese and other foreign cultural elements were introduced steadily from the thirteenth century onward, and were adopted without significant change by the Japanese.

    (e)   a predominantly aristocratic and wealthy class of Japanese, which gained from capitalistic enterprise as well as feudal privilege, was well able to endow the arts and letters.

9.   Between the tenth and the end of the sixteenth centuries the economy of Japan was

   *(a)   based on a manorial economy in which large estates were worked by small farmers in virtual serfdom, since, in return for protection, they relinquished their properties to powerful neighbors who became the "great lords."

    (b)   isolated from the economies of other Far Eastern and western countries, since trade with them was insignificant until the fifteenth century.

    (c)   a barter, or exchange economy, which preempted diversification of production, limited marketing activities, and did not include any true capitalistic enterprises.

    (d)   at best static and at worst regressive in comparison with the economies of other Asian and western countries during the Later Middle Ages.

    (e)   crippled by the country's preoccupation with military matters, which greatly reduced the number of merchants until the peaceful era of the daimyo.

10.   *All but one* of the following occurred in Japanese society during the age of confusion and turmoil. Mark the exception.

    (a)   Strong feudal "great lords" emerged as a class, and their initial administrative authority over large territories eventually became hereditary.

   *(b)   There was a dramatic improvement in the status of women, from a position of abject subordination to male authority to one of romantic adulation and relative equality, as can be seen in mid-fifteenth century literature.

    (c)   Certain nobles exploited the fear and apprehension aroused by unstable political institutions to attain prestige and material wealth at the expense of the lesser aristocracy and peasantry, whose services they claimed in return for protection.

    (d)   Feudal retainers and robber monks engaged in robbery and pillage within a state of near-anarchy.

(e)   A code of valor, loyalty, and honor toward lords developed, which dicta-
ted that a samurai defend or avenge his lord, even at the cost of his life
or the lives of his family.

11.   Although Japanese and western feudalism were not identical, a striking parallel
between the two is evident in

(a)   poems of romantic love that characterized women as marvelous beings
who could grant intense spiritual and sensual satisfaction.

(b)   the development of a feudal class that avidly participated in capitalistic
enterprises.

(c)   the formation of massive armies recruited by and standing under the
command of the emperor.

(d)   the independent, equal status of the higher clergy and the aristocracy.

*(e)   the leadership of land owner warriors over a subservient peasantry, with
governmental power exercised by the warriors as if it were a private right.

12.   Who or what was chiefly responsible for state formation in sub-Saharan Africa?

*(a)   Traders from Europe and North Africa, and, to a lesser extent, from
regions near the Persian Gulf and northwestern India, wanted the natural
riches of the vast continent. Recognizing this, leaders of African clans
and city-states organized in order to control and benefit from the trade
in minerals and precious metals.

(b)   Migrating tribesmen and non-African immigrants, who had been exposed
to more developed civilizations, poured into western and sub-Saharan
Africa after 900 A.D.

(c)   Muslim and Christian rulers, moved by missionary fervor, promoted prose-
lytism among African non-believers.

(d)   Tribal leaders were willing to accept the rule of a divinely inspired king
for the sake of mutual defense.

(e)   The knowledge of earlier great empires on the continent, transmitted from
generation to generation by tribal *griots*, inspired some groups to unite
and form kingdoms from autonomous city-states.

13.   Below are brief descriptions of several African kingdoms. Mark the one whose
development was motivated by increased demands for raw materials on the part
of Indian Ocean traders.

(a)   Known by the eighth century as the world's major gold exporter, this
territorial empire succumbed to outside pressure in the thirteenth century.

(b)   As in Muslim India, slaves in Muslim Africa could assume high administrative and military responsibilities here and, as happened on at least one
occasion, could usurp supreme governing authority.

(c) Trade centers established at the forests' edge challenged this people to build mini-kingdoms in order to effectively control trade in the area.

*(d) Rulers of this territorial kingdom, rich in copper and gold, commanded enormous economic and military power after consolidating their states in the thirteenth century.

(e) This kingdom became a missionary agent of Christianity in the fourteenth and fifteenth centuries with the conquest of pagan states to the west of its borders.

14. Carefully reread question 13. Identify the five states and their order of presentation by choosing one of the lists below:

(a) Mwenemupata empire; Benin; Ifé; Songhay; Ghana.

*(b) Ghana; Songhay; Akan; Mwenemupata empire; Ethiopia.

(c) Songhay; Ifé; Ghana; Benin; Hansa.

(d) Akan; Sofala; Kilwa; Mwenemupata empire; Ethiopia.

(e) Sofala; Mali; Benin; Ghana; Songhay.

15. Among the various reasons for the disintegration of the great Mongol empire, the most decisive one might be

(a) the defeat of Kublai Khan's troops during landing operations on the shores of Japan in 1274 and 1281.

*(b) the vast geographic extent of the empire, which impeded effective centralized administration and enforcement of cultural or religious conformity.

(c) the alliance between the rulers of Rajputana and the Muslim and Hindu kings in the Deccan, which succeeded in converting growing popular discontent into a unified liberation movement.

(d) the unbearable burden of terror as a matter of administrative policy in areas under Mongol domination.

(e) the Chinese uprising against the conquerors under the leadership of a "soldier of Fortune," the founder of the Ming Dynasty.

IDENTIFICATIONS

Rajputana	Nun-Shogun
Raziya	Daigo II
Nalanda	Kamakura
Tamerlane	Daimyo
"Five Dynasties"	"Askia"

Grand Canal   Sunjata
Marco Polo   *Griot*
Chu-Hsi

TRUE OR FALSE

T   1.   Unlike the rigid caste-bound Hindu societies, Islamic communities were essentially democratic. If one could prove oneself a capable administrator, any upstart might be accepted as legitimate sovereign.

F   2.   Hindu converts to Islam were not accepted on an equal basis by the dominant Muslim faction.

F   3.   Two independent Muslim kingdoms came into existence in the Deccan in the fourteenth century.

T   4.   With the reopening of the caravan routes in the fifteenth century, the Ming government restricted seaborne travel and effectively isolated China.

T   5.   The mariner compass, in use since the eleventh century, greatly contributed to the development and expansion of Chinese navigation, especially in the late fourteenth century.

F   6.   A disproportionately large number of extant Chinese works of art were produced during the Sung and Yüan periods.

T   7.   At the end of the sixteenth century the Tokugawa family completely reorganized the Shogunate, arresting political deterioration that was approaching anarchy.

F   8.   Only the bejeweled hilts and ornate scabbards of swords used by the Japanese nobility were produced in Japan. The curved blades were imported from Toledo and Damascus, where metalworking was more advanced.

F   9.   Hausaland shared a common border, language, and cultural heritage with the population of the Mali Empire from the late fifteenth to the late sixteenth century.

T   10.   The foundations of a great Muslim university were laid early in the fourteenth century at the Sankore mosque in Timbuktu.

DISCUSSION AND/OR ESSAY QUESTIONS

1.   Explain the roles of religion and commerce in the development of territorial empires and their civilizations in sub-Saharan Africa. Discuss the nature of the changes wrought by these forces in the societies in question. Give specific examples.

2.   How did Japan happen to develop a political and social organization remarkably similar to that of Western Europe's feudal system? Discuss the tensions and

conflicts that this system produced, but also consider the constructive forces that emerged, and how these significantly changed Japanese society.

3. "The truth has been made manifest ... No more writing is needed." How does this assertion reflect the teachings of the Neo-Confucian school? Did this attitude freeze political, economic, and cultural progress? How did talented individuals respond to the challenge of nostalgic orthodoxy?

4. Is Wang An-shih correct in stating that his proposals follow genuine Confucian principles adapted to the needs of his time? Why can we say that his over-all program approximates a kind of state socialism? How does this program compare with the radical reform program of Wang Mang during the Han Dynasty 1000 years earlier?

5. Discuss the impact of the rise of Muslim kingdoms in India on Indian culture and society. Indicate which changes had a lasting effect on the society and which did not.

SUGGESTED FILMS

INDIA

The Cross in the Lotus. 23 min. Color. National Council of Churches Broadcasting and Film Commission (1972).

Forgotten Empire. 12 min. B/w. National Education and Information Films, Ltd. (Bombay) (n.d.).

CHIINA

Chinese Ceramics. 18 min. Color. Unijapan Films (Tokyo) (1970).

The Forbidden City. 16 min. Color. National Broadcasting Co., Educational Enterprises (n.d.).

Story of Chinese Art. 20 min. Color. McGraw-Hill Textfilms (1952).

JAPAN

Architecture of Japan. 20 min. B/w; c. Association Films, Inc. (n.d.).

Buddhism. Part II. 15 min. Color. Doubleday Multimedia (1968).

Japan: An Historical Overview. 14 min. B/w; c. Coronet Instructional Films (1964).

The Japanese Sword as the Soul of the Samurai. 24 min. Color. Independent Film Producers Co. (1970).

AFRICA

City-States of East Africa. 30 min. B/w. Holt, Rinehart and Winston (1969).

Ethiopia: The Hidden Empire. 51 min. Color. Films Incorporated (1970).

Ethiopia: Cultures in Change. 20 min. Color. Films Incorporated (1971).

Kingdoms of the Western Sudan. 30 min. B/w. Holt, Rinehart and Winston (1969).

Negro Kingdoms of Africa's Golden Age. 17 min. Color. Atlantis Productions, Incorporated (1968).

CHAPTER 18. THE CIVILIZATION OF THE RENAISSANCE
(c. 1350-c. 1600)   563

Outline

MULTIPLE CHOICE
Choose the best response.

1. The Neoplatonists of Florence

    (a) emphasized mysticism and intuition in their philosophy and claimed that the world is inhabited by spirits and maintained in perfect harmony by supernatural forces.

    *(b) were members of a loosely defined organization of intellectuals under the patronage of Cosimo de' Medici for the sole purpose of popularizing the different themes of ancient thought.

    (c) closely followed the scholastic philosophy of St. Thomas Acquinas in coordinating the secular aspects of their intellectual and artistic endeavors with beliefs still maintained concerning divine revelation.

    (d) considered the universe a well-ordered mechanism in which there was no place for an omnipotent creator.

    (e) dismissed religion as unscientific superstition, the product of custom and habits, and an institution that impeded humans in their quest for ultimate truth.

2. The exciting achievements of the Renaissance between 1350 and 1600 were due to a growth in all of the following *except*

    (a) classical learning that followed rediscovery and popularization of classical Roman and Greek treatises, both scientific and philosophical, which in turn influenced and considerably altered existing ideas and modes of expression after 1350.

    (b) urban sophistication, providing an atmosphere conducive to experimentation with new expressions in thought and art.

(c)   intellectualism and urbanity, which to a large extent freed medieval culture from the nearly exclusive service of religion that earlier cultures had known.

*(d)   a fundamentally anti-Christian, almost pagan, outlook that expressed itself in a large corpus of art and literature and succeeded in preparing Europe for the Protestant Revolution.

(e)   an optimistic, naturalistic, and individualistic outlook on life.

3.   The common Renaissance intellectual ideal, humanism,

(a)   concentrated on finding appropriate answers to aid humanity in its struggle and hope for eternal salvation.

(b)   emphasized a university curriculum that was considerably altered from Scholasticism but that still stressed the precedence of soul over body.

*(c)   firmly attested the dignity of man, who was the most excellent of God's creatures below the angels, as well as the nobility and possibilities of the human race.

(d)   successfully combined the tenets of Scholastic philosophy with the new interest in Aristotelian concepts of fully human life in relation to the experiential world.

(e)   intended equally to make people more eloquent and moral and to encourage the use of scientific observations and experimentations to improve earthly life.

4.   Which of the following statements does *not* correctly describe secularism as a developing trend of the Renaissance?

(a)   In the greatest artistic and literary achievements of the age, the laity had an edge over the clergy.

(b)   Although international humanism largely depended on the use of Latin, the use of the vernacular for an ever-increasing proportion of literature and statesmanship diminished the importance of the ancient, official language of the Church.

(c)   The preference of ancient Roman traditions—reflected in a number of municipal schools and the secular curricula introduced into the universities—inclined Italy to more secular influences earlier than other European regions.

(d)   Nonreligious themes in art and literature corresponded well to the aesthetic demands of a literate laity.

*(e)   Initially influenced by Italian secularism, northern Europe surpassed Italy in its separation of humanistic concerns from organized religion.

5. "Renaissance man" is

   (a) an abstract term coined by humanist philosophers by which they characterized anyone dedicated to the ultimate Renaissance ideals.

   *(b) a person who is accomplished in many different pursuits and is also brave, witty, and "courteous," that is, civilized and learned.

   (c) Leonardo da Vinci, who was painter, musician, architect, writer, engineer, inventor, and naturalist.

   (d) a powerful, colossal, and magnificent male figure carved by Michelangelo in stone as an expression of his philosophy.

   (e) a group of rich and powerful merchant princes of the Italian cities whose portraits reflect all that was valued during the Renaissance.

6. Which of the following statements is *incorrect*?

   (a) The harmony of the universe is reflected in the human body, the parts of which are in perfect relation to one another and to the whole. Therefore, reasoned the Renaissance architect, architecture should represent the same harmony in its constituent parts and their interrelationship with the whole.

   (b) To find the "pure form" Michelangelo preferred sculpture to painting and so produced a number of allegorical figures that best expressed his philosophical thought.

   (c) Leonardo da Vinci's use of his technical skills to imitate nature with absolute precision seem to represent his conviction that works of art should depict a harmonious and well-ordered universe.

   (d) The influence of Italian philosophical traditions, combined with Germanic realism and earlier forms of Christian mysticism, lends a distinctive quality to Dürer's and Hans Holbein's work.

   *(e) By initiating a program of humanistic studies, Petrarch clearly established the Scholastic foundations of the Renaissance philosophy.

7. Which development most fully represents Renaissance religiosity?

   (a) The practical humanists of the English Renaissance were interested in more rational forms of Christianity without the dominance of Scholastic logic.

   (b) Inquisitorial control over free speculation did not extinguish cultural and artistic achievements, nor did it concern itself with the spontaneous upsurge of nonheretical religious fervor among European Catholics and Protestants.

   *(c) Neoplatonistic-humanistic influence during the Renaissance did not eliminate otherworldly concerns of people, but, rather, emphasized humanity's ennobled and spiritualized position in the universe.

   (d) Civic humanists' undrestanding of human action as a struggle to gain mastery over the earth relegated their concern with organized religion to a secondary position.

(e)   Many humanists considered asceticism and contemplation essential to move away from mere ethics in order to achieve union with God.

8. Curioristy about the inner workings of human nature is emphasized by which of the following characteristics of the Renaissance?

(a)   Symbolism and allegory in art and literature were often used as vehicles to express a fascination with peoples' emotions, basic values, and capacities for abstract thought, all things beyond the pale of human understanding.

(b)   A cynical yet realistic view of the baser attributes of human nature motivated Machiavelli to describe the practices of successful government as these actually occurred.

(c)   By portraying humans with absolute physical exactitude, Masaccio and Leonardo da Vinci rendered an interpretation of the human psyche that transcended mere representation.

(d)   While thinkers and writers were casting theories to probe the causes of human actions, scientists were insisting on finding observable, measurable causes and effects in the world of nature.

*(e)   All of the above.

9. Erasmus, an incarnation of the finest ideals of the northern Renaissance, maintained that

(a)   the concepts of humanitarianism and universal toleration clearly demand that the Church canonize the great thinkers of the classical past, first among these being Cicero and Socrates.

*(b)   misery and injustice are due to ignorance and superstition and can be eliminated by liberality of mind, reasonable action, and manifestations of essential human goodness.

(c)   emphasis upon scientific research will create better living conditions and will promote people's interests in literature and moral philosophy.

(d)   Protestant revolutionism is the only possible means to reform the institutional Church and return it to the simple teachings of Jesus.

(e)   Christian rulers are duty-bound to lead crusades against irrational, intolerant, and superstitiously extravagant princes of the Church.

10. The end of the Renaissance in Italy was least influenced by

(a)   the French invasion of 1494 and Spanish involvement in the Italian-French conflict, which created chaotic conditions not compatible with flourishing intellectual and artistic activity.

(b)   the shift of eastern trade to the Atlantic that gradually diminished Italian supremacy in world trade and eliminated a vital financial asset, one that had supported much Renaissance accomplishment and that might have mitigated the effect of costly wars.

(c)   the so-called Catholic Reformation, establishing unbearable controls over artistic expression and formerly free intellectual speculation.

(d)   Spanish puppets appointed by Charles V as ruling princes who patronized the arts yet did not consider Italy the nation of their allegiance nor its traditions their primary concern.

*(e)   the secularization of the papacy by Nicholas V and his successors, a move that was resolutely opposed by humanist artists and thinkers.

11.   Sometimes the theories of Montaigne and Erasmus did not correspond, as in the view that

    (a)   the ideals of toleration of all races and religious are dictated by basic human reasoning.

    (b)   the fickleness and failure of human institutions does not warrant violence and war among systems, classes, and nations.

    *(c)   asceticism is not a superior good and so men should not deny their physical natures or pretend that anything connected with sense experience is sinful.

    (d)   liberality of mind, reason, and conciliation are needed to combat rigorous beliefs about proper human action that actually end in fanaticism.

    (e)   none of the above.

12.   Which of the following developments offers the *best* explanation for advances made in the sciences during the Renaissance?

    (a)   The educational programs of the humanists encouraged the development of the sciences as a reaction against the "vain speculations" of the Scholastics.

    (b)   Popular Neoplatonic theories provided the basis for integration of abstract theories with practical, empirical, and strictly rational thought.

    *(c)   The publication of Archimedes' mathematical and physical treatises in 1543 encouraged a view that the world of nature operates on the basis of mechanical forces and is not driven by supernatural power.

    (d)   Rational humanism dismissed alchemy and astrology as superstition.

    (e)   The publication of Ptolemy's heliocentric theories both challenged the traditional geocentric theories of the Church and gave the impetus for observations and experimentation by Copernicus.

13.   The heliocentric idea of the Copernican Revolution

    (a)   was due to the discovery of the telescope having a magnifying power of thirty times and by which the moons of Jupiter, the rings of Saturn, and the spots on the sun could be observed.

*(b) originated in the reinterpretation of old astronomical evidence by Copernicus, who was greatly inspired by Neoplatonic assumptions concerning shape, motion, and the relation of the sun to the planets.

(c) was primarily due to mathematical experimentation and observations of Danish scientist Tycho Brahe.

(d) had its foundation in the laws of the planets, which stated that the earth and planets move on elliptical paths around the sun and at the uniform velocity.

(e) began with the discovery of the Milky Way as a collection of celestial bodies independent from our solar system.

14. Within the literature and philosophy produced by English writers of the Renaissance all the following trends were represented *except*

(a) moral allegory, used as a device for motivating people to embrace the virtues of chivalry.

(b) an intense love of all things human and sensuous, as well as the profound analysis of human character.

*(c) a concern with practical aspects of science beyond the limits of alchemy, astrology, and medicine.

(d) the humanist ideals of noble humanity and the obligation to be tolerant.

(e) the analysis and indictment of social, political, and economic abuses of the time.

15. One statement below does *not* apply to western European music of the fifteenth and sixteenth centuries.

*(a) Stimulated by the discovery of ancient tonal modes, music, as well as the visual arts, was dominated by the study of ancient models.

(b) Music was an essential element in the cultural background of an educated person, of whom proficiency—such as the ability to read a part at sight— was expected.

(c) Highly complicated contrapuntal motets and polyphonic settings of the Ordinary of the Mass provided emotionally satisfactory background music for liturgical services in the Church.

(d) Application of similar principles of musical composition to the secular madrigal, ballad and part song, and the sacred motet and chason substantially diminished the distinction between the sacred and the profane.

(e) During the fifteenth and sixteenth centuries regional and national schools of music with affinity to Renaissance art and literature centers became institutionalized in the cathedral choirs and the permanent musical ensembles of the ducal and royal courts.

IDENTIFICATIONS

Italian or Petrarchan sonnets
Discourses on Livy
Chiaroscuro
Statues "in the round"
Roman Inquisition
Index of Prohibited Books
Letters of Obscure Men
Praise of Folly

abbey of Thélème
Oath of Supremacy
Utopia
Doctor Faustus
*Dissertation upon the Movement
    of the Heart*
History of Italy
Ars Nova

TRUE OR FALSE

T   1. Discord among the Italian states and the interference of France and Spain
        in Italian affairs were instrumental in establishing the short-lived Republic
        of Florence.

F   2. The philosophical basis of much of Botticelli's work is directed primarily
        against Savonarola of Ferrara.

T   3. Michelangelo was one of the architects of St. Peter's Church in Rome.

T   4. The mechanistic interpretation of the universe, which took hold in some
        scientific circles after the mid-sixteenth century, insisted upon finding
        observable and measurable causes and effects in the world of nature.

F   5. Galileo's conclusion that "every weight tends to fall toward the center by
        the shortest way" was the first step toward discovery of the law of gravity.

F   6. Distrust of human nature and disillusionment with the scheme of the
        universe led Shakespeare to the writing of his sonnets.

T   7. The Florentine humanists Leonardo Bruni and Leon Battista Alberti
        argued that their basic nature equips people for action, usefulness to their
        society, and service of the state.

F   8. By painting idyllic landscapes and symphonies of color, members of the
        Venetian school successfully integrated philosophical and pyschological
        themes with human sensuality.

T   9. Many soldiers in the Spanish armies of Charles V came from Germany
        and the Low Countries.

T   10. Hans Holbein was one of the few artists who devoted his talents to the
        cause of Protestantism.

DISCUSSION AND/OR ESSAY QUESTIONS

1. "If there were any essential differences between the English literature of the
    Renaissance and that produced during the late Middle Ages, they would consist

in a bolder individualism, a stronger sense of national pride, and a deeper interest in the themes of philosophic import." Explain and provide appropriate evidence.

2. What are the essential differences between high-medieval and Renaissance thought and art?

3. "What a piece of work is man, how noble in reason, how infinite in faculty, in form and moving, how express and admirable in action, how like an angel in apprehension, how like a god: the beauty of the world, the paragon of animals."
   —Shakespeare, *Hamlet*, II, 2
   How does Renaissance art fulfill the ideas above?

4. What were the reasons for the spread of the Renaissance outside Italy? What were the specific differences between northern European and Italian Renaissance thought and art?

5. One of the most brilliant aspects of Renaissance activity is music, which was "no longer regarded merely as a diversion or an adjunct to worship but as an independent art." Explain.

SUGGESTED FILMS

Botticelli (1444-1510). 10 min. Color. Time-Life Films, Inc. (1970).

The Ceiling of the Sistine Chapel. 11 min. B/w. Macmillan Films, Inc. (1956).

The Christians: Princes and Prelates (1309-1519). 39 min. Color. McGraw-Hill Films (1979).

Civilization: The Hero As Artist. 2 parts, each 26 min. Color. Time-Life Films, Inc. (1970).

Civilization: Man—Measure of All Things. 2 parts, each 26 min. Color. Time-Life Films, Inc. (1970).

Dürer and the Renaissance. 14 min. Color. McGraw-Hill Films (1962).

Ecce Homo. 9 min. Color. Roland Films (1970).

El-Greco. 28 min. Color. Graphic Curriculum, Inc. (1970).

El-Greco. 11 min. Color. Pictura Films Corporation (1965).

Erasmus, the Voice of Reason. 25 min. B/w. (Available for rental from the University of Utah; see *Educational Film Locator*) (n.d.).

Flanders in the 15th C.—the First Oil Paintings. 25 min. Color. Radim Films, Inc. (1965).

1492. 54 min. Color. McGraw-Hill Films (1965).

Francis Bacon. 31 min. B/w. Time-Life Films, Inc. (1969).

Galileo: The Challenge of Reason. 26 min. Color. Learnex Corporation of Florida. (1970).

I, Leonardo da Vinci. 54 min. Color. McGraw-Hill Films (1966).

Music in the Art of the Renaissance. 28 min. Color. Fran (Paul E.) (1971).

Raphael. 20 min. B/w. Time-Life Films, Inc. (1970).

The Secret of Michelangelo: Every Man's Dream. 51 min. Color. Association of Instructional Materials (n.d.).

The Sonnets: Shakespeare's Moods of Love. 21 min. Color. Learnex Corporation of Florida (1972).

The Spirit of the Renaissance. 31 min. Color. (From the Humanities—Philosophy and Political Thought series.) Encyclopaedia Britannica Educational Corp./Films (1971).

Touring Great Cities: Amsterdam. 40 min. Color. Time-Life Films, Inc. (1977).

Touring Great Cities: London. 40 min. Color. Time-Life Films, Inc. (1977).

Venice—the Great Renaissance Merchant State. 20 min. Color. Benchmark Films, Inc. (n.d.).

William Beaumont. 23 min. Color. University of California, Extension Media Center (1976).

William Harvey. 19 min. Color. University of California, Extension Media Center (1974).

Outline

MULTIPLE CHOICE
Choose the best response.

1.   Although not really a part of the Renaissance, the growth of the Reformation
     movement accompanied Renaissance activity. Which of the following is *not*
     representative of common denominators to the Renaissance and the Reforma-
     tion? Both

     (a)   returned to common sources of civilization, the roots of which were buried
           in antiquity or in the earliest centuries of the Middle Ages.

     (b)   had a background in the growth of trade and urban society and the result-
           ant rapid economic development in Europe.

    *(c)   affected equally the daily life and experiences of aristocrats and the
           common man.

     (d)   were products of the emerging current of individualism, which asserted
           rights of freedom and human dignity.

     (e)   were concerned with religion, although religious preoccupations during
           the Reformation had comparatively little in common with those of the
           Renaissance.

2.   What would most warrant the statements: "The gateway to the modern world
     is the Reformation?"

     (a)   With its emotional and less rational approach to prevailing theological
           trends, the Reformation appealed to the religious, economic, and,
           occasionally, political yearnings of aristocrats and the common man,
           usually by reacting against the established Roman Church.

     (b)   Unwilling to compromise, the chief thinkers and leaders of the Reforma-
           tion broke with the religious traditions of the past.

     (c)   In its appeal to the emerging spirit of national consciousness among
           northern Europeans, the Reformation provided Europe with alternative,
           national religions.

141

    (d)   The objections raised by Reformers against the Church of Rome fostered a general attitude of resentment against a structured ecclesiastical system in northern Europe.

  *(e)   All of the above.

3.   One of the following statements incorrectly implies that the religious cause of the Protestant Revolution was

    (a)   a reaction against the worldliness of some popes and bishops and rebellion against abuses in the Church.

    (b)   the widespread appeal of Augustianian doctrines, which stressed spiritual rather than material realities and seemed best suited to an age in which people were routinely exposed to forces beyond their control.

  *(c)   tied to the strong influence of the thought of northern humanism, which, through the writings of Erasmus and More, was linked to Pauline Christianity.

    (d)   particular rejection of Catholic reformers who preached the Scholastic doctrines of St. Thomas.

    (e)   a desire to return to the simplicity of more primitive Christianity as sanctioned in the Bible and by the fathers of the Church.

4.   The political causes of the Protestant Revolution included

    (a)   the development of a spontaneous sense of national pride and a growing spirit of independence among all peoples outside Italy, a process begun during the late Middle Ages.

    (b)   a powerful resentment of an ecclesiastical system that was largely Italian in character yet exercised substantial authority within the developing national states.

    (c)   the rise of absolute monarchs whose political ambitions could not tolerate the exclusion of religion from their control.

    (d)   the revival of Roman law which suggested that people had delegated all their power to a ruler whose authority should not be challenged by the head of a foreign religion.

  *(e)   all of the above.

5.   Augustinianism, the Reformers' religious ideal, rested upon

    (a)   a belief in the necessity of good works to supplement faith and complete the Christian code of conduct.

    (b)   a belief that the sacraments were essential to the communication of God's grace to humanity.

(c)   the authority of priests—derived from the Apostle Peter—to forgive sins and perform the miracle of the Eucharist.

(d)   the concept of heavenly grace without which humans were believed incapable of avoiding evil and, therefore, without which they would have no chance for eternal salvation.

*(e)   conceptions of original sin and the omnipotence of God, who has pre-destined the fate of human beings regardless of their deeds.

6.   St. Thomas's theological system, which became the popular religious doctrine during the late Middle Ages and against which Reformers rebelled, taught that

*(a)   humans are endowed with freedom of will to choose between good and evil.

(b)   sinners do not need the ministrations of a priest in order to gain God's saving grace.

(c)   faith in an omnipotent God suffices to shed the bondage of human depravity.

(d)   veneration of relics and invocations of the saints will not procure salvation.

(e)   sacraments are mere symbols and, therefore, are unnecessary appendages to essential, true faith.

7.   Scholastic philosophers' arguments concerning business are described by the following statements. Which one is *incorrect*?

(a)   The charging of interest on loans is sinful. It is contrary to nature since it enables the lender to live without labor.

(b)   Merchants and manufacturers should be satisfied with "wages" as recompense for the services they render.

(c)   All excess profit is to be distributed to the poor and needy.

*(d)   Only Muslims and Jews should be permitted to engage in moneylending because they are not members of the Church.

(e)   To take advantage of a business rival or a wage earner is contrary to laws of morality.

8.   Obsessed with the idea of his sinfulness, Luther finally concluded that

(a)   salvation lies in good works.

*(b)   by faith, and faith alone, rather than by good works humans can be justified in the sight of God.

(c)   the sacraments of Baptism and Eucharist are instruments essential to God's imparting grace to humans.

(d)   in order to merit salvation, one's love of God has to be continually demonstrated by extreme ascetic practices and contemplative life.

(e)   just as Christ humbled himself on the cross for the benefit of humanity, humans must humble themselves in this life to gain benefits in an afterlife.

9.   The Anabaptists taught that

    (a)   the sacrament of Baptism is ineffectual and should, therefore, be eliminated entirely from the rites of the Church.

  *(b)   the clergy's traditional role in guiding people toward slavation is useless and ineffective; rather, every individual should follow the guidance of the "inner light."

    (c)   —when necessary—each person should be willing to take up arms and fight for the creation of a new Jerusalem upon earth.

    (d)   all goods owned by individuals were not to be shared by the community.

    (e)   God's revelation to humanity ceased with the last book of the New Testament.

10.   The most feasible explanation for the success of Calvin's concept of predestination is hinted at by which of the following statements?

    (a)   The universe is utterly depending on the will of the Almighty.

  *(b)   Evidence that a person is one of God's elect might be indicated by relative success in life through moral conduct, active piety, and zeal.

    (c)   Humans are predestined by God's will, some for eternal salvation and others for the torments of hell.

    (d)   Nothing can alter the otherworldly fate of human beings, neither good works nor divine grace.

    (e)   Only the Congregation of the Clergy is able to exemplify proper human conduct on this earth.

11.   As an essential part of the great religious movement of the late Middle Ages, the inception of the Catholic Reformation

    (a)   or the so-called Counter-Reformation, originated with military campaigns of popes to check the growth of Protestantism.

    (b)   was fueled by Cardinal Ximenes's teachings: With the aid of the Jesuits Ximenes implemented reform programs in order to eliminate abuses in the Iberian Church.

  *(c)   in the late fifteenth century began with the persistence of pious Catholics in Spain and Italy who wanted both to make the priests of their Church more worthy of their calling and to strengthen religious conviction among the faithful.

(d) was focused primarily on heretics, Jews, and Muslims in southern Europe.

(e) none of the above.

12. Meeting at intervals between 1545 and 1643, the popes and their bishops attending the Council of Trent responded to inroads made by the Protestant Revolution upon Catholic congregations. The final resolution of the council

(a) suggested means for conciliation with all Protestant churches with the goal of reestablishing conformity and unity of beliefs.

(b) permitted and even encouraged the growth of Protestantism as a national church so long as mutual cooperation could be maintained.

*(c) redefined Catholic doctrine and reinstituted discipline in the Church.

(d) maintained both the council's superiority as the Church's governing body and the bishops' equality with the pope.

(e) suppressed inquisition in Spain and Italy and requested that the various Protestant churches likewise abolish their own inquisitional organizations.

13. The Society of Jesus was

(a) one of the chivalrous orders established to offer military assistance in enforcing decisions of the Council of Trent concerning various devotions and doctrines.

*(b) a new clerical order founded by Ignatius Loyola for the purpose of serving the Catholic Reformation through preaching, teaching, and missionary work.

(c) a militant religious organization under the iron discipline of the Calvinist congregation of the clergy in Geneva.

(d) an armed force whose companies were commanded by the Professed of the Four Vows.

(e) none of the above.

14. The German Peasants' Revolt of 1524-1525 was

(a) the first mass revolt in European history in which the lower classes sought redress of their economic and political grievances.

(b) an attempt of the urban working masses to wrest political rights from the Church and then delegate these to themselves and the peasants.

(c) a clash between workers in the German cities and German knights under the leadership of Ulrich von Hutten.

*(d) a desperate move, inspired in part by Luther's teachings, agains the rising cost of living and against concentration of land.

(e)   the first great Anabaptist attempt to create an idealistic new city of Jerusalem.

15.   As indicated in *all but one* of the statements below, the Reformers' thought and action affected European society in ways both negative and positive.

    (a)   To achieve conformity of faith, methods of inquisition and censorship of books were used by both Catholics and Protestants.

    *(b)   The recently formed religious sects were zealous in sending missionaries to proselytize newly discovered lands.

    (c)   Religious intolerance in various European states resulted in wars, revolts, and expulsion of dissenters until ca. 1800.

    (d)   The spread of education, which had been initiated in the thirteenth and fourteenth centuries, was given support by most of the religious reformers.

    (e)   New political concepts that gave foundations to truly democratic governments, which would take fuller form in modern times, were asserted and sometimes practiced by Jesuit and Protestant philosophers and activists.

IDENTIFICATIONS

Dispensation	New Act of Supremacy
Indulgence	Peace of Augsburg
Treasury of Merits	Huguenots
Statutes of Provisors	Edict of Nantes
and Praemunire	Congregation of the Index
Annates	*Institutes of the Christian Religion*
Against the Thievish, Murderous	Schmalkaldic War
Hordes of Peasants	Mennonites
Münster, A.D. 1534	

TRUE OR FALSE

T   1.   Certain Jesuit philosophers taught that the law of nature puts literature on the power of rulers, that authority of the secular ruler is derived from the people, and that tyrants may be killed in extraordinary circumstances.

F   2.   Basic political changes during the late Middle Ages and parallel growth of economic interests in Europe were the main causes that sparked an emerging religious movement of Europe into a full-scale Protestant Revolution.

T   3.   A law of 1438 in France abolished papal rights to raise revenue there and gave power to civil magistrates to regulate religious affairs in their administrative districts.

T   4.   Ulrich von Hutten and Franz von Sickingen, leaders of the rebellion of knights, dreamed of a united Germany freed from interference by the Church.

F   5.   Thomas Munzer started the Peasants' Revolt in 1524 at Martin Luther's instigation.

T   6.   Calvinist theology required a life of piety and morality and encouraged its followers to engage in worldly activities for the glory of God.

F   7.   Independence of Swiss cantons was first achieved after the appearance of Zwingli and Calvin.

T   8.   The revolt of the Netherlands resulted in the establishment of the independent Dutch Republic, freed from Spanish dominion.

F   9.   Michael Servetus was a victim of the Roman Inquisition.

F   10. In 1521 the Imperial Diet at Worms granted full freedom of conscience to all Germans.

DISCUSSION AND/OR ESSAY QUESTIONS

1.   The culture of the Renaissance was accompanied by the movement of the Reformation, although one cannot justifiably conclude that the Reformation was a part of the Renaissance. How does the Renaissance concept of religion differ from the religious spirit of the Reformers?

2.   Why did Augustinianism have such appeal for Luther and his followers?

3.   Describe the process by which the Church in England became Protestant.

4.   What are the economic causes for the emergence and success of Protestantism in Germany?

5.   What are the essential and specific differences between Calvinism and Lutheranism?

SUGGESTED FILMS

The Christians: Protest and Reform (1485-1561). 39 min. Color. McGraw-Hill Films (1979).

Civilization: Protest and Communication. 2 parts, each 26 min. Color. Time-Life Films, Inc. (1970).

English History: Tudor Period. 11 min. B/w; c. Coronet Instructional Films (1954).

John Calvin. 29 min. B/w. (From the Christian Philosophy series.) University of Utah, Educational Media Center (1962).

Matthew Merian. 14 min. B/w. Roland Films. (n.d.).

M. Luther and the Protestant Reformation. 30 min. B/w. Time-Life Films, Inc. (1969).

The Reformation. 14 min. B/w; c. Coronet Instructional Films (1955).

The Reformation–Age of Revolt. 24 min. Color. (From the Humanities–Philosophy and Political Thought series.) Encyclopedia Educational Corp./Films (1973).

Outline

MULTIPLE CHOICE
Choose the best response.

1. What motivation did kings have during the fifteenth and sixteenth centuries and
    afterward to commission mariners to initiate voyages of discovery?

    (a) Adventurous persons were willing to take extraordinary risks to find
         untapped sources of wealth, gain personal fame, and advance the mercan-
         tilist ambitions of their national monarchies.

    (b) Motivated by the momentum of religious fervor, many pious individuals
         had joined mendicant orders and had volunteered to work as missionaries
         among the "heathen" for the glory of God and their kings.

    (c) Neoplatonic concepts of the universe that still flourished in the fifteenth
         century impressed humanists—among them some of the European kings—
         to try to disprove the theory that the earth is flat.

    *(d) Discovering a new route to the Orient would mean that the claimants of
         such a route could challenge the monopoly of Venice and Genoa in the
         Mediterranean trade with the East.

    (e) Recent discovery of the compass and the astrolabe had allowed experienced
         sailors to undertake voyages into the open sea, a challenge that had been
         inconceivable in earlier times.

2. Which of the following was *not* a result of the overseas expansion?

    (a) The spirit of competition between north Italian commercial cities, the
         Hansa League and newly emerging commercial centers of northern Europe
         decreased when the volume of commercial goods and demand for these
         goods increased.

    (b) The Mediterranean trade that Italian cities maintained was expanded
         across the seven seas into a world enterprsie.

    (c)   The centers and activity of European commerce shifted to those states adjacent to the Atlantic, first to Portugal and Spain and later to England, France, and Holland.

*(d)   Increased economic opportunity, technological discoveries, and better and cheaper methods of production revolutionized European economic life.

    (e)   Revolutionary improvements in agricultural techniques and the introduction of new crops imported from the colonies were chief among changes in Europe that allowed the Industrial Revolution of the nineteenth century to develop.

3.   Which of the following statements can be considered a positive effect—at least in some respects—of overseas expansion in starting the Commercial Revolution in Europe?

    (a)   Massive imports of silver from Mexico, Peru, and Bolivia initiated a tremendous inflation which proportionately reduced workers' and peasants' buying power and contributed to numerous bankruptcies in major medieval businesses.

    (b)   Germany's silver-mining industry was ruined by the depreciation of silver, and, consequently, the foundations of the German economy were shattered.

    (c)   Initial Spanish economic preeminence could not be maintained because Spain was unable to provide the manufactured goods needed by European colonists in the Western world.

*(d)   Agricultural specialization in the latter part of the late Middle Ages and the resultant growth of northern cities created new commercial and trade centers, with easy access to New World colonies.

    (e)   New markets and new opportunities contributed to the development of a capitalistic mentality, which ruthlessly introduced revolutionary changes in economics while seeking efficiency and profits.

4.   The Commercial Revolution included all the following characteristics *except*

    (a)   development of capitalism as an economic system and new business organizations, both for the sake of profit.

    (b)   the growth of private and government banks to serve the monetary needs of individuals and the national states.

    (c)   changes in the modes of production that substantially increased the volume of commodities for markets and reduced costs.

*(d)   legislation that stabilized wild fluctuations in prices and profits, introduced a completely new, carefully balanced relationship between employer and employee, and provided living wages to urban and rural workers.

(e) steps toward adoption of a standard monetary system by most states, an innovation that greatly contributed to a more efficient money economy.

5. Which statement concerning the Commercial Revolution is correct?

*(c) The domestic, or putting-out, system guaranteed the greatest degree of freedom to the worker and eliminated fear of dismissal from employment for petty reasons.

(b) The guild system provided adequate defense against the attempts of dishonest employers to cheat workers out of their wages or to pay them in goods.

(c) All individuals had sufficient opportunities to acquire raw materials and tools that enabled them to start their own, even if small, businesses and eventually enter the rising middle class.

(d) The economic well-being of most individuals rose once equal distribution of profits in the joint-stock companies was instituted.

(e) Technological advances in new industries substantially reduced the risks of accidents connected with manufacturing.

6. All but one of the following statements describe the impact of the Commercial Revolution on the lower classes. What is the exception?

(a) Being dependent upon the capitalists, workers under the domestic system were unable to organize effectively for common action and so were occasionally forced to work in central shops and comply with fixed routines, not much differently from workers in early modern factories.

(b) In order to provide manpower for economic and military growth of the nation, French laws provided economic advantages to the heads of large families.

(c) Economic boom and recession cycles, as well as liberal extensions of credit and frequent defaults on loans, wrought impoverishment in the cities and brought vagrancy and banditry to the rural areas.

(d) Although improvements were made in the living conditions of most Europeans, slavery and serfdom were resurrected in the colonies and in the eastern parts of Europe.

*(e) Many Europeans found relief from oppressive economic conditions by joining various monastic orders as monks or nuns.

7. Mercantilist attitudes toward the lower classes are best explained in which of the following theories?

(a) Government should guard the life of its citizens, provide free medical care, and take care of the poor.

(b)   Newly explored territories should be settled by citizens in order to develop colonies and so provide raw materials for the production of commodities in the homeland.

(c)   Enclosures will improve landlords' flexibility to experiment with new and better farming methods and will eventually increase agricultural production without the help of tenant farmers and peasants.

(d)   Some advocates of mercantilist policy urged governments to initiate public-works projects and provide funds for the relief of the poor.

*(e)   All the statements above. Each considers the lower classes necessary to secure the wealth of the nation and, thus, to make it strong.

8.   The economic system of mercantilism was

(a)   a set of economic and political doctrines and practices that accompanied the later stages of the Commercial Revolution.

(b)   a policy of the newly emerging, wealthy middle-class merchants and manufacturers who encouraged and supported trade directed by the state.

(c)   a system of government intervention to promote national prosperity, to increase the power of the state, and to make the state respected throughout the world.

(d)   a policy to protect infant industries committed to production of commodities for profit, thereby helping the state reach national self-sufficiency.

*(e)   all of the above.

9.   With one exception, the majority of those who wrote on mercantilism

(a)   supported the growth of absolute monarchy instead of feudalism's weak, decentralized structure of governance.

(b)   advocated a policy somewhat similar to modern concepts of government spending in order to stimulate business.

(c)   were interested in various theories by which a favorable balance of trade could be devised.

*(d)   argued that a favorable balance of trade is possible only through international cooperation of colonial powers.

(e)   wished to increase the prosperity of all classes within the country.

10.   The policies of mercantilism were brought to full realization in

(a)   the administration of Queen Elizabeth I of England, who strengthened English colonies, gave monopolistic privileges to the trading companies, and generally controlled the economic activities of all citizens.

(b)   the absolutism of the Spanish kings, who used to their best advantage the flow of silver and gold from the kingdom's newly acquired colonies.

(c) the Hohenzollern kings of Prussia, who intervened and controlled the economic sphere in Germany in order to maintain the strongest and best-equipped standing army in Europe.

*(d) Jean Baptiste Colbert's application of mercantilistic principles to increase the wealth and power of France and to gain his absolute sovereign's approval.

(e) the successful economic expansion of the British and the Dutch East India Companies, which controlled territories larger than those of the chartering homelands.

11. The governments of England, France, Spain, and the various German kingdoms and principalities applied mercantilistic principles to their economies. Which statement does *not* apply to all of the above-mentioned states?

(a) Various tariffs and bounties controlled the export and import of goods, with the chief aim of maintaining a balance of trade favorable to the homeland.

*(b) Colonies and colonial empires were essential to the realization of a true mercantilistic philosophy.

(c) To gain self-sufficiency, industries were fostered and manufacturers were occasionally subsidized and often extensively regulated.

(d) Regulations and laws tended to interfere in the most private affairs of people on the precept that these measures were necessary to secure a reliable work force for local industry and agriculture.

(e) The power of money was esteemed, and profit and acquisition of wealth were encouraged throughout the time of the Commercial Revolution. By these gratuitous means the state's power and the absolute ruler's fame were seen to increase also.

12. Which statement describes a decisive result of the Commercial Revolution?

(a) By the end of the eighteenth century international ownership within joint-stock companies had overstepped national boundaries and had substantially weakened local and regional loyalties.

*(b) The rise of a well-to-do European middle class transferred European cultural values to the colonies, which were soon regarded as appendages to Europe.

(c) Increased concern for the well-being of the working classes and interest in incorporating new technological discoveries into the manufacturing process all but eliminated the incentive or perceived need to use slaves within the work force.

(d) International economic cooperation eased tensions between states and diffused the religious strife of the Reformation period.

(e)   A substantial rise in standards of living enabled the lower classes to voice their grievances, receive a hearing, and then effectively cooperate through elected representatives in the governmental procesess of their various national states.

13.   Which of the following long-range results of the Commercial Revolution had the greatest impact on the nineteenth century?

(a)   Many elements of the Commercial Revolution were responsible for the introduction of a capitalist mentality and the rise of a class of capitalists who constantly sought opportunities to invest their surplus profits.

(b)   Colonial empires provided certain commodities at reasonable prices to all segments of the homeland populations, products that until the seventeenth century were luxuries because of their absence from or scarcity in Europe.

(c)   A growing demand for manufactured goods established a trend toward the adoption of a factory method of production, which, coupled with technological improvements, inevitably led to the Industrial Revolution.

(d)   Mercantilist policy encouraged new industries that were totally independent from the medieval guild system.

*(e)   New crops and farming methods radically reduced the mortality rate due to starvation, and population started to increase in the nineteenth century as never before.

14.   The enclosure movement is best described in which statement?

*(a)   The enclosure movement—one of the significant effects of the Commercial Revolution—may be regarded as the fencing off of lands without regard for the traditional holdings of the peasants.

(b)   The necessity of "scientific farming" and sheep raising for profit motivated landlords to set aside certain lands for such purposes.

(c)   Parliamentary "acts of enclosure" in England redistributed all lands into fenced parcels among landowning aristocrats without the consent of the Crown and Parliament.

(d)   Cooperation between landlords and dependent peasants, according to contemporary practices of mercantilistic paternalism, brought about an agricultural revolution that was a prerequisite for the success of the Industrial Revolution.

(e)   None of the above.

15.   The new society of the Commercial Revolution is *best* characterized by the

(a)   increase of population in the cities and the emergence of new urban centers.

(b)   disappearance of small shops and the subsequent emergence of large mechanized factories.

(c)   triumph of urbanism, which provided income and leisure time and managed to structure the beginnings of economic and social equality among all classes.

*(d) pursuit of self-interest and egosim along with an indifference to human suffering that did not permit generosity toward less fortunate human beings.

(e)   reduction in the agricultural work force since commercial and industrial centers could support practically unlimited numbers of people.

IDENTIFICATIONS

Tariffs and bounties
Astrolabe
The Fuggers of Augsburg
Merchant Adventurers
Statism
Bullionism
The first and second
   Navigation Acts
Cameralists

Dynamic economy
Economic nationalism
The Mississippi Bubble and the
   South Sea Bubble
Jean Bodin and Thomas Hobbes
Chippendale and Hepplewhite
Coffee house
The London Company

TRUE OR FALSE

F   1.   Rapid advances in geographic knowledge and technological expertise after 1490 made it possible for European travelers to reach America and the Far East.

F   2.   A uniform monetary system was established in France by Cartier after the discovery and exploitation of the St. Lawrence River area.

T   3.   The English queen Elizabeth I authorized justices of the peace to fix prices, regulate hours of labor, and—to eliminate idleness—compel every able-bodied person to work.

F   4.   As a result of the Commercial Revolution, the economic power of the middle classes easily turned into political supremacy by the end of the seventeenth century.

F   5.   Enslavement of Native Americans was unsuccessful because of their fierce resistance and outstanding tactical ability against European military forces.

T   6.   Mercantilistic imperialism revolved around the notion that colonies exist for the benefit of the homeland and, therefore, must not engage in manufacture and/or shipping, potential sources of profit that the mother country reserves for itself.

F 7. The mining and smelting industries remained under the traditional operation of the ironmongers' guild.

T 8. "Turnip" Townshend was one of the first advocates of the eighteenth-century English enclosure movement.

F 9. The credit facilities provided by modern banking did not yet exist in sixteenth- and seventeenth-century finance.

F 10. Regulated companies were formed through the issues of shares of capital to a considerable number of investors.

DISCUSSION AND/OR ESSAY QUESTIONS

1. "The ordinary means therefore to encrease our wealth and treasure is by *Forraign Trade*, wherein wee must ever observe this rule: to sell more to strangers yearly than wee consume of theirs in value."
   —Thomas Mun, *England's Treasure by Forraign Trade*
   How does this quotation represent English mercantilism?

2. Define *capitalism*. How did concepts of capitalism influence the development of the banking industry and industrial production during the sixteenth and seventeenth centuries?

3. Discuss the origin and purpose of the various business organizations during the Commercial Revolution. What was their role in the development of the colonies? What was their contribution to mercantilistic concepts and practices?

4. Detail the deliberate mercantilistic policies of Jean Baptiste Colbert.

5. Discuss the agricultural revolution during the eighteenth century. How can this revolution be considered a necessary prerequisite for the Industrial Revolution?

SUGGESTED FILMS

The Age of Exploration and Expansion. 17 min. Color. Centron Educational Films (1971).

The Christians: The Conquest of Souls (1492-1588). 39 min. Color. McGraw-Hill Films (1979).

The Christians: In Search of Tolerance (1526-1682). 39 min. Color. McGraw-Hill Films (1979).

Civilization: Grandeur and Obedience. 2 parts, each 26 min. Color. Time-Life-Films, Inc. (1970).

Colonial Expansion of European Nations. 13 min. B/w; c. Coronet Instructional Films (1955).

Cortez and the Legend. 52 min. Color. McGraw-Hill Films (1968).

South to the Strait of Magellan. 12 min. Color. Association–Sterling Films (1975).

Ten Who Dared: Christopher Columbus. 30 min. Color. Time-Life Films, Inc. (1977).

Ten Who Dared: Francisco Pizarro. 30 min. Color. Time-Life Films, Inc. (1977).

Outline

MULTIPLE CHOICE

Choose the best response.

1. With one exception, all the following correctly assert that in the later Middle Ages strong monarchs in western Europe

    (a) both eliminated regional fragmentation and opposition of the provincial nobility and, as absolute rulers, attempted to develop untrammeled monarchical power in place of the decentralized medieval system.

    (b) enhanced their political power by the adoption of prevailing mercantilistic theories and through the royal support they extended to the merchant-class practitioners of these theories.

    (c) expanded bureaucracy in their governments, especially in military and foreign-policy operations, with the aid of increased revenues from colonies and new taxable industries.

    *(d) were greatly influenced by the philosophical and theological arguments of the humanists, who argued for the exercise of unlimited authority as a divinely granted duty.

    (e) fostered Protestant ideals in order to eliminate the last vestiges of a waning papal overlordship and to gain full control over religious as well as civil affairs.

2. In the most general terms, absoulte monarchs

    (a) ruled arbitrarily, like oriental pharaohs or caliphs, in imitation of the despotic administration of the Ottoman Empire.

    (b) completely controlled their aristocracies and merchant classes by issuing decrees that did not require justification and, therefore, could be readily enforced.

*(c)   usually respected due process of law and tradition, which they broke only in exceptional circumstances.

(d)   interfered in the lives of their citizens, much as modern dictators have done, with the intention of elevating people from a "solitary, poor, nasty, brutish" existence.

(e)   maintained a loyal military organization that doubled as a domestic police force able to implement the monarchs' edicts.

3.   Absolutistic tendencies were defeated before 1789 in England alone, because

(a)   the Commercial Revolution had greatly aided the growth of a new class of English merchants and entrepreneurs, whose wealth and commercial success provided the tax base of royal appropriations.

(b)   the geographic isolation and sea shelter of England eliminated the need or justification to maintain huge, professional armies, which rulers might then have used to control domestic protests.

(c)   the lack of consistent religious policy in England was provocation for radical Protestants to protest royal whims.

*(d)   no other country had a group similar to Parliament that was involved in the royal decision-making process and could stand as an effective barrier to potential absolutism.

(e)   the ideals of limited government as expressed in the Magna Carta were never entirely destroyed during the period of royal dynastic absolutism, and extreme absolutistic principles did not appeal to the English, usually not even to traditionalist adherents of the monarchy.

4.   Responsibility for the outbreak of civil strife in England that led to the abolition of absolute royal power rests *mainly* with

(a)   members of the Parliament. For some time parliamentary representatives had permitted the Tudor monarchs to regulate their consciences through cajolery, bullying, or flattery, thus abdicating their duties as representatives and granting monarchs substantial, if not nominal, absolute power.

(b)   James I and Charles I. These monarchs insisted that the English accept the theories of monarchical absolute power and attempted to actualize the broad-sweeping powers these theories implied.

(c)   radical Protestants. These Protestants, later evolving into several factions, had come under Calvinist influence while in France during the reign of Mary Tudor and considered the Elizabethan Compromise unsatisfactory.

(d)   Sabbatarian Puritans and Scottish Presbyterians. These sects resented the imposition of an arbitrary system of religious administration under Charles I.

*(e) members of the House of Commons. Many House representatives were small landholders, tradesmen and manufacturers, either Puritan or Presbyterian, or else sympathetic to Calvinistic theories of predestination, economic success, and social activism.

5. The failure of the Puritan Revolution was due to

(a) active resistance by the chief Catholic and Anglican nobles and landowners who wished to revenge the execution of Charles I.

(b) armed rebellion instigated by the 143 Presbyterians protesting the Protectorate of Richard Cromwell and supported by dismissed members of the Rump Parliament.

(c) the radical political and economic platforms of the Levelers and Diggers, which were given a sympathetic hearing by the majority of the population.

*(d) general dissatisfaction with the administration of Oliver Cromwell which was more sovereign and absolute than that of any Stuart monarch.

(e) most people's desire for relief from the austerities of the Calvinist life style forced upon them by zealots and enforced by soldiers.

6. From an international perspective, which conclusion is acceptable? The Glorious Revolution

(a) motivated the English Parliament to pass numerous laws to safeguard the rights of the English and to protect citizens from monarchical autocracy.

(b) established the Parliament's authority over the king in all legislative and juridical matters.

*(c) established the ideal of limited government in England and inspired many opponents of absolutism to create governments according to the English example.

(d) eliminated the theory of divine right of kings, since the Parliament was clearly responsible for the crowning of William and Mary, whom it decided upon as successors to James II.

(e) prepared the way for royal succession based upon parliamentary consensus.

7. What European political belief might be considered an influencing factor in establishing the independent authority of the U.S. Supreme Court?

(a) Only the law of God contains those universal principles of elementary justice and morality that are above the laws of peoples.

*(b) When an act of a parliament violates the conclusions of common right and reason, the common law will be applied and will adjudge such an act void.

(c) A governmental agency—whether a ruler or a parliament—to whom people have voluntarily surrendered part or all of their rights has thus been invested with unlimited authority to govern.

(d) Sovereignty inheres in the people, and government should rest on the consent of the governed.

(e) The law of nature provides equal political rights for individuals, rights that can be safeguarded only by an authoritative governing body that operates with the consent of the governed.

8. Which of the following political ideologies *least* reflects the exalted notions Louis XIV had of himself as an absolute monarch?

(a) Princes are bound only by the natural and moral laws of God, and, therefore, no legislative body has the right to impose limits on their power.

*(b) Predestined for eternal bliss, the prince is God's chosen instrument for fulfilling His plans on earth and must rule absolutely, without interference or opposition from subjects.

(c) Only a single ruler endowed with absolute power will be able to help the nation grow strong, independent, and self-sufficient.

(d) Since people at the beginnings of organized society gave up all their rights to the ruler in exchange for an expected degree of security, the ruler is entitled to govern despotically.

(e) Regardless of whether people initially surrendered their rights voluntarily or were compelled to do so for the sake of social order, continued order in society is impossible without the investment of unlimited authority in a ruler.

9. Assertion of which claim contributed most effectively to the erosion of absolutism?

(a) Just as it is blasphemous to dispute what God can do, so it is presumptuous and contemptible to dispute what a king can do.

(b) "The powers that be are ordained of God."

*(c) As the chosen people of God, Calvinists must play a part in the drama of the universe for the furtherance of God's plans.

(d) Kings are justly called gods, for they resemble in their actions divine power upon earth.

(e) The authority of the king is clearly derived from God, and the supreme obligation of people is to obey divine authority.

10. The growth of royal absolutism resulted in wars prompted by the

(a) militant policies of the Duke of Guise, leader of the Huguenots, with full support of English Puritans and Scottish Presbyterians.

(b) European merchant classes' greed for increased profits that motivated them to participate in liberating Netherland deep-water ports from the punitive tariffs of Philip II.

(c)   defensive measures taken by the Holy Roman emperor, Ferdinand I, against Mongol and Turkish invasions.

*(d)   religious differences and dynastic ambitions, which continued to be major factors in the progression of struggles for supremacy among powerful European autocrats.

(e)   Hapsburg rulers' new acquisitions in Spain, which had given them tactical advantages for gaining ascendancy over France.

11.   A most significant result of the Seven Years' War was the

(a)   equal division of Silesia between Prussia and Austria.

*(b)   loss of the French Empire in America and the emergence of Britain as the supreme colonial power of the world.

(c)   end of religious warfare in Europe and the onset of comparative peace throughout the world.

(d)   resolution of all differences between the Bourbons and the Hapsburgs, achieved when the Hapsburgs assented to Bourbon succession to the Spanish throne.

(e)   incorporation of Lithuania into greater Russia and the ultimate withdrawal of the Mongols beyond the Ural Range.

12.   One of the outcomes of the age of absolutism was the development of the modern state system, best characterized by

(a)   broadening of the tax power and the extension of judicial authority, first steps in achieving sovereignty in the modern sense.

*(b)   the principle that all states, as established by the Treaty of Westphalia, were equal and independent, whether small or large, and able to pursue independent foreign policy and use diplomacy to avoid war.

(c)   the repudiation of the authority of a universal church and the acquisition of complete power by princes and kings.

(d)   successful governmental intervention in the national economies to increase the power of a state and make it respected throughout the world.

(e)   none of the above.

13.   Which of the statements below does *not* describe consequences of the War of the Spanish Succession?

(a)   The war left France and Great Britain the two major powers in Europe.

(b)   It gave Britain the authority—stipulated in the Asiento—to provide Spanish America with slaves and opened the way for British merchants to make Britain the richest nation on earth.

*(c)   Religious contention between nations was halted, and the power of rulers over the Church was firmly established by the Peace of Utrecht.

(d)   The claims of smaller nations to sovereign equality with their larger and more powerful neighbors seemed less meaningful after the War of the Spanish Succession and its intense competitions for control of the world's commerce and seas.

(e)   The importance of Holland and Spain as world powers abated after the war, while the Hohenzollerns of Brandenburg were elevated to kings of Prussia.

14.   With one exception, each of the following is a general characteristic of governmental politics formulated by the so-called enlightened despots, who

(a)   followed the new rationalist philosophers in France and wanted to implement reforms based on reason.

(b)   were directed in their governmental practices by what they conceived to be the highest ideals of reason and justice.

(c)   attempted to lower the status of nobles, reduce the power of the clergy, and improve living conditions for the masses both of cities and of rural communities.

(d)   aimed to make education available to all persons, regardless of social or economic background.

*(e)   earnestly endeavored by diplomatic and military means to force colonial powers to abolish slavery.

15.   Which of the following statements *best* describes the results of Russian absolutism?

(a)   The development of Russia as a national state was greatly impeded by Mongol threats during the High and later Middle Ages.

(b)   The Europeanization of Russia was initiated by Ivan the Great, who claimed himself the sovereign of "all Russia" by incorporating Lithuania, Poland, and Hungary into his domain.

(c)   Peter the Great established close contacts with the West after defeating the Teutonic Knights and pushing the Tartars out of northern Russia.

(d)   Extravagance and cruelty characterizes the enlightened despotism of Catherine the Great, which was based on absolutism with force, the secret police, and extensive bureaucracy.

*(e)   While Peter the Great introduced Russia to Western ideas, Catherine the Great succeeded in making Russia into a great power in European affairs.

IDENTIFICATIONS

Despot
Totalitarianism
Puritans
Separatists
Gunpowder Plot
Petition of Rights
Instrument of Government
The cabinet system

Concordat of Bologna
Intendants
"Invincible Armada"
Drang nach Osten
Leviathan
Law of War and Peace
Treaty of Westphalia

TRUE OR FALSE

F　1. For not accepting Anglicanism, John Hampden was convicted by the royal court of Charles I, and after execution was venerated as a martyr and a symbol of resistance to autocratic royal power.

T　2. Poland was dismembered by Catherine the Great, Frederick the Great, and Maria Theresa at the end of the Seven Years' War.

F　3. Frederick the Great, convinced by the new rationalist philosophy of his friend, the French philosopher Voltaire, tolerated all religious beliefs.

F　4. The term "absolutism" as practiced in western Europe is synonymous with "despotism" and "totalitarianism."

T　5. One of the most unpopular methods Charles I used to collect revenues was the "ship money," a special tax collected from all seaboard cities and inland counties for the maintenance of the royal navy.

F　6. As a result of the Glorious Revolution the Toleration Act granted religious liberty to all Christians.

F　7. The Bill of Rights reasserted all stipulations of the Petition of Right of 1628.

T　8. The Act of Settlement of 1701 assured the succession of Protestants to the throne of England.

F　9. English victory in the Seven Years' War obliterated Hohenzollern plans for future colonial expansion.

F　10. "Quieta non movere" was a political principle of King George III of England, with which he succeeded in maintaining English supremacy in the world.

DISCUSSION AND/OR ESSAY QUESTIONS

1. "There are four essential characteristics or qualities of royal authority. First, royal authority is sacred.

Second, it is paternal.

Third, it is absolute.

Fourth, it is subject to reason."

    —Jacques Bossuet, *Politics Drawn from the Very Words of Holy Scripture*
How does the statement above reflect the last three Bourbon kings' practices of absolutism? Did these practices effect the French Revolution? Why?

2. Describe the major features of the struggle between the Hapsburgs and the Bourbons. What were the reasons for the struggle, and how were the problems resolved?

3. To what degree did religion influence the outcome of the struggle between king and Parliament in England?

4. Discuss the development of absolutism in Prussia, Austria, and Russia. Why do we consider some of the rulers in these countries enlightened monarchs?

5. How did the age of absolutism contribute to the development of the modern state system?

SUGGESTED FILMS

The Age of Absolute Monarchs in Europe. 14 min. B/w; c. Coronet Instructional Films (1965).

Age of Elizabeth. 30 min. Color. Encyclopaedia Britannica Educational Corp./Films (1959).

Catherine the Great—a Profile in Power. 26 min. Color. Learning Corporation of America (1976).

The Christians: Politeness and Enthusiasm (1689-1791). 39 min. Color. McGraw-Hill Films (1979).

English History: Absolutism and Civil War. 11 min. B/w; c. Coronet Instructional Films (1958).

The London of William Hogarth. 27 min. B/w. McGraw-Hill Films (1956).

Puritan Revolution: Cromwell and the Rise of Parliamentary Democracy. 33 min. Color. Learning Corporation of America (1972).

Racine. 20 min. B/w. McGraw-Hill Films (1969).

Royal Rococo (1725-1850). 12 min. Color. Time-Life Films, Inc. (1970).

The Sun King. 30 min. B/w. National Education TV, Inc.; Indiana University Audio-Visual Center (1965).

Outline

MULTIPLE CHOICE

Choose the best response.

1.   Locke's approach to knowledge is stated in one of the following.

   (a)   One must directly observe nature, precisely note facts about things, and, by induction, discover laws that govern them.

   (b)   By building upon simple, self-evident truths, one can deduce a sound body of universal knowledge.

   (c)   There are no self-evident truths inherent in the mind; the origin of all knowledge is sense perception.

   *(d)   Reason has the power to combine and coordinate impressions received from the senses and, in this manner, form a body of general truth.

   (e)   The universe, as well as humanity, is assumed to be governed by a set of rational, natural laws, knowledge of which will assure the progress of the human race.

2.   A high point in the mechanistic interpretations of the universe is to be found in which of the following propositions?

   (a)   The whole universe can be defined by extension and motion, and human behavior flows automatically from internal and external stimuli.

   (b)   The universe is but a beautiful machine with a fixed and harmonious order that humans cannot change.

   (c)   Since there is nothing spiritual anywhere in the universe that the mind can discover, the universe, as well as humanity, can be explained in terms of its incessant mechanical operations.

166

*(d)   All measurable motion within the universe is assumed to be an attraction of every particle of matter to every other particle of matter according to the measurable force of gravity.

(e)   Careful investigation will assist men and women in mastering the world in which they live.

3.   Which of the following theories most thoroughly challenged and modified traditional ideas concerning God, human existence, and the universe during the age of the intellectual revolution?

(a)   Human beings must doubt all knowledge received from past thinkers because former seekers of truth had been prisoners of preconceived notions concerning truth, or else were sidetracked by inadequate Scholastic logic.

(b)   By means of the mathematical instrument of pure deduction, humans must systematically question, in terms of self-evident truth, each sense impression received.

(c)   Geometry, not authority, tradition, or syllogistic logic, can furnish the only proper methods to discover philosophical truth.

(d)   Since the human mind at birth is a *tabula rasa*, reasonable men and women cannot live intelligently on the basis of beliefs that are the fortuitous combinations of "reason."

*(e)   It is the task of philosophers, scientists, and all thoughtful people to rethink the validity of opinions received from the past and to shape the future of society according to rational conclusions.

4.   The baroque style developed

*(a)   from artists', thinkers', and writers' inspiration to selectively adopt classical concepts and combine these forms by using imaginative ways to enhance the classical ideals of grandeur, order, and reason.

(b)   in the work of Lorenzo Bernini and Christopher Wren as an architectural style intended to inspire reverence and respect for the Catholic and Reformed churches.

(c)   within the courts of Louis XIV and other absolute rulers, who wanted to express the absolute power invested in the person of the king and to emphasize the formality of his station.

(d)   in the work of Peter Paul Rubens and his followers, who wished to please contemporary affluent merchants and nobles and to gloriously represent the increased prosperity of their day.

(e)   among the artists of the intellectual revolution, who followed contemporary popular conceptions concerning received knowledge and who rejected Renaissance formalism and exaggerated naturalism.

5. One of the following is *not* a trend characteristic of the Enlightenment:

   (a) the emphasis upon the rejection of superstition in the classical tradition, while ignoring elements in that tradition that emanated from ignorance and intolerance.

   (b) the insistence upon the dramatic, robust vitality of the age as seen in the operas of Monteverdi, the paintings of Rubens, and the architecture of Bernini.

   (c) the extraordinary confidence in the inclination and ability of men and women to examine their world critically, but the dismissal of the possibility of "heaven" as unknowable.

   *(d) an assertion of the natural superiority of Western society over all other less developed societies.

   (e) the inherent belief in the power of knowledge by which the world of the future might be progressively improved.

6. Popular beliefs of the seventeenth and eighteenth centuries were challenged by prominent thinkers. Which statement correctly reflects one of these challenges?

   *(a) The revival of reason and the influence of scientists gradually worked to eliminate superstitions and mass accusations of witchcraft.

   (b) Both Isaac Newton and Francis Bacon raised their voices against superstition and the cruelty of various churches which tortured those who dared to question the churches' traditional opinions transmitted as doctrine.

   (c) At Calvin's insistence, witch trials were eliminated among all Protestants in Geneva, as well as among the Huguenots in France and the Puritans elsewhere.

   (d) Theologians in the various doctrinal camps tended to ascribe the victories of their opponents to Satan and Satan's representatives on earth, who were said to have assumed human form.

   (e) A defender of royal absolutism, the French philosopher Jean Bodin insisted on legislation outlawing witch trials.

7. Which statement correctly describes the cause of one social problem of the Enlightenment?

   *(a) Rank and privilege bound together the world of the Enlightenment in which a free-lance, independent status for the artist, i.e., one not dependent on a wealthy patron, was virtually unheard of.

   (b) While humanitarianism undermined serfdom in the East, it paved the way for slavery in the West.

   (c) Maritime states enforced bans on the slave trade and, in a gesture of social concern, declared all slaves in the colonial empires free.

(d) Voltaire and nearly all of his contemporaries in intellectual circles advocated diffusion of the new enlightened doctrines among the citizenry, so that people might be liberated from the ignorance and depravity of survival ethics.

(e) Spinoza's new interpretation of God, grounded in reason rather than faith, encouraged a mutually tolerant attitude between Jews and Christians in his community in the Netherlands.

8. With one exception, the following statements describe achievements made in music during the seventeenth and eighteenth centuries. Composers

(a) insisted upon the use of a primary voice, accompanied by traditional Renaissance musical instruments, in order to better express the dramatic, intense feelings of the individual.

(b) experimented with new forms of musical expression and, in the eighteenth century, perfected the opera and the classical forms of concerto, oratorio, and sonata.

(c) greatly enhanced the aesthetic quality of liturgical services by the choral works composed for performance in churches and featuring solo parts and instrumental accompaniment.

(d) —by reconciling baroque and rococo styles with individualistic, preromantic forms—had created a classical era of music manifest in chamber and orchestral music and dramatic operas.

*(e) helped maintain and transfer intact the traditions of Franco-Flemish polyphonic music to the modern age.

9. Which of the following statements indicates the close relationship of musical development to the intellectual revolution and the Enlightenment? Musical compositions of the seventeenth and eighteenth centuries

(a) symbolize local aspirations, pride, and aesthetic preferences and yet also have a universal appeal—that is, an appeal that supersedes regional or national boundaries.

(b) reflect the power and complexity of the baroque style and the refinement and charm of the rococo.

*(c) introduced dramatic changes in musical structure and composition that mirrored shifts occurring in the intellectual world.

(d) proliferated liturgical composition, such as cantatas, oratorios, Passions, and Masses, for Sunday and holy-day services.

(e) none of the above.

10. The concepts of the intellectual revolution appearing in the compositions of Johann Sebastian Bach are *best* reflected in

(a) his use of the operatic form as a mode of musical expression from which his successors were to derive the form of sonatas, quartets, concertos, and symphonies.

(b) the pattern of a symphony orchestra, which he introduced and which was to remain basically unaltered to the present time.

*(c) the great attention Bach paid to rational order and mathematical harmony in his music, concepts that lay at the heart of the intellectual revolution.

(d) his devotion to German Protestantism, which motivated him to compose church music exclusively for use during Protestant services.

(e) his successful combination of various stylistic characteristics already indigenous to eighteenth-century music and his creation of new and formal levels of chamber and orchestral music.

11. Thinkers of the Enlightenment perceived human beings as

(a) the only possible reason for a supernaturally directed universe as was conceived by medieval theologians.

(b) emotional believers in God, whom they saw as interested in their personal history and destiny and who centered the universe upon human life alone.

*(c) only a link in the rationally ordered chain of beings that included all living things.

(d) bundles of feelings, animal urges, and fears that, according to Rousseau, must be controlled by means of a rational approach to life.

(e) ignorant fools, at least the majority of humans, hopelessly enmeshed in a world of darkness and superstition they themselves had devised.

12. Which argument does *not* fit Deist theories?

(a) God is simply the prime mover of an ordered universe and the force that had devised its laws—laws not beyond human comprehension.

(b) Human beings have the freedom and rational ability to choose between good and evil.

(c) Divine predestination of humans for either salvation or eternal damnation violates the human dignity reason bestows on all human beings.

*(d) There are no absolute standards of good and evil. Good is merely that which gives pleasure; evil, that which brings pain.

(e) God cannot be petitioned and persuaded to interfere with the operation of natural laws to benefit any one person.

13. Which viewpoint represents the Enlightenment's optimistic belief in continuous human progress?

(a) Even the ills of the world work to the advantage of humanity in this, the best of all possible worlds.

*(b) The discovery of the laws of nature, which can be formulated as precisely as mathematical principles, and the application of these laws to politics and other human institutions or needs, will ensure progress.

(c) The truths of reason and science, if taught to the masses, will eventually free the world from any traces of ignorance.

(d) Only by the application of reason to the problems of society can a general social improvement result.

(e) Educational reform will lead the masses to liberty and equality and will eliminate the necessity for any restrictions on personal freedom.

14. Which of the following statements is *incorrect*? Scientific research in the seventeenth and eighteenth centuries

(a) was encouraged by rulers because the discoveries were of great practical value to the advancement of mercantilistic policies followed by the rulers.

*(b) was pursued exclusively at the great universities, which were heavily endowed by merchants and entrepreneurs hoping to increase their profits through discoveries and inventions.

(c) was motivated by a belief that the understanding and harnessing of nature's laws can contribute to human progress and generally to the betterment of human living conditions.

(d) gave firm foundations to physics, chemistry, and medicine as independent and rapidly expanding fields of study.

(e) became truly international in scope as governments lent their support to scientific inquiry in the hope that new discoveries would yield immediate and practical applications.

15. The impact of the Enlightenment on the future political development of Europe is most clearly seen in which development?

(a) Agitation for new criminal laws and more liberal prison conditions spawned a new penal philosophy incorporating concepts of crime prevention and rehabilitation rather than vengeance.

*(b) Rousseau's political philosophy and his call for liberty and equality inspired the ideal of majority rule.

(c) Social order maintained by natural law and a view to practical experience did not bring an end to feudalistic customs, nor did it abolish privilege enjoyed by accident of birth.

(d) A general revulsion against wars developed into a European attitude of pacifism and led to workable plans for creating a League of Nations that could forbid or defend national monarchies against blatant aggression.

(e)   Serious attempts by intellectuals and various religious groups to expose the evils of slavery soon led to its abolition in Europe.

IDENTIFICATIONS

Novum Organum	Phlogiston theory
Inductive method	Leyden jar
Deductive method	Neo-Palladianism
Encyclopedists	Petit Trianon and Sans Souci
Crimes and Punishments	*Opera buffa*
Quietists	Monody
Royal Society of London	*The Outline of the Progress of*
Sceptical Chymist	*the Human Mind*

TRUE OR FALSE

T   1.   Locke's *Treatise of Civil Government* posited a political philosophy based on natural law, which was used to justify, among other insurrections, the American Revolution.

T   2.   According to Locke, if there is evil in the world, it is not the result of a divine plan, but rather of an environment human beings can change.

F   3.   The Cartesian ideas describe the concepts of Francis Bacon concerning true knowledge.

F   4.   Henry Cavendish and Joseph Priestley provided the names for hydrogen and oxygen.

F   5.   In his natural history, Georges Buffon recognizes the close relationship between humans and higher animals and clearly defines the theory that links human evolution to that of animals.

T   6.   Alexander Pope suggested that men and women study the inflexible laws of nature and, by following them, manage to bring order into human affairs.

T   7.   It was Joseph Haydn who firmly established the stylistic principles of symphonic composition.

F   8.   Rococo is a regional variation of the baroque style that is best represented by the remodeled Hampton Court of King William of England.

T   9.   Enlightenment study of contemporary civilizations other than that of civilized western Europe prompted several anthropological treatments that extolled once supposed inferior, "native" civilizations above that of Europe.

F   10.   The optimism implicit in Voltaire's writings was accepted and expanded by other theorists in the eighteenth century who believed in the progress of humanity.

DISCUSSION AND/OR ESSAY QUESTIONS

1. Why and how did Voltaire epitomize the Enlightenment as Luther had the Reformation and Michelangelo the Renaissance?

2. How did Mozart embody the aristocratic spirit and Haydn that of the liberated plebeian?

3. Describe the major achievements of medical research during the intellectual revolution. Who were the major figures, and what did they contribute to modern medicine?

4. How is optimism and belief in human progress represented in the literature of the intellectual revolution?

5. How did classicism affect the development of thought, literature, art, and music during the Enlightenment?

SUGGESTED FILMS

Benjamin Franklin—Scientist, Statesman, Scholar, and Sage. 30 min. Color. Handel Film Corporation (1969).

Bernini's Rome. 30 min. Color. National Education TV, Inc. (1966).

Captain James Cook. 30 min. Color. Time-Life Films, Inc. (1977).

Caravaggio and the Baroque. 14 min. Color. McGraw-Hill Films (1961).

Civilization: The Light of Experience. 2 parts, each 26 min. Color. Time-Life Films, Inc. (1970).

Civilization: The Pursuit of Happiness. 2 parts, each 26 min. Color. Time-Life Films, Inc. (1970).

Civilization: The Smile of Reason. 2 parts, each 26 min. Color. Time-Life Films, Inc. (1970).

Rembrandt: Painter of Man. 19 min. Color. Perspective Films (1958).

Rubens. 45 min. B/w. Macmillan Films, Inc. (1950).

Touring Great Cities: Venice. 40 min. Color. Time-Life Films, Inc. (1977).

Touring Great Cities: Vienna. 40 min. Color. Time-Life Films, Inc. (1977).

Voltaire Presents Candide: An Introduction to the Age of Enlightenment. 34 min. Color. (From the Humanities—Philosophy and Political Thought series.) Encyclopaedia Britannica Educational Corp./Films (n.d.).

Outline

MULTIPLE CHOICE

Choose the best response.

1. The three centuries between 1500 and 1800 witnessed an advancement of civilization in sub-Saharan Africa because commercial contacts with Europe

    *(a)   stimulated centralization of African authority in some areas which in turn fostered native artistic vitality—forces which supplied the bases of even greater cultural achievement after 1800.

    (b)   fostered economic rivalries and precipitated destructive civil wars between African tribal states that vied for European trade advantage.

    (c)   after 1505 were based on principles much different from those that had first brought Europeans to Africa; prospects of lucrative trade in arms, munitions, and humans supplanted religion and common intellectual interests as the primary motives of interchange.

    (d)   impoverished Africa with an influx of largely non-productive goods in exchange for its gold, copper, ivory, ebony, and slaves.

    (e)   reoriented West African trade toward the Americas via Atlantic routes.

2. Which of the following statements gives the most *fundamental* explanation for the development of territorial states and empires in sub-Saharan Africa after 1500?

    (a)   After 1500, some African kingdoms, whose rulers foresaw the dangers of the Atlantic trade, sought to defend themselves against the intrusive Europeans by creating highly centralized territorial empires.

    (b)   In most cases, failure to keep Europeans or Muslim foreigners at arms length regarding control of trade and political advice resulted in erosion of power and the eventual collapse of African kingdoms.

    (c)   Before 1505 many African leaders received Europeans with enthusiasm, hoping to learn the agricultural, industrial, and warfare technology that might bring about a rapid advancement of their people.

174

*(d) Indigenous traders and tribal chiefs, striving for a share of the oceanic trade, were motivated to reorganize politically and economically, first to withstand the force of local rivalries, then to profit from the shift in markets. This reorientation, in its early stages, had little to do with foreign intervention, especially among the interior African states between 1730 and 1800.

(e) Some cautious African leaders reasoned that political and economic ruin were likely to follow European intrigue at their courts and marketplaces, and could only be avoided through an isolationist, state-controlled political and economic system.

3. *One* of the following was not found in the culture of the sub-Sahara between 1500 and 1800; namely,

(a) sculpture in brass, bronze, ivory, and, most importantly, in wood among the peoples of the forest civilizations.

(b) magnificent cities laid out in a gridiron pattern, with broad, tree-lined streets, and mud or reed palaces with multi-colored, stylized facades.

(c) performances by professional acrobats, dancers, and musicians that often criticized government policies or social conventions.

(d) pictorial tapestries and fine raffia cloth stamped with distinctly symbolic motifs, variously surrealistic, expressionistic, abstract, and naturalistic.

*(e) massive stone fortifications constructed according to the medieval European pattern and decorated with intricately-done scenes from heroic ancestral tradition.

4. Mogul cultural development in India included all of the following, *except*

(a) the development of some of the world's greatest cities of the seventeenth century—with sumptuous palaces and costly buildings done in the distinctive Indo-Muslim style of architecture—which testified to multi-ethnic influence and Hindu and Jain ideology.

*(b) the strong influence of contemporary Persian art among the masses of the Hindu populace, which had the effect of lowering formerly exacting artistic standards to satisfy the demand for ephemeral household decorations.

(c) a religious philosophy based on the concepts of brotherhood, oneness of God, and charity.

(d) impressive achievements in literature stimulated by royal patronage and enriched by the availability of a variety of vital languages including those spoken at court, those used to record the sacred texts, and those used by administrators in the provinces.

(e) the emergence of a "camp language," called Urdu, whose vocabulary includes many Persian and Arabic words, and which is written in Arabic script following the basic grammatical structure of Hindi.

5. The Mogul rule is best characterized by

   (a) revolts and fratricidal wars among princes who competed for the right of succession.

   *(b) the development of a successful pattern of government, yet one inevitably menaced by court intrigues and resisted by defiant and powerful Indian groups that held conflicting political and religious ideologies.

   (c) successful integration of many Indian peoples regardless of their religious professions or social status, under Indian rulers of mixed ethnic backgrounds.

   (d) continuous efforts to establish, by any and all means possible, conformity to and orthodoxy within Islam.

   (e) destructive wars waged to extend the Empire's limits to encompass heretical Muslim states and territories of non-believers, and to eradicate rival religious ideologies in the process.

6. The greatest long-term effect of the Ch'ing Dynasty was that it

   (a) gave rise to hostility against northerners among the southern Chinese, since taxation policies and expenditures clearly favored the north.

   (b) repeated the Mogul dynastic tactic of destruction and terror, although it did not completely uproot traditional Chinese governmental practices in favor of arbitrary autocracy.

   (c) reached a zenith of governmental efficiency during the reigns of two very able, long-lived emperors, between 1661 and 1796.

   *(d) provided generally stable if not entirely benevolent governments that created one of the best-governed and most civilized states of the eighteenth century world.

   (e) succeeded in holding European traders and adventurers within bounds—that is, prevented serious exploitation of the Chinese—and dealt effectively with Russian encroachment on the Manchurian border.

7. With *one exception*, Manchu society

   (a) experienced an unprecedented population explosion, which forced the Chinese to improvise and hastily implement new farming methods, resulting in floods and serious soil erosion that long afterward menaced agriculture.

   *(b) was centered around a single standard of morality and, since continuance of the civil service exams kept China a meritocracy, accorded Manchus and Chinese, northerners and southerners, men and women alike equal access to key administrative posts.

(c) remained basically unaltered in organization and structure between the seventeenth and nineteenth centuries, untouched by the benefits and pitfalls of industrial revolution.

(d) was free of extreme factionalism and civil war and, once having dealt with the European presence, was able to make substantial material progress.

(e) was generally conservative, tending to venerate ancient authorities and adhere rigidly to traditional social institutions.

8. The characteristics of Manchu culture included all the following, *except*

(a) the development of a school of philosophy to study the ancient classics objectively and scientifically.

(b) a lack of originality in most of the products of culture.

(c) a rigid adherence to Confucian orthodoxy as interpreted by Chu-Hsi.

(d) freshness and originality in the literary medium of the novel, which reached a higher degree of excellence than it had even under the Ming Dynasty.

*(e) attempts to rehabilitate society by applying ancient Buddhist and Taoist doctrines to social criticism.

9. The political achievements of Ieyasu and his successors are correctly represented in which statement?

(a) Japan's feudal institutions were systematized to ensure that government would remain decentralized.

(b) The conquest of Korea and of substantial territory in northern China and Manchuria provided the necessary raw materials for Japan to sustain an industrial revolution like that of Western Europe.

*(c) Japan was united under a common central authority supported by a large and well-organized bureaucracy.

(d) Although the emperor's sanctity and inviolability were considered paramount, the imperial court and nobility shared the responsibility for administrative matters but had no influence in military matters.

(e) Heavy stone castles were built according to Portuguese models, and housed officers of the new regime; it was military rule alone that kept peace in the outlying areas and transmitted urban culture to rural outposts.

10. One important feature of Tokugawa society that expresses a *recurrent* theme in Japanese history is

(a) the elevation of the samurai to the highest social category, with the expectation that they, in turn, would excel in literature and art.

*(b)   a hierarchical structure that theoretically, albeit not in practice, replicated the traditional Chinese social arrangement.

(c)   a slow rate of population growth, apparently more often a result of deliberate family planning than of scarce resources.

(d)   the rising esteem of manufacturing, trade, and transport occupations, in spite of their ranking at the bottom of the social pyramid, and the contributions made by these to the changing face of Japan's economy and its urban centers.

(e)   the decline of the daimyo and their retainers concomitant to the rise of merchant classes, and the breakdown in class distinctions that followed.

11.   Which statement does *not* describe a distinctively Japanese cultural achievement during the Tokugawa era?

(a)   The tastes of the new middle class in the populous commercial and industrial centers fostered the development of new trends in art, literature, and the field of entertainment.

(b)   Realistic folk art, enlivened by humor and caricature, gained wide acceptance through the medium of the wood-block print.

(c)   A new form of drama evolved, the Kabuki, which offered popular entertainment to the middle and lower classes.

*(d)   Interest in the Confucian classics was heightened by refugee scholars from China; they were encouraged by the Shoguns, who sought by this means to reinforce principles of virtue, especially obedience, among civilians as well as the military.

(e)   Creative talents in Japan catered to bourgeois tastes by the production of racy novels and piquant satires.

12.   The nature of European contact with India, the Far East, and Africa is *best* reflected in

(a)   cultivation of new crops in these regions, which often enabled the indigenous population to sustain much higher population densities than previously.

(b)   an emphasis upon long distance trade, which encouraged the exchange of ideas among the peoples of the various regions.

(c)   the reaction of non-European governments, which set up rigid trade restrictions and almost totally excluded European traders from the Far East.

(d)   the widespread acceptance of Western religion, books, and ideas, and an apparent demand for western products and technology among the ruling classes of the non-western states.

*(e) the passage of control of Eastern waters from Arab to European navigators, which ultimately triggered Chinese prejudice against the "Ocean Devils," Japan's isolationism, and the transformation of Africa into an exploited satellite of Europe's economic system.

13. Of the following, one was *not* a product of European relations with India, the Far East, or Africa; namely,

(a) the spread of disease, including fatal malaria and yellow fever, among European travellers and potential colonists.

(b) the fashionable craze in western Europe during the 1700s for Chinese-style gardens, pagodas, lacquer, incense, and, especially, porcelain.

(c) the influence, however limited or superficial, of Confucian texts and the mythical "Chinese sage," who deists and Enlightenment philosophers cited in support of their own theories.

*(d) the strong influence of Asian and African dramatic forms on the development of nineteenth century European drama of the bourgeoisie.

(e) the cubist tradition, first born not in early twentieth century Europe, but in West African forest societies centuries before.

14. Which statement concerning the discovery and use of gunpowder, firearms, and munitions in India, the Far East, and Africa indicates its most important consequence?

(a) Discovered and used by the Chinese in firecrackers in the era of the Ch'in, gunpowder was first employed by the Mongols in the thirteenth century to make primitive bombs, propelled, perhaps, by catapults.

(b) The sale of arms and munitions in effect forced a number of African states to engage in slave raiding and trading, or else face political and possibly economic ruin at the hands of cunning European "advisors."

(c) Firearms acquired from the Portuguese played a great role in the feudal battles of late sixteenth-century Japan, and, in that instance, contributed to the political stability that came with the victorious Tokugawa Shogunate.

(d) Portuguese artillery assisted the Ming armies in their attempt to resist Manchu attacks, setting a precedent for the use of gunpowder as a destructive force.

*(e) All of the above contributed to the creation of a staggering demand for arms by the eighteenth century and turned armaments into the single most important trade commodity of its time.

15. Which of the following statements most accurately reflects advances made by African civilizations during the period of intensifying European contact from 1500 to 1800?

    (a)   Africa's real economic growth was spurred by the expansion of trade with Europe.

    (b)   African contact with the European capitalist system contributed to the process of state formation and to the development of long-term political stability.

    *(c)   Despite the disruptive influences fostered by the Europeans these three centuries witnessed steady artistic advancement in African societies.

    (d)   The growth of long-distance trade led to the introduction of new food crops from Asia which enabled some regions of the African continent to sustain higher population densities and to the introduction of European medical practices which effectively eliminated disease as a major determinent in African history.

    (e)   The accessibility of European markets enabled African societies to develop their natural resources for the benefit of the indigenous population.

IDENTIFICATIONS

The "Great Mogul"	Yoruba civilization
Peacock Throne	Oni of Ifé
Tulsi Das	Fort Jesus
"Ocean Devils"	Shona armies
The Manchu Treaty of 1689	Omani
"Han Learning" scholars	"Floating world"
Kabuki	Sikhs
Edo	

TRUE OR FALSE

F   1.   The criminal code of Akbar surpassed in its ferocity that of the European nations of the late sixteenth century.

F   2.   Nanak's doctrines of the brotherhood of man, belief in one God, and the duty to perform acts of charity were derived from the teachings of Mencius and Chu-Hsi.

T   3.   The revolution that eventually overthrew the Manchu Dynasty originated in southern China.

T   4.   Many French Jesuits were engaged at the Manchu court as instructors in science, mathematics, and cartography.

F   5.   Social and economic changes in China were triggered by an industrial and commercial revolution during the Manchu period.

T   6.   Under the Tokugawa Shogunate feudal institutions remained intact, but served the interests of a strong central government.

F   7.   Christian missionaries were responsible for instigating the peasant rebellion of 1637 in Japan.

T   8.   Initiated by amoral white slave traffickers and carried out by their black collaborators, Africa's lamentable human losses became America's gains.

T   9.   A national military draft of both men and women was instituted in the kingdom of Dahomey in the eighteenth century.

F   10.   Soon after the Moroccan invasion of Songhay, Islam became the primary factor in the social and cultural development of virtually all of sub-Saharan Africa.

DISCUSSION AND/OR ESSAY QUESTIONS

1.   Why did Sir Thomas Roe urge his countrymen to seek profit "at sea and in quiet trade," and to remember that "war and traffic are incompatible"? Judging by the conduct of the East India Company and the Royal African Company in the latter seventeenth century, did the English comply with the letter or the spirit of Roe's advice? Distinguish between instances of "quiet trade" in the sense of a lack of open conflict and genuine peacetime trade. What underlying social problems were being created by England's "quiet trade" overseas between 1600 and 1900?

2.   How did contacts with European missionaries, traders, and adventurers affect Indian, Chinese, and Japanese societies? Include a discussion of responses by the governments of these countries to the foreign presence. What were the short- and long-term results?

3.   Why does it appear that the Tokugawa Shoguns could have provided the foundation for a structure different from and better than a duplicate of Western industrialized society? Is it correct to assume that they initiated Japan's transformation into a modern state? At the crossroads, i.e., when Japan might have achieved an organization superior to that of the industrialized West, but instead experienced the imperial restoration, what internal and external pressures made the Tokugawa appear inadequate?

4.   What were the reasons for internal discontent in China during the Manchu period and in Japan during the Tokugawa Shogunate? Can you find similar elements in Indian resistance to Mogul rule? Discuss instances where the lack of governmental policy, e.g., an inability to respond to problems, proved fatal to the regime, as well as those times when specific policies antagonized the populace.

5.   "The exchange of guns, powder, alcoholic beverages, and cheaply manufactured textiles for humans, gold, ivory, pepper, and palm oil stimulated the centralization of African authority in some areas and contributed to the growth of empires."

In what areas of Africa was authority centralized by reason of the conditions of trade? Identify the political, social, and economic structures of territorial empires that arose as a result of contact with Europe, and discuss their positive and negative attributes.

SUGGESTED FILMS

INDIA

The Exploration of Prince Henry. 13 min. B/w; c. McGraw-Hill Textfilms (1959).

Four Centuries Ago. 19 min. Color. National Education and Information Films, Ltd. (Bombay) (n.d.).

The Great Mogul. 30 min. Color. Time-Life Films, Inc. (1969).

India's History: Mogul Empire to European Colonization. 11 min. Coronet Instructional Films (1956).

Mughal Glory. 19 min. Color. National Education and Information Films, Ltd. (Bombay) (n.d.).

Taj Mahal. 14 min. Color. National Education and Information Films, Ltd. (Bombay) (n.d.).

AFRICA

Ancient Kingdoms in Northeast Africa. 30 min. B/w. Holt, Rinehart and Winston, (1969).

The Slave Coast. 50 min. Color. Westinghouse Broadcasting Productions (1972).

The Slave Trade Begins. 30 min. B/w. Holt, Rinehart and Winston (1969).

The Story of Ghana. 20 min. B/w. Peter M. Robeck and Co., Inc. (Distributed by Time-Life) (n.d.).

Outline

MULTIPLE CHOICE
Choose the best response.

1.   Which of the following reforms of Napoleon exerted the *greatest* influence on
the European states?

  (a)   A universal system of education under the supervision of a national
        university.

  *(b)   A body of laws, called the Code of Napoleon, based on the principles of
        legal uniformity and individual property rights propogated by the French
        Revolution.

  (c)   The system of meritocracy, which opened careers to all talented persons
        regardless of birth or background.

  (d)   Abolition of all manorial privileges, local liberties, and exemptions from
        taxation or civic service formerly granted to the nobility and clergy.

  (e)   A workable agreement for government to cooperate with the Church in
        order to secure domestic tranquility and international solidarity.

2.   Which statement *best* describes the social conditions in France in the 1780s that
triggered the revolution?

  (a)   Overlapping functions of the regional governments and conflicts of juris-
        diction between various departments severely curtailed attempts by the
        king's ministers to strengthen absolutism.

  (b)   Ancient privileges of exemption from taxation reduced revenues at a time
        when the peasantry and the middle class increasingly carried the state's
        financial burden.

  *(c)   Many were unwilling to compromise traditional or acquired rights con-
        cerning tax exemption and wished to pursue commercial advantage by
        eliminating mercantilistic restrictions.

(d) The gradations of social status that separated the nobility from the rest of the French population was resented by merchants and the lower classes.

(e) Ideas and theories of class conflict, which were derived from the works of Enlightenment theorists, greatly appealed to those who, for various reasons, resented government controls or who were dissatisfied with things as they were in prerevolutionary France.

3. By insisting on traditional rights, which class of people was chiefly instrumental in aggravating conditions that led to the French Revolution?

(a) The nobles of the robe, many of whom accumulated substantial wealth in land, property, or investments, which they intended to protect against the king's punitive taxation plans.

(b) The peasants, who resented the duties of an outmoded manorial system.

*(c) The nobles of the sword, who made use of the parlements, the intendancies, and the provincial estates to protect their own privileges.

(d) Business and professional classes, whose demands for political power were interdicted by the traditional discrimination of a social pecking order.

(e) The bishops, archbishops, and cardinals, who satisfied their financial obligations to the state by an annual "free gift," but did not wish to ease the economic plight of the urban poor.

4. The liberal political theory of some revolutionaries of the French Revolution was based on *all but one* of the following.

(a) The law of nature puts automatic limitations on every branch of government. Any attempt at governmental restriction of individual freedom is illegal.

(b) The authority of government should be broken up into its three natural functions in order to prevent the absolute supremacy of the majority over an unwilling minority.

(c) All people are endowed by nature with equal rights to life, liberty, and property, and governments' jurisdictions are confined to the protection of such rights.

*(d) The ideal form of government, suitable for all peoples under all conditions imaginable, is based on the parliamentary rule by the middle class.

(e) The powers of government should not extend beyond the absolute minimum consistent with personal security, and all individuals should be permitted to pursue their own devices.

5. The political theorists of the French Revolution disagreed in regard to which concept of government?

(a) Governmental power is limited by the will of the governed.

(b)   If dissatisfied, the governed may take effective measures of resistance against the offensive government and have the right to rebel, or dissolve or overthrow it.

(c)   It is the natural right of every person to establish some form of government by voluntary contract between governors and governed groups of people.

*(d)   By means of a social contract, individuals have given up all rights to the people collectively and mutually agree to submit to the general will, since the voice of the people is the "voice of God."

(e)   Human beings' natural rights include life and liberty, which are to be protected by rational laws equally applied to all.

6. The political theorists of the French Revolution agreed that the state is

*(a)   a civil society in which the government—a necessary evil—has been established with legitimate powers limited to the enforcement of natural rights or the general will.

(b)   nothing but the combined powers of all members of society, and its authority no more than that which its constituents possessed within the state of nature but gave up to the community.

(c)   a politically organized community, sovereign in its function to express the general will.

(d)   a community in which sovereignty has to be adapted—with or without the agreement of the people—to harmonize with physical conditions and the level of social advancement experienced by particular communities.

(e)   an organization in which individual interests are protected and advanced by a limited government agreed upon by all members.

7. What viewpoint was *not* a direct influence of the Enlightenment on the concepts of political theorists of the French Revolution?

(a)   Just as nature is governed by rational, universal laws, a set of natural, rational laws also governs the politics of nations on earth.

(b)   Since the universe can be explained as operating mechanically, all human actions, appetites, and aversions also have a mechanistic explanation, the knowledge of which will result in humanity's mastery of the world.

(c)   The laws of nature reasonably limit the dimensions of constituted authority and prohibit arbitrariness in the use of power.

(d)   Improvement of human conditions is possible only if people learn nature's laws and workings and put these to use to ensure human progress.

*(e)   Governments established by social contract will provide people with that relief and support they had formerly sought by their supplication to a supernatural deity.

8. The immediate cause of the French Revolution was the

   (a) determination of the nobles of the robe and the nobles of the sword to force the king to grant them further concessions.

   (b) rise in prices, especially in the cost of bread—representing approximately 80 percent of a poor family's income—and the resultant rioting in Paris.

   (c) uprising in Paris of the sans-culottes, who, fearing reprisals by the aristocracy or king for their recent demands of government reform, stormed and destroyed the Bastille on July 14, 1789.

   *(d) inability of the king to stave off imminent bankruptcy of the state, even by the imposition of a vexing stamp duty and annual tax on produce.

   (e) women's march on Versailles and their success in returning the king and queen to Paris.

9. Which of the following statements is *incorrect*? The constitution

   (a) of the National Assembly converted the government into a limited monarchy, in which the right to vote was allowed only to those who paid a certain amount of taxes.

   (b) enacted in 1790 provided that all bishops and priests be elected by the people and subject to the authority of the state.

   *(c) drafted by the National Convention assured universal manhood suffrage, which was implemented and successfully enforced by the Committee of Public Safety.

   (d) of the National Convention granted suffrage to all adult male citizens who could read and write, permitting them the right to vote for electors, who in turn chose members to a legislative assembly. Eligibility for electorship was tied to status as a proprietor with a minimum annual income, according to the constitution.

   (e) of the First Consul, by providing for indirect election, reasserted that political power must remain in the hands of middle-class entrepreneurs and profesionalss.

10. The Declaration of Pillnitz by Austria and Prussia in 1791 and the subsequent declaration of war by the French assembly in 1792 resulted in all the following *except* the

    (a) persecution of intellectuals, politicians, and businessmen who initially had been sympathetic to the revolutionaries' cause.

    *(b) strengthening of bonds between the Girondist and Jacobin factions whose cooperation in the new National Convention was instrumental in achieving final victory for the equalitarian-minded middle class in the revolution.

    (c) increased importance of *émigre* nobles at the various courts of Europe. These Frenchmen worked in the manner of a fifth column, encouraging

European governments to adopt antirevolutionary policies in general and to oppose France in particular.

(d) legal persecution of philosophical radicals in England who endorsed the overthrow of privilege and absolutism.

(e) growth of English patriotism, working in opposition to subversive French ideas thought to endanger national survival.

11. Which statement correctly identifies the reason for the onset of the second, so-called "radical" stage of the French Revolution following the sessions of the Constituent Assembly?

*(a) Despite the Constituent Assembly's accomplishments, dissatisfaction increased among the politically literate urban classes, who felt that the assembly had not addressed itself to their concerns and political aspirations.

(b) Counterrevolutionary activity among religious officials who resented the secularization of the Church by the National Assembly.

(c) Economic privations of the peasantry were not solved by the abolition of manorial dues and the elimination of aristocratic exemptions from taxation.

(d) The urban mobs could not be satisfied in the face of steadily rising inflation merely by lofty ideals such as those embodied in the Declaration of the Rights of Man and of the Citizen.

(e) The Constituent Assembly had drafted legislation that most benefited the men and women of the middle class.

12. The decline of the National Convention can be best explained by one of the following statements.

(a) Price fixings, confiscation of property, and the constant threat of execution alienated the merchant classes, originally supporters of the revolution.

*(b) Dissatisfaction with increasing inflation, rather than the Terror, eroded support of commoners, the social sector that had given the radical element their power and support base in the convention.

(c) Continuous attempts of sabotage by rightist and leftist enemies, as well as revolutionaries more radical than themselves eroded the authority of the National Convention and its Committee on Public Safety.

(d) Foreign intrigue continued in spite of spectacular military successes by the National Guard.

(e) New legislation that nullified the ancient tradition of primogeniture and introduction of an incomprehensible metric system as the standard measure for business transactions evoked universal resentment from the French citizenry.

13. Napoleon Bonaparte gained power in France primarily because

   (a) the Committee of Public Safety was unable to cope with attacks by the coalition of European states.

   (b) commoners and peasants resented the political victory of the prosperous classes to whom special privileges were given in the constitution of 1795.

   (c) "Gracchus" Babeuf effectively campaigned to abolish private property and parliamentary government.

   *(d) the directors were unable to cope with domestic difficulties—including severe inflation—and foreign policy.

   (e) he gained the general support of the population, which yearned for order and stability after the excesses of the Terror.

14. At Napoleon's order, central European countries revolutionized their governments in all the following ways *except* by

   (a) organizing a new governmental administration under strict supervision from Paris.

   (b) the obliteration of manorial courts and the elimination of church courts.

   *(c) agreeing to join in a European tariff-free custom union designed to stimulate manufacture of goods and trade on the Continent.

   (d) the codification of laws according to the Napoleonic system.

   (e) applying the principles that had already transformed postrevolutionary France.

15. Napoleon's eventual defeat was primarily due to

   *(a) his obsessive self-confidence and his assumption of invincibility consequent to his role as savior of France.

   (b) his "Continental System," which the French navy could not enforce, and the subsequent British naval blockade of the Continent that effectively countered Napoleon's plans.

   (c) the overextension of the military in unwarranted expansionist ventures, and the ultimate disastrous defeat in Russia as a consequence of this.

   (d) his attempt to unite Europe in a fashion modeled after the ancient Roman Empire—an ambition indicated in many symbols of Napoleon's empire.

   (e) an alliance of European powers, whose military might eventually overcame that of France when Napoleon's supply of men and materials was shown to have its limits.

IDENTIFICATIONS

Taille	Estates General
Gabelle	Departments
Nobles of the robe	*Reflections on the Revolution*
Generalities	*in France*
Second Treatise of Civil	*The Rights of Man*
Government	Declaration of the Rights of Man
Spirit of Laws	and of the Citizen
Inquiry into the Nature and Causes	Jacobins
of the Wealth of Nations	*Enragés*
Discourse on the Origin of Inequality	

TRUE OR FALSE

F   1.   The clergy and nobility were exempt from indirect taxes during the reign of Louis XVI, causing discontent among the peasants and the middle classes.

T   2.   On the eve of the revolution, the vast majority of French peasants were free and many owned the land they cultivated.

F   3.   The new French constitution of 1791 granted seats in the assembly to the king's ministers and veto power over all legislation to the king.

F   4.   The Constituent Assembly abolished the French monarchy on September 21, 1792, and declared France a Republic.

T   5.   Many of John Locke's ideas had been incorporated into the American Declaration of Independence and later influenced the thinking of the French middle class during the French Revolution.

T   6.   Rousseau argued that the sovereign power of the state has no limitations whatsoever.

F   7.   The thirteen *parlements* of France were regional assemblies of elected representatives, exercising both judicial and legislative power.

T   8.   The *assignats* were paper money issued by the National Assembly as collateral for the confiscated Church land.

F   9.   The urban mobs and the oppressed peasants had received the most benefits at the end of the first stage of the French Revolution.

F   10.   The Girondists were members of a Parisian political club and introduced radical republicanism into the second stage of the French Revolution.

DISCUSSION AND/OR ESSAY QUESTIONS

1. What was the impact of the French Revolution on European society? What changes or achievements of the revolution were transferred to Europe in general?

2. What was the role of the urban masses in the affairs of 1789 and 1793 and in the Girondist-fueled provincial rebellions of 1793?

3. How did leaders of the French Revolution deal with the problem of the Church at various stages of the revolution? Why was there a need to introduce Reason as a divinity? Why was there a need still later to substitute a deistic divinity for Reason?

4. What economic problems contributed to the outbreak of the French Revolution? How did its leaders solve these problems? Concentrate especially on the hardships caused by continuous inflation.

5. The Abbé Sieyès was one of the most articulate spokesmen of the third estate. How do his statements below reflect the benefits and pitfalls of the revolution?

" 'What is the third estate?' asked the Abbé Sieyès. . . . The answer he gave . . . 'everything.' "

"When . . . the Abbé Sieyès was asked what he had done to distinguish himself during the Terror, he responded dryly, 'I lived.' "

"Abbé Siéyès . . . declared for counterrevolution in the name of virtual dictatorship: 'Confidence from below, authority from above.' "

SUGGESTED FILMS

Civilization: The Worship of Nature. 2 parts, each 26 min. Color. Time-Life Films, Inc. (1970).

Francisco Goya y Lucientes. 26 min. Color. Pyramid Films (1974).

French Revolution. 16 min. Color. Coronet Instructional Films (1957).

The French Revolution: The Bastille. 22 min. Color. Learning Corporation of America (1970).

The French Revolution: The Terror. 28 min. Color. Learning Corporation of America (1970).

Goya: The Disasters of War. 20 min. B/w. Film Images (1952).

The Hundred Days: Napoleon—from Elba to Waterloo. 40 min. Color. Time-Life Films, Inc. (1969).

The Napoleonic Era. 14 min. Color. Coronet Instructional Films (1957).

Thomas Paine. 13 min. Color. Encyclopaedia Britannica Educational Corp./Films (1975).

Outline

MULTIPLE CHOICE
Choose the best response.

1.   In the middle of the eighteenth century Europe was especially primed for the
     Industrial Revolution because

     (a)   —according to modern terminology—it was an "underdeveloped" agricul-
           tural area where the illiterate masses were ready to better their living
           conditions.

     (b)   its predominantly rural, handicraft economy provided an impetus for the
           establishment of a new, urban economy, based on machine-driven manu-
           facturing.

    *(c)   the Commercial Revolution had established European merchants and
           men of commerce as the world's foremost manufacturers and traders.

     (d)   the retrogressive, paternalistic regulations of national economics were
           overthrown shortly after the French Revolution.

     (e)   following the ideas of the Enlightenment, the new, urban middle classes
           believed that the application of the laws of nature in designing institutions
           to meet human needs would ensure progress of the human race.

2.   By the end of the eighteenth century the various revolutionary changes that had
     transpired in European practices and thought resulted in

     (a)   a consensus among middle-class manufacturers, traders, and professionals
           that the world is predictable, rational, and stable.

     (b)   absolute rulers' reliance upon an increasingly influential and thriving
           commercial class, which could achieve the ideals of mercantilism and
           strengthen the national economy.

     (c)   a new contractual understanding between rulers and entrepreneurs concern-
           ing the inviolability of private property, whether in land or in commerce.

     (d)   recognition of an expanding world market, confidence in human progress,
           and hopes for indefinite prosperity.

191

*(e)   the growing influence of a class of capitalists who not only believed in the presuppositions above but tried to implement them to their best advantage through commercial activity.

3.   Which contention is an *inappropriate* explanation for why the Industrial Revolution took place in Europe first rather than elsewhere?

(a)   Overseas expansion opened new markets in India, Africa, and North and South America to European trade.

(b)   New markets were compelled to follow European economic practices and to accommodate Europe's demands for raw materials.

*(c)   Only the United States was able to escape the dictates of European market demands and compete on equal footing with European capitalists in the world market.

(d)   Continuing growth of European populations provided an ever-increasing domestic market for manufactured goods.

(e)   The surplus population was absorbed into the labor force either within mushrooming industries or the new manufactures being established in industrial centers.

4.   With one exception, the origins of the Industrial Revolution are to be found in England for the following reasons:

(a)   a relatively high standard of living, due to an abundance of imported raw materials and manufactured goods.

(b)   enclosure of fields, pastures, and waste lands that when cultivated provided a sufficient food supply for increasing urban populations.

(c)   expanding colonial possessions and the emphasis on trade, which supplied the capital necessary to finance new enterprises.

*(d)   a number of bills that were received sympathetically by the Parliament to encourage the development of factory industry.

(e)   Habits of mind or ideologies among the English people that encouraged capital investments and perceived the pursuit of wealth as a worthy goal in life.

5.   England's eighteenth-century Industrial Revolution occurred by reason of one of the following advantages:

(a)   the growth of population and the concurrent expansion of domestic and foreign markets for more manufactured goods.

(b)   constantly improving systems of transportation for the delivery of goods to markets and raw materials to manufacturers.

(c)   overseas territorial gains after the wars in which England participated, as well as a large merchant fleet and a navy that had penetrated hitherto unexploited territories in search of new resources.

*(d)   the parliamentary system that—without interference from capricious rulers—fully supported England's interests and economic fortune through pertinent legislation.

(e)   London's development as the world center of trade, finance, and manufacturing.

6. What can be considered the most important cause of the revolutionary changes in the textile industry?

(a)   Cotton produced tougher thread than did wool fiber and could withstand the rough treatment of early weaving machinery.

*(b)   Labor-saving machinery and the introduction of medium- to large-size mills could meet increased demands at dramatically reduced costs.

(c)   Light cotton materials were especially suited for use in the tropical climates of India, Africa, and Central America.

(d)   Cotton materials were cheap enough to be bought by millions who never before used washable clothes.

(e)   The growth in textile manufacture contributed to discoveries of new production methods suitable for other industries as well.

7. Industrialization in England resulted in all the following *except*

(a)   the increased production of goods in all industries to meet the needs of apparently insatiable markets.

(b)   the reinvestment of profits from manufacturing, and the production of new and more sophisticated goods.

(c)   the expansion of the trades according to industrial and market demands.

(d)   new methods of production that reduced the costs of goods and speeded up their manufacture.

*(e)   the elimination of social distinctions between the middle and working classes.

8. Changes in production methods and marketing techniques in England can be considered truly "revolutionary" because they

(a)   corresponded to theoretical and technological conclusions derived from pure scientific research.

*(b)   represented the spontaneous response of the English to the demands and needs of the world, with the result that the life style of people across the globe was changed.

(c)   displaced a greater part of the rural population to the cities by 1850, where those who had migrated comprised a substantial part of the work force.

(d)   would have been impossible without the British educational system, which produced a well-trained elite of managers and technocrats.

(e)   further strengthened Sir Robert Walpole's cabinet system, especially during the reign of King George III (1760-1820).

9.   The lack of vigorous industrialization on the Continent before 1815 is *best* explained by which circumstances?

(a)   Manufacturing was determined by regional variances in the availability of raw materials, access to markets and traditionalism, specialization and lack of adaptability.

(b)   The scarcity of raw materials and the lack of abundant supplies of fuel prohibited large-scale expansion of industries.

(c)   With the exception of France, central Europe consisted of small principalities with their own set of tolls and tariffs, which impeded commercial activity over long distances.

*(d)   The French Revolution and the Napoleonic wars interrupted the growth of mechanization in industry, which had begun in Europe during the 1780s.

(e)   Capital on the Continent was dispersed in small-scale enterprises, the owners of which appear to have lacked the entrepreneurial spirit of their English counterparts.

10.   Continental industrialization after 1815 was due to each of the following *except*

*(a)   the technical advice of British experts, who flocked to European industrial centers after Napoleon's defeat.

(b)   the abolition of the trade guilds and the removal of a great number of tariffs that had barred intracontinental trade.

(c)   the population increase in countries with established commercial and industrial bases that provided increased numbers of producers and consumers.

(d)   improvement of road systems and opening of canals, combined with the introduction of rail transport in the 1840s.

(e)   state intervention with financial assistance to stimulate industrial change and commercial expansion.

11.   Which of the following statements is characteristic of continental industrialization during the first half of the nineteenth century?

    (a)   Continental manufacturers rejected technological innovation because they found local methods of production entirely satisfactory.

*(b)   As a result of industrialization and urbanization, combined with increased demands for manufactured goods, the iron industry took the lead over the textile industry, since England was less entrenched in world markets for this manufacture.

    (c)   With the discovery of the rich coal deposits in the Rhineland, the entire French iron production was mechanized by steam engines.

    (d)   The use of imported machinery from England was prohibited by most European governments aiming to encourage machine construction in their respective states.

    (e)   The continental textile industry neglected the production of cotton goods because it could not compete with cheap and well-made British products.

12.   Which statement identifies the *most* significant effect that the spread of railways had in furthering the aims of industrialization? The construction of railroads

    (a)   stimulated the production of such quantities of goods that the West's industrialization could be completed.

    (b)   increased the demand for coal and manufactured goods, while it decreased the time necessary for the sale of goods it brought to market.

*(c)   made Europe and England into the most industrially advanced areas of the globe and the producers of the world.

    (d)   allowed the transport of great quantities of goods quickly and cheaply across long distances.

    (e)   offered capitalists the opportunity to invest their surplus profits and to expect a decent return sooner than before the rise of marketing by rail.

13.   Which of the following statements incorrectly describes some of the results of industrialization in Europe between 1850 and 1870?

    (a)   Improved transportation systems permitted the relatively uncomplicated transit of goods in both domestic and foreign markets.

    (b)   Restrictive regulations, such as those under the guild system, were removed from business practices, and membership in the trades was opened to all who had the talent.

    (c)   Entrepreneurs could develop resources as they saw fit, without interference from government.

*(d)   The discovery of new sources of coal in France and Germany put the Continent ahead of England in industrialization.

    (e)   Trade with Africa, Australia, and America roughly divided the world between producers of manufactured goods and suppliers of raw materials.

14. Basic presuppositions of an industrial revolution include all the following *except*

    (a) a transportation system of roads, navigable rivers, and harbors that can assure the smooth transport of raw materials and manufactured goods over land and sea.

    (b) markets for the sale of goods, under an authority that can provide financial and legal security.

    (c) manufacturing centers with sufficient supplies and a reliable work force.

    (d) a commercial class and entrepreneurs, who are willing to invest in new manufacturing and trade ventures with expectations for reasonable capital returns.

    *(e) a lack of personal ambition and determination to gain the greatest profit from resources invested.

15. One of the following cannot be considered a result of the Industrial Revolution.

    (a) The trade of hand-loom weavers became increasingly less renumerative as the textile-machinery inventions of the eighteenth century were popularized.

    (b) A new class of proud workers—the English navvies—played a legendary role in the development of the railroad industry.

    *(c) Only a small fraction of Europe's population remained in the rural areas, as agriculture became significantly mechanized.

    (d) The benefits of industrialization could not reach areas without industrial and manufacturing bases, such as Italy, Spain, and Ireland.

    (e) Slavery and serfdom were continued as a way of life in the cotton fields of the American South and in the wheat fields of the Ukraine.

IDENTIFICATIONS

Zollverein	Pas-de-Calais
Spinning jenny	Continental System
Spinning mule	Laissez faire
Cotton gin	State intervention
Thomas Newcomen	Thomas Brassey
James Watt	Société Générale
Investment banks	Calico
George Stephenson	

TRUE OR FALSE

T   1.   Enclosure acts were passed by the English Parliament to support the aggressive capitalistic aims of the English aristocracy, in order to ensure specialization and large-scale production in agriculture.

F   2.   By 1850 steam engines had entirely replaced water as the principal energy source of European industry.

T   3.   By 1815 cotton goods represented 40 percent of the value of all domestic goods exported from Great Britain.

F   4.   Old tools and the methods of traditional home industry were replaced immediately when factory-based industry was introduced.

T   5.   In 1852 Britain exported about half of its total iron production of approximately 2 million tons.

T   6.   Ultimate success of the Industrial Revolution largely depended upon the availability of a cheap, new source of energy: coal.

T   7.   Richard Arkwright's water frame made possible the production of fair-quality warp and woof in large quantities.

F   8.   With the single exception of the United States, world-wide construction of railways was financed by the various governments.

F   9.   British manufacturers were free under the law to export innovative machinery along with the technical personnel to operate the machines.

T   10.   The silk and lace industries in France and Belgium gained international reputation during the reign of Louis XIV.

DISCUSSION AND/OR ESSAY QUESTIONS

1. " 'It is our vanity which urges us on,' the economist Adam Smith, defender of laissez faire capitalism, declared. 'And thank God,' Smith implied, 'for our blessed vanity!' "

   How does this quotation reflect the English aristocracy's attitude toward individuals' active involvement in the growth of prosperity for the country as a whole?

2. Why was the Industrial Revolution in England as profound and long lasting as the revolution that occurred simultaneously in France?

3. What were the essential differences in the social, economic, and political conditions and attitudes in England as opposed to the Continent at the beginning of the Industrial Revolution?

4. How did the development of the textile industry initiate profound changes in other industries? Give examples from the progress of the textile industry in several European states.

5. Why was England able to remain the pacesetter in the Industrial Revolution until 1879?

SUGGESTED FILMS

An Age of Revolutions. 26 min. Color. International Film Bureau (1976).

At the Foot of the Tree—a Homage to Steinlen. 24 min. B/w. Roland Films (n.d.).

Civilization: Heroic Materialism. 2 parts, each 26 min. Color. Time-Life Films, Inc. (1970).

Market Society and How It Grew. 2 parts, each 29 min. B/w. National Education TV, Inc. (1963).

Story of Electricity. 11 min. B/w. Knowledge Builders (1941).

Outline

MULTIPLE CHOICE
Choose the best response.

1. The theory of history formulated by Marx had great appeal for the working
    classes chiefly because

    (a) *The Communist Manifesto*, published at the height of revolutionary agita-
         tion on the Continent, called upon the workers of the world to unite.

    (b) it made workers conscious of how urban living and factory work aggravates
         their disaffection toward institutions that fail to recognize workers'
         humanity.

    (c) the Communist League succeeded in organizing the ever-debased working
         classes of Europe for the overthrow of the bourgeoisie.

    *(d) it provided a potential sense of ultimate, near-utopian purpose to the
         proletariat that predicated triumph by their class at the end of an
         inevitable revolutionary process.

    (e) of the inability of most critics of industrialization to come up with
         satisfactory alternative explanations that could render the working
         class experience understandable.

2. The social theories of Marx include all the following *except*

    (a) just as feudalism and manorialism were vanquished by capitalism, so
         capitalism, too, will be vanquished by communism.

    *(b) respect for property, which Marx defined inclusively as the right to life,
         liberty, and estate.

    (c) the overthrow of the bourgeoisie, viewed as an inevitable outcome of laws
         of the dialectic process operative in history.

(d)   a "dictatorship of the proletariat," which will eliminate the last vestiges of bourgeois tradition and create a truly classless civilization.

(e)   that concentration of capitalist economic power into fewer and fewer hands will proportionately increase the opposition of an alienated, disenfranchised proletariat.

3.   The Marxist theory of history is

(a)   the precise application of the German philosopher Georg Wilhelm Hegel's notions about the motive force of ideas in constant conflict with each other.

(b)   a reaction against doctrinaire Augustinianism and a response to the last vestiges of mercantilism.

(c)   an arbitrary interpretation of the synthesis occurring between ideas in continuous antithetical relationship with each other.

*(d)   an adaptation of a particular theory of progress that sees history as a dialectical process, marked by conflicts and resolutions, in terms of economic forces.

(e)   derived from radical ideas of utopian thinkers, who taught that society can be both industrial and humane.

4.   Which of the following theories is in harmony with the nineteenth-century middle-class worldview?

*(a)   Industrial entrepreneurship and a standardized, centralized financial system will contribute to the increase of wealth and the proliferation of human happiness throughout the world.

(b)   Free schooling, equality of the sexes, and the reward of workers solely on the basis of actual labor were to be features of a reorganized society.

(c)   A system of workshops governed by workers was assumed to lead to the withering and eventual disappearance of capitalist society.

(d)   Universal manhood suffrage and the resultant control of the state by the working classes was to be the only solution for the problems caused by industrialization.

(e)   Although production is governed by unchangeable laws, society can regulate the just redistribution of wealth for the benefit of the majority of the people.

5.   Middle-class art in the nineteenth century

(a)   attacked the values of an industrialized bourgeoisie with the aim of popularizing elements essential to the initiation of change in society.

*(b) was artificial and decorative, and was expected to tell a story or preach the triumph of middle-class morality.

(c) rejected the artistic techniques of the Renaissance and used rococo models as an expression of social protest.

(d) imitated baroque examples in order to satirize social and political evils and to ridicule corruption and hypocrisy.

(e) —under the leading example of Dante Gabriel Rossetti—disdained sentimental and pietistic conventionality.

6. Which statement is *incorrect* in describing the theories of John Stuart Mill?

*(a) Only by following the thought of earlier rational philosophers of France is implementation of economic reforms based on the immutable laws of nature possible.

(b) The worker will share in the more general increase in living standards if the working day is shortened.

(c) Either the government or society must abolish the wage system and create cooperatives in order to grant the workers the fruits of their labor.

(d) John Stuart Mill believed that the government should take preliminary steps to redistribute wealth by taxing inheritances and by appropriating unearned accumulations of land holdings.

(e) Although Mill repudiated a number of the most sacred premises of the classical schoool he favored legislative interference under certain circumstances, thus expanding classical notions of departure from laissez-faire economics.

7. Except for one of the following, the tenets of classical liberal economics were accepted by the middle class as their own because the theories

(a) rationalized middle-class ascendancy over an older society of the landholders and the urban poor.

(b) absolved the middle class from responsibility for poverty and from the burden of supporting the urban unemployed.

*(c) acknowledged the necessity of reorganizing society on the basis of cooperation, with rewards given to workers solely for actual labor performed.

(d) insisted that the interests of the community were nothing more than the sum of individual interests, which were to be curtailed only if these interests interfered with those of the majority.

(e) argued that unfettered individualism will further industrialization, the progress of which will, in turn, afford the greatest happiness to the greatest number.

8. Which statement expresses a postulate of Adam Smith's theories that followers of the classical-liberal ideology conveniently neglected?

   (a) General prosperity can best be promoted by allowing all individuals to pursue their own interests so long as they do not trespass upon the equal rights of others to do the same.

  *(b) State intervention is necessary to prevent injustice, to advance education, to protect public health, and to maintain enterprises that would not be established by private capital.

   (c) Free competition and free trade will ensure maximum production according to demand and will provide the greatest benefits to the most people.

   (d) As in each sphere of the universe, the laws of nature that govern economics must be recognized and respected.

   (e) Individuals must be free to negotiate contracts without outside interference.

9. Which of the following statements is *not* a rationalization of conflicting interests in middle-class prosperity and ascendancy?

   (a) Laws of nature have set limits for the progress of mankind toward happiness and wealth, and, therefore, poverty and pain are inescapable.

  *(b) Understanding of the present world will lead to an improved world in the future, in which the redistribution of wealth will secure a stable and beneficent society.

   (c) Extreme interventionist policies will inhibit the distribution of industrialization's very benefits, while more temperate, socially useful laws are sufficient to curtail individual greed and pave the way for a stable and beneficent society.

   (d) It is industrialization and the factory system that have introduced the last "positive" stage in world history, and schemes designed to help the poor will only hobble the capital means that now operate to increase the happiness of many, and more productive, members of society.

   (e) The middle class has a leading role in securing, through the means of production, commerce, and finance, happiness for the majority of the world's population.

10. The most significant result of early nineteenth-century European industrialization is expressed in which statement?

   (a) Hardship caused by the stress of agricultural capitalism and its inadequate response to the needs of rural populations compelled millions throughout Europe to seek better conditions in the cities.

   (b) Low pay, unemployment, and the stress of urban factory life turned millions of men and women into machinelike beings who had little time to think about anything but the source of their next meal.

(c) Critics as well as supporters of industrialization construed radically different, new worldviews, which they presented to nineteenth-century Europe as sociohistorical philosophies ripe for application to current politics.

(d) Most governments, trying to cope with overpopulation and underemployment, encouraged emigration to the Americas.

*(e) By mid-century men and women began to perceive themselves as part of a class, different from and in opposition to another class.

11. Agricultural capitalism might be best defined as the

*(a) investment of capital to transform small land holdings into large tracts in order to meet market demands for food and obtain the greatest possible profits that the market will allow.

(b) elimination of the last vestiges of feudal responsibilities lords had in relation to vassals and serfs, making possible salaried labor employed according to seasonal need.

(c) enclosure of lands to improve agricultural production scientifically.

(d) legislation allowing landowners of the old society to turn their land into a negotiable commodity.

(e) none of the above.

12. The economic position of the working class is described correctly in which statement?

*(a) The increase of population brought underemployment and, in its wake, poverty to rural and urban laborers.

(b) The availability of cheaper food, improved agricultural technology, and the introduction of the potato in Europe all but eliminated hunger and starvation.

(c) Cholera, typhus, and tuberculosis were successfully controlled in manufacturing centers during the early decades of the nineteenth century through the construction of adequate sewage systems and fresh-water facilities.

(d) Many capitalists recognized and met their responsibility to postindustrial society by initiating improvements in working conditions and funding welfare programs in their communities.

(e) The building of crowded, single-family dwellings and townhouses adjacent to the factories greatly alleviated the psychological stress of first-generation workers.

13. Middle-class success in nineteenth-century Europe is best accounted for by which statements?

*(a) Obedience to similar standards and aspirations bound members of the

middle class to the same values and, in part because of this solidarity, guaranteed the ascendancy of their interests over those of the old aristocratic society of land and of the poor.

(b) The middle-class belief that intelligence and dedication to work will advance one's position in terms of responsibility and personal profit remained a myth for the great majority.

(c) An examination system allowed middle-class youngsters to enter government bureaucracies and to advance therein, while most working-class children, lacking the recourse to education that enabled social mobility, seemed predestined to become cheap labor in the factories.

(d) With the exception of a few, short-lived attempts to establish governments comprised of independent workers' cooperatives, management of cities was, for the most part, in middle-class hands.

(e) Set apart from the unpleasant sights and smells of industrialized urbanization, both the residential areas housing the middle class and the cities' landmarks reflected the middle-class social triumph over the older aristocracy and the poor.

14. Regarding mobility within the emerging urban middle class, the classes of workers, and the landed aristocracy, one statement below *incorrectly* implies that: social mobility was

(a) possible in the various subgroups and categories within a class, but far less common between classes.

(b) practically impossible without education—an expensive and mostly unattainable luxury for the children of workers, and thought to be unnecessary for women.

(c) often counterbalanced by downward movement among members of the working class due to technological changes that rendered certain skills obsolete.

*(d) available only to women of the working class, whose employment in the factories gave them full equality with men.

(e) far more difficult on the Continent than in Britain, especially for the middle class to enter the aristocracy, since social distinction between nobility and commoners was a jealously guarded tradition on the Continent.

15. Which statement properly describes the stress that urban factory life caused workers?

(a) The trauma of migration to the city was somewhat eased when workers settled either among relatives who had already made the transition or friends who worked in the same trade.

(b) Employment of women and children weakened and disrupted the traditionally strong family unit.

(c) Urban factory life—that required each worker to respond to the discipline of the whistle—created psychological stresses unknown to people accustomed to working at their own pace.

(d) Adjustment to long factory hours and new physical working conditions was as difficult and as oppressive as adjustment to urban living.

*(e) All of the above.

IDENTIFICATIONS

Regulated lands
Junkers
William Gladstone
Self Help
"Angel in the House"
Essay on Population
*The Principles of Morals
    and Legislation*
Nassau Senior

Positivism
Hiram Powers
Honoré Daumier
"Associations of Production"
Bourgeoisie
*The Condition of the Working Class
    in England in 1844*
The Human Comedy

TRUE OR FALSE

T 1. Some European governments attempted to solve the problem of population growth in the years between 1800 and 1850 by passing laws raising the age of marriage.

F 2. Following the example of European legislation, the Russian government introduced laws that turned land into a negotiable commodity.

F 3. The most radically capitalist element of French society was the rural middle class.

T 4. Law in most European countries in the early nineteenth century tolerated a husband's infidelity, yet ruthlessly punished a wife for a similar deed.

T 5. Family vacations were a nineteenth-century middle-class invention.

F 6. European working-class conditions and mobility during the years 1800-1850 were singularly similar qualitatively as well as quanitatively.

T 7. Utilitarianism provided the theoretical bases for governmental interventionist reforms, as well as for unfettered individualism according to the principles of laissez faire.

F 8. Pietistic naturalism and obsession with morality, in combination with innocuous social protest, was preferred by European middle-class people in the nineteenth century.

F   9.   The theories of the French politician and journalist Louis Blanc were greatly influenced by the Positivistic interpretation of progress within the history of the world.

T   10.   The parents of Karl Marx and Friedrich Engels were wealthy middle-class industrialists.

DISCUSSION AND/OR ESSAY QUESTIONS

1. What were the reasons for the growth of European populations during the early nineteenth century? What were the means by which nature or governments acted to slow down the increase in population?

2. How were middle-class women of the nineteenth century treated, and what was generally expected of them? How were working-class women treated, and how were they expected to cope with the hardships that faced them, particularly if they were poor?

3. Compare middle-class and working-class living conditions in early ninteenth-century Europe.

4. The middle-class worldview, though highly rationalized, occasionally permitted members of the middle class to perceive the conflict of their interests with those of the working class. By mouthing popularizations of some contemporary economic theorists, the middle class managed to cast aside self-doubt concerning its role and responsibility in shaping society. What were some initial perceptions of conflict of interest, and what theories were appropriated by many middle-class Europeans to assure themselves that their vision was right and should be realized?

5. Did the standard of living rise or fall in Europe during the first half-century of the Industrial Revolution?

SUGGESTED FILMS

Balzac. 23 min. B/w. Film Images, a Division of Radim Films, Inc. (1950).

The Changing World of Charles Dickens. 27 min. Color. Learnex Corporation of Florida (1969).

Civilization: The Fallacies of Hope. 2 parts, each 26 min. Color. Time-Life Films, Inc. (1970).

Daumier (1808-1879). 14 min. B/w. Roland Films (1970).

Karl Marx–His Work and Background. 30 min. B/w. Institute on Communism and Constitutional Democracy, Vanderbilt Univresity (1964).

Pre-Raphaelite Revolt. 30 min. Color. Films, Inc. (1971).

Outline

MULTIPLE CHOICE
Choose the best response.

1. In order to achieve lasting peace, representatives of European powers at the Congress of Vienna considered each of the following political measures *except* one.

    (a) Most governments intended to restore and/or maintain domestic and international order by any means possible after the revolutionary upheavals of the preceding years.

    (b) Stern reactionary policy against liberal doctrines was thought to preempt the outbreak of domestic disturbances.

    (c) By forming alliances, the participating states agreed to cooperate in the suppression of any uprising that might attempt to overthrow legitimate governments, i.e., those having dominion at the time of the congress.

    (d) Although the boundaries of France were to remain essentially the same, the congress negotiators drew up strong barriers to contain French territorial ambitions.

    *(e) As a token of their consensus that the new international order was to be based upon the Christian precepts of justice and peace, and in order to encourage free exchange of goods and ideas, participating governments abolished all tariff barriers.

2. Legitimacy, the guiding principle of the Congress of Vienna,

    (a) allowed the territorial expansion of Prussia and Russia into Saxony and Poland, respectively.

    *(b) was a concept invented by Talleyrand to protect French interests against decisions by the congress, and, in turn, was accepted by Metternich as a convenient apology for the restoration of European monarchies and the return of a prerevolutionary status quo.

    (c) guaranteed the maintenance of the kingdoms of Saxony, Würtemberg, and Bavaria as a bulwark against the growth of Prussian and Russian power.

(d)   transferred control of French dominions in South Africa, South America, and Ceylon to Britain.

(e)   encouraged the independence movement of smaller nations under foreign rule at the time of the congress and the restoration of national dynasties.

3.   Metternich's conservative foreign policy is best indicated by his

(a)   secret alliance with France and England to prevent Russian expansion.

(b)   distrust of Great Britain, where the liberal movement was gaining momentum by the late 1820s.

*(d)   hatred of any change in the status quo, as well as his suspicion that the tsar's devotion to "liberty" and "enlightenment" might be a clever plot to extend Russian supremacy over Europe.

(d)   support of the Anglo-Russian-French naval intervention in the Greeks' war of liberation against the Turks.

(e)   repression of the *Carbonari* movement despite French and English refusal to endorse the Troppau agreement to defend international order and suppress revolutions.

4.   The earliest evidence that the Quintuple Alliance could not preserve the principle of status-quo government is indicated by the

(a)   reciprocal distrust and suspicion apparent among the allies that could never by fully overcome.

(b)   creation of a constitutional monarchy in Belgium as a buffer state between France and Holland, as a result of insurrection by Belgian liberal and nationalist elements.

*(c)   successful Greek nationalist rebellion against Turkish domination, in which the support of Russia, England, and France had been instrumental.

(d)   sympathy of the politically powerful English Whigs toward the working classes and their support of political and social reform.

(e)   socialist and anarchist agitation in France for the establishment of a republic.

5.   As a reaction against the intransigent policies adopted by the allies in the international conferences that followed the Congress of Vienna

(a)   young liberals attempted to force various European kings—and occasionally succeeded in doing so—to devise constitutions modeled after that of the French constitution of 1789-1791.

*(b)   middle-class liberals were more determined than ever to fight against the status quo and to form and support governments that would implement the doctrines of classical economists.

(c) most colonial areas achieved independence, recognized and supported as they were by British commercial interests and through the British navy, without significant opposition from the mother countries.

(d) nationalists throughout the world organized themselves, according to the examples of the American and French Revolutions, to gain independence for their countries.

(e) working-class people, by rioting and insurrection, pressed their demands for equality, representation, and participation in political life.

6. The interests of the Whigs and the Tories in England after 1815 differed in regard to which of the following policies:

(a) staunch defense of the status quo and opposition to all democratic notions.

(b) liberalization of the Corn Laws, which, until the 1820s, had excessively favored the prices set by landed aristocracy.

(c) streamlined practices in criminal law, including the abolition of capital punishment for approximately one hundred offenses.

(d) legislation that permitted participation in political life to all members of various Protestant sects other than Anglican and to Roman Catholics.

*(e) insistence on the traditional representation of landowners—whose interests were regarded as coincidental with those of the nation as a whole—in the House of Commons.

7. As its most significant constitutional change, the Reform Bill of 1832

(a) completely destroyed the traditional notion of parliamentary representation according to the interests of landed property.

*(b) complied with the interests of middle-class industrialists by admitting them into junior partnership with the landed oligarchy.

(c) redistributed parliamentary seats from the rural south to the industrial areas in the north, and granted representation to artisan and tradesman leadership of the working classes.

(d) extended the franchise, yet did so without any carefully prescribed limitations that stipulated property-ownership requirements.

(e) toppled the landed, aristocratic government of the conservative Tories and brought in a new, liberal Whig government under Lord Grey.

8. Both the Revolution of 1830 in Paris and the English Reform Bill of 1832

(a) created equal electoral districts based on population density and granted the franchise to the majority of the male population.

(b) provided leadership to the emerging working classes, whose interests were ably represented by the newly elected middle-class members.

(c)   introduced that positive stage in the history of the world of which Auguste Comte spoke and which, according to him, was not possible without the turmoil of industrialization.

*(d)   served primarily the concerns and interests of the industrial middle class.

(e)   contributed in an organized fashion to the distribution of industrialization's benefits and the spread of general happiness.

9.   Which of the following events was *not* directly and immediately inspired by the successes of the 1830 revolution in Paris?

    (a)   Middle- and working-class radicals in England relentlessly pressed for liberal reforms, which came to be realized, in part, in 1832.

    (b)   Polish nationalists rose against Tsar Nicholas I, who ruthlessly crushed the insurrection with Russian troops and absorbed Poland into the tsarist empire.

    (c)   King Louis Philippe agreed to support the principles most desired by the middle class: equality, meritocracy, a two-chamber parliament, and limitations on the franchise.

    *(d)   Karl Marx moved to Paris and established the Communist League to achieve the overthrow of the middle class.

    (e)   Belgian nationalists and liberals succeeded in gaining independence from the Dutch—the Netherlands' appropriations of Belgium having been one of the settlements of the Congress of Vienna—and establishing a constitutional monarchy.

10.   Which was *not* an accomplishment of the British Parliament after the Reform Bill of 1832?

    (a)   According to liberal notions of efficiency, new laws were passed—almost without dissent—regulating the treatment of paupers.

    (b)   Sir Robert Peel, as prime minister, split his own Conservative party when he tried to have the Corn Laws repealed in 1846.

    (c)   The eloquence of William Wilberforce and devotion to the tenets of Christianity among many members of the urban middle class motivated the Parliament to abolish the slave trade in British colonies in 1833.

    *(d)   Drafted by Jeremy Bentham's former private secretary, Edwin Chadwick, the Education Act virtually guaranteed primary education to all.

    (e)   In a series of factory acts, working hours in some trades were limited to ten hours a day by 1847, and some gains were also made in limiting women and child labor in the mines.

11.   Which of the following statements points to some similarity in the reasons for domestic upheavals in France and England in the 1830s?

(a)   Trade unions were organized in the belief that workers would be able to overthrow the last vestiges of bourgeois class interests and might gain relief from economic hardship in a classless society.

*(b)   Radical members of the lower middle and working classes felt increasingly dissatisfied with the results of middle-class liberalism, which they had initially supported and for which, in France, they risked their lives.

(c)   Following the theories of radical socialists, secret societies aimed to create genuine republics by calling for universal manhood suffrage that could transfer the control of the state to the majority working classes.

(d)   The bourgeoisie and the working classes joined in their opposition to constitutional monarchy and demanded the abolition of parliamentary governments.

(e)   The working classes demanded political reforms that could have given them, and millions of others, representation in the government, a representation based on class interests, not any democratic ideology.

12.   Louis Napoleon Bonaparte's early popularity, in the years following his election as president and later emperor of France, is best explained by

*(a)   his programs, which catered to middle-class as well as workers' interests and promised the opportunity for material prosperity for all segments of the population.

(b)   the alliance of the middle class with the radicals during the reign of Philippe Auguste, neither one of whom would have been able to bring him to power.

(c)   a desire for order after generations of political misadventures, which motivated the French people to overlook controls placed on the free press and on the universities and to welcome, instead, repression of political opposition.

(d)   patriots' and hero worshipers' vision of France as a great world power, and a general yearning for a resurgence of national glory under the namesake and relative of Napoleon I.

(e)   the support extended by Catholics, socialists, and anarchists, with whom he had established close personal relationships.

13.   The Reform Bill of 1867 was passed for all the following reasons *except*

(a)   the emergence of a new class of skilled "labor aristocrats" who benefited most from increases in demand for technical expertise in an industrialized system and, therefore, accepted many liberal economic, middle-class principles as their own.

(b)   the demand for direct participation in the governmental process by responsible workers, whose loyalty to the state could not be questioned.

   (c)   the union between the labor aristocracy and those middle-class reformers who considered many national institutions to be remnants of aristocratic privilege.

  *(d)   Liberal, i.e., Whig, reaction against Conservative opposition in the Parliament.

   (e)   organization of the Reform League, which campaigned throughout the country for new legislation and new parliamentary representatives who would listen to the reformers' case.

14.   The triumph of the liberal principles—free trade, representative government, and general prosperity—is best represented in which of the following achievements:

  *(a)   The English Reform Bill of 1867, which opened the House of Commons to the working class without revolution.

   (b)   the English Reform Bill of 1832, which assumed that middle-class representatives in government could represent working-class interests as well.

   (c)   Thomas Attwood's theories, expressed in his "Political Union of the Lower and Middle Classes of the People," which remained the basis for all reforms providing the enfranchisement of the working classes.

   (d)   gains by the revolutionaries of February 1848, who forced the French provisional government to declare universal manhood suffrage.

   (e)   the French Revolution of 1830, which extended the franchise to 200,000 workers, artisans, students, and writers.

15.   The most fundamental concern(s) of nineteenth-century middle-class liberalism was (were)

   (a)   order and liberty under either a constitutional monarchy or a democracy.

   (b)   devotion to Christian ideals of peace and justice for all.

  *(c)   a governmental system based on representation of middle-class interests, the belief in individualism, and the pursuance of classical liberal economic doctrines.

   (d)   a government that would value the development of commerce and industry and understand their contribution to national glory.

   (e)   accommodation of working-class demands in order to achieve liberal economic goals.

IDENTIFICATIONS

Holy Alliance	Lord Shaftesbury
Carbonari	Constitution of 1814
Six Acts	*Conspiracy of Equals*

Peterloo
Decembrists
Third Section
Carlist Wars
Luddites

The Extinction of Pauperism
Crédit Mobilier
Limited liability
Mechanics Institutes

TRUE OR FALSE

T 1. Prince Metternich was ready at one time to restore Napoleon as emperor of France under Hapsburg protection.

F 2. The independent Dutch Republic was restored by the Congress of Vienna, held after Napoleon's exile.

F 3. At Troppau, in 1820, members of the Quintuple Alliance agreed to come to each other's aid to suppress revolts directed against international order.

T 4. The liberal belief that poverty was a person's own fault and, in the end, was an individual and not an institutional problem was based on Thomas Malthus's theories.

T 5. As indemnity for damages wrought by the Napoleonic Wars, the French had to pay substantial amounts of money to the victorious allies and had to give up all territories conquered between 1789 and 1814.

F 6. Louis Napoleon Bonaparte expanded the French educational system by establishing elementary schools in every village and providing trade schools and teacher-training institutes in larger towns.

F 7. The six points of the "People's Charter" included the demand for a written constitution.

T 8. French liberalism during Louis Napoleon's reign condoned "democracy" in name only, taking the greatest freedom enjoyed by a citizenry to be the freedom to structure economics and to manage one's own fiscal affairs.

T 9. The February 1848 revolution in France was a catalyst for uprisings throughout Europe.

F 10. The toleration of individual preference in religious belief at the universities of Oxford and Cambridge was the driving force behind the passage of the Reform Bill of 1867.

DISCUSSION AND/OR ESSAY QUESTIONS

1. "Politicians in Britain in the 1860s were confronted by a situation not unlike that which had faced Guizot in France in 1848."

Compare the conditions in France and England that contributed to nineteenth-century reforms in both countries.

2. What was the role of the French middle class in triggering the revolutions of 1830 and 1848?

3. How did trade unions develop in England after 1832? Name the various organizations and describe the reasons for their defeat.

4. How did the liberal preoccupation with individualism and governmental nonintervention in private lives deal with the problems of poverty? Why was the English poor law ineffective?

5. Why was nineteenth-century liberalism strongest in France and in England?

SUGGESTED FILMS

English History: Nineteneth Century Reforms. 13 min. B/w. Coronet Instructional Films (1959).

Outline

MULTIPLE CHOICE
Choose the best response.

1. Nineteenth-century nationalism was all of the following *except*

    (a) a reaction of middle-class liberals against the repressive policy of status-quo government, and middle-class support of all regional movements that acknowledged, at least in part, the doctrines of classical economists.

    (b) the assumption made by the middle classes in Germany, Austria, Poland, and Italy that liberal reforms can be achieved by political unity based on the traditions of national identity.

    (c) a sentiment derived from the romantic notions of a heroic past, of historical progress, and of the predictability of a nation's destiny.

    *(d) an irresistible force and intellectual movement, first manifest in the French Revolution, that later reacted against Prince Metternich's particular brand of rationalism as displayed in the works of the Congress of Vienna.

    (e) the essential basis of gradual nation-building, which still maintained the general balance of international power as of 1815 without creating a need for major readjustments in that balance.

2. Which statement *best* reflects romanticism's view of history?

    (a) At the end of a revolutionary process the ever debased working classes will inevitably overthrow the bourgeoisie.

    *(b) The experiences of the past should be made to function as a means to understand the present and to plan for the future.

    (c) The fabric of society cannot be destroyed simply by disregarding religion, since religion is an individual experience and not an expression of national heritage.

    (d) The superiority of German *Volksgeist*, expressed in its customs, traditions, and history, will eventually prevail in the world.

215

     (e)   Social and political institutions must evolve organically and in a manner suitable to the genius of the people.

3.   Which of the following conceptions of history is *not* representative of thought in the age of nationalism and romanticism?

     (a)   The history of European civilization is a progressive development stemming from regional variables and the unique cultural characteristics of the common people.

     (b)   Emphasis on tangible reality rather than on beliefs as the organizing principles of society will ensure that progress of society through the "metaphysical" and "religious" stages and into the "positive" stage—one that will assure the middle class a leading role in this culmination of world history—during the industrial epoch.

     (c)   History is a dialectical process, marked by conflicts and resolutions in terms of economic forces, that will result in the inevitable triumph of the proletariat.

     (d)   History is the organic deveoplment of social and political institutions, marked by conflicts and resolutions in terms of the motive force of ideas, that will inevitably create unified nation-states.

   *(e)   There are immutable laws in every sphere of the universe that set stubborn limits to the progress of humanity in reaching for happiness and wealth.

4.   In question 3 above specific views of history formulated by various philosophers and/or economic theorists are contained in each response option. Which list below is the proper ordering of thinkers that corresponds to their theories as presented in succession above?

     (a)   Hegel, Bentham, Engels, Herder, Hobbes.

     (b)   Ricardo, Bentham, Marx, Rousseau, Locke.

   *(c)   Herder, Comte, Marx, Hegel, Hobbes.

     (d)   Fichte, Comte, Hegel, Marx, Chateaubriand.

     (e)   Coleridge, Rousseau, Marx, Herder, Hegel.

5.   Which of the following is compatible with the ideas of the eighteenth-century Enlightenment?

     (a)   Men and women are free to view life according to individual reactions and are not bound to see it in terms of a set of rational precepts.

   *(b)   Nature is best perceived by reason. Only through reason can one explain order in and the laws of the universe and, ultimately, improve individual life.

(c) Institutions and laws cannot be measured exclusively by considerations of their usefulness, since only that which is more or less mysterious can render things beautiful, pleasing, and grand.

(d) A person's own inherited personality combines with sensory experience to form the basis of individual creativity.

(e) There are limits to human knowledge, and, beyond these limits, there is a world of "things in themselves" that are unknowable.

6. For most representatives of the romantic movement the concept of freedom was the

(a) subordination of the human spirit to the spirit of a whole people, to which individuals are bound by tradition, customs, and history.

*(b) total absence of restraints on the human spirit, in order that individuals be able to transcend the limitations of the physical world and achieve self-fulfillment.

(c) self-imposed duty that forces one to act according to the dictates of practical reason and to live in a manner consistent with the "categorical imperative."

(d) absence of social disorder, which can be gained only by submission to the naturally evolved laws and customs of the state.

(e) absence of all restraints that might impede the development of national identity and that are alien to local social conventions.

7. Romantic writers and artists strove for creativity unfettered by national conventions. Which statement contradicts this position? Romantic writers and artists

(a) concerned themselves with the experiences of individuals, which transcended national boundaries and nation-building politics.

(b) denied the necessity of sacrificing individual freedom to restrictive metaphysical and political conventions.

(c) —as radical individualists—broke with the past, its assumptions, and its stereotypes.

*(d) supported national aggrandizement by claiming that men and women had a duty to an authority higher than themselves.

(e) worshiped—although they could not analyze—the "genius" that, they claimed, must be allowed to make its own rules.

8. The 1848 uprisings were triggered by

(a) the British government's treatment of Chartist demonstrators in front of the Parliament, since the demands for reform that Chartism articulated had become extremely popular throughout Europe.

(b) persuasive influences of the French radical and middle-class reformers on European delegations and political refugees residing in France, who claimed to represent the oppressed of all European nationalities.

*(c) the success of the February revolution in Paris, leading to the abdication of Louis Philippe and demands for the establishment of a republic.

(d) the publication of the *Communist Manifesto*, which called upon the workers of the world to unite.

(e) a Hungarian nationalist uprising under the leadership of Louis Kossuth, demanding an independent, republican government in Hungary.

9. Which statements concerning the initial successes of one of the revolutions of 1848 is true?

(a) By yielding to the popularly elected legislative assembly at Frankfurt, King Frederick William of Prussia allowed the unification of the various German principalities and kingdoms.

*(b) Under pressure by his own liberal government, Ferdinand of Austria was forced to grant major concessions to the Hungarian and Czech nationalists.

(c) Daniel O'Connell's Irish nationalist movement abolished the union that the English had imposed on Ireland in 1801.

(d) The Austrians' defeat by the combined Italian forces unified Italy under the rule of King Charles Albert of Sardinia.

(e) The republican form of government became the model government sought initially by all revolutionary movements in Europe.

10. The Austrian "restoration" of the Empire in 1849 included all but one of the following.

(a) After the removal of the liberal government that had ruled Vienna since March 1848, the state was centralized within one political system and under a uniform code of laws.

*(b) Bohemia and Hungary retained some privileges even though subordinate to the central authority of the emperor and his prime minister, Felix von Schwarzenberg.

(c) The administration of the empire was greatly facilitated by the construction of railways and road systems.

(d) Peasants loyal to the empire were permitted to retain their newly gained freedom from serfdom.

(e) Because of the new protectionist tariffs levied against foreign goods, the building of factories and the growth of domestic manufacture was encouraged.

11. Economic nationalism is

    (a) a response of nationalists to the internationalism of liberal, free-tade economics.

    (b) best represented in the protectionist Prussian *Zollverein*, established to protect property without ever interfering with the operation of the economic process.

    (c) an abstract science of immutable laws that are equally applicable to the economy of every national state.

    (d) the freedom of each national state to engage in the production of those things it is best fitted to produce, and the freedom to competitively market and trade these commodities.

    *(e) a theory rooted in the particular needs and national experiences of individual countries.

12. Bismarck's overall *Realpolitik* is best exemplified by his

    (a) success in combining liberal and Prussian nationalistic concepts in furthering the cause of the Prussian monarchy.

    (b) total dedication to making Prussia more powerful by bringing other German states under Prussian rule.

    *(c) practice of politics on Prussia's behalf, politics based not on idealistic concepts but, rather, on the hard-headed reality of current domestic and international affairs.

    (d) clever manipulation of the German masses so as to make apparent their differing needs and interests in opposition to landlords and capitalists, enabling Bismarck to use popular support to insulate the central government against upper-class influence.

    (e) total disregard of the ideological and moral implications of his actions.

13. The unification of Germany was achieved for all the following reasons *except*

    (a) the success of Bismarck's *Realpolitik* in building Prussia into a powerful national state.

    (b) the elimination of the Germanic Confederation in 1866 and the undermining of Austrian leadership among German states thereafter.

    (c) the unification of all German states north of the Main River within the North German Confederation headed by Prussia.

    *(d) the Hungarian uprising against Austria after the Seven Weeks' War, a revolt that prevented any military cooperation between France and Austria against common enemies.

(e) the Franco-Prussian War, which rallied the formerly reluctant southern German states to the cause of Prussia and which insured German victory.

14. The unification of Italy was primarily due to

(a) the activities of liberal and nationalist reformers who aimed to restore Italy to its glorious past.

(b) British liberal support and financing of Mazzini and his *Carbonari*, whose propaganda attempted to create a united Italian republic.

(c) religious-minded patriots, who wished to create an Italian confederation under the papacy.

*(d) the successes of Camillo di Cavour and Giuseppe Garibaldi, coupled with the French defeat in the Franco-Prussian War.

(e) Prussian pressure on Austria to cede Venetia to Italy after the Seven Weeks' War.

15. Nation-building in the United States can be best understood in terms of governmental policy that

(a) established a republic committed to the promotion of a stable society and the protection of private property.

*(b) was directed toward the cultural assimilation of immigrants, who were encouraged to commit themselves to their adopted nation.

(c) opposed the unlimited sovereignty of the majority that fostered a political system based in principle on the virtue and talents of political officeholders and that sought to provide personal liberty for all.

(d) promoted political equality for all, universal manhood suffrage, and the election of government officials.

(e) stated specifically that each person is a citizen of the United States and not of any individual state or territory.

IDENTIFICATIONS

Ideas for a Philosophy of Human History
Volksgeist
The Genius of Christianity
Addresess to the German Nation
Monumenta Germaniae Historiae
Risorgimento
A Vindication of the Rights of Women

Sorrows of Werther
Confederation of the Rhine
Municipal Ordinance of 1808
Landtag
German Confederation
Adam Mickiewiez
The Ems dispatch
Law of Papal Guaranties

TRUE OR FALSE

T 1. Georg Wilhelm Hegel reasoned that men and women can be truly free only within the protective institutions of the state.

F 2. Regarding self-realization as humanity's ultimate goal, and not merely that of a few people, all romantic thinkers insisted upon the subordination of the human spirit to the spirit of the whole people.

T 3. German educational institutions were considered to be ideal agencies for the dissemination of the doctrines of Fichte and Savigny.

F 4. Frederick William IV, a devotee of liberal principles, openly declared himself in favor of constitutionalism—a central doctrine of liberalism.

F 5. Pan-Slavism was an almost exclusively cultural nationalism movement of all Slavic groups in Europe after 1848 under the leadership of the Hungarian radical nationalist Louis Kossuth.

F 6. Joseph Mazzini's Young Italy Society wished to unite all Italians in some form of constitutional monarchy.

T 7. Magyar nation-building was thwarted by Josef von Jellachich, a Croatian nationalist who launched a counteruprising against Magyar nationalist aims and whom the emperor named as commander of the military forces sent against the Magyars.

F 8. The whole unification movement in Italy was characterized by a desire for a constitutional monarchy or a confederation under the presidency of the pope.

T 9. By the theory of a recurring clash between "thesis" and "antithesis" that will each time eventuate in a "synthesis," Hegel predicted the unification of Germany.

T 10. The Emperor Ferdinand actually encouraged disunity along national lines in order to catalyze events that could restore the territorial integrity of his empire.

DISCUSSION AND/OR ESSAY QUESTIONS

1. "The paradox of nationalism, as it manifested itself in central Europe, was that as soon as a cultural majority had declared itself an independent or semi-independent state, other cultural minorities within that new state complained bitterly about their newly institutionalized inferiority."

   Illustrate the quotation above with appropriate examples from Germany and Austria.

2. Delineate the aims and the results of the Frankfurt Assembly. How did the delegates cope with their dual goal of liberalism and nationalism?

3. How did romantic art support nationalism in literature, in painting, and in music?

4. How did romanticism support internationalism in literature, in painting, and in music?

5. How do Kant's theories of knowledge, authority, and freedom reflect the theories of the Enlightenment and the theories of romanticism?

SUGGESTED FILMS

Beethoven and His Music. 14 min. B/w; c. Coronet Instructional Films (1954).

Bismarck—Germany from Blood and Iron. 30 min. Color. Learning Corporation of America (1976).

The Civil War: A House Divided. 25 min. Color. McGraw-Hill Films (1968).

1848. 22 min. B/w. Radim Films, Inc. (1949).

1848: Revolutions of 1848. 11 films, each 25 min. (Series appears in The British National Film Catalogue, Vol. 15, 1977; London: British Film Institute, 1978.)

English Literature: Romantic Period. 14 min. Color. Coronet Instructional Films (1957).

Eugène Delacroix. 26 min. Color. Pyramid Films (1974).

Jacques Louis David. 26 min. Color. Pyramid Films (1974).

James Mallard William Turner. 26 min. Color. Pyramid Films (1974).

Thomas Jefferson. 28 min. Color. Handel Film Corporation (1966).

The War of 1812. 14 min. B/w; c. Coronet Instructional Films (1958).

William Blake. 26 min. Color. Pyramid Films (1974).

Outline

MULTIPLE CHOICE
Choose the best response.

1.   Industrial development between 1870 and 1914 is *not* characterized by

   (a)   increased international economic competition between the industrial
          nations, ideologically linked with concerns about national security and
          a political balance of power.

   (b)   a complete reorganization of the capitalist system and the development
          of "scientific" production and techniques for the management of labor.

   (c)   the inception of a consumer-oriented society, interdependent with a series
          of new technologies, new products, and new energy sources.

   *(d)   the westernization of less developed or colonial territories, brought about
          by the deeply penetrating influence of industrial civilization upon indige-
          nous cultures.

   (e)   development of industrial-imperial nations, which tenuously held the
          entire world in their possession by the strength of their military and
          economic might.

2.   Which statement *incorrectly* describes why German industrial and commercial
     enterprises could successfully compete with those of the British after 1870?

   (a)   Using the improved Bessemer method, Germany was able to produce
          twice as much steel as Britain by 1914.

   (b)   In sales of organic compounds and electrical equipment, German firms
          consistently outstripped the British companies across the globe.

   *(c)   By 1900 the overall volume of German trade surpassed that of the British
          in Australia, South America, China, and Britain itself.

(d) Germany's output of manufactured goods increased sixfold between 1870 and 1913.

(e) Most German industries rationalized design and standardized parts so that efficiency in production would be enhanced.

3. Which educational theory or practice was instrumental in the successful German challenge to British industrial and commercial leadership?

(a) At a very late date (1880) public elementary education was made obligatory in Britain.

(b) Prussia's system of primary education, compulsory in most areas of that nation since the eighteenth century, was considered vital to nation-building and to the dissemination of doctrines that inculcated a sense of duty to the nation.

*(c) Well-organized institutions for technical instruction supplied German industry and commerce with literate workers, well-trained technicians, and creative scientists.

(d) In the view of the British middle class during the late nineteenth century, the goal of education was the formation of "gentlemen," whose chosen careers were increasingly political or administrative. This often meant that talented Englishmen would assume positions in the imperial bureaucracy rather than engage in entrepreneurial experimentation.

(e) Europeans, in general, were willing to have the state establish educational systems, whose aims included the training of elites capable of assisting national industrial development.

4. Britain's inability to counter the German challenge in manufacturing and commerce is best accounted for by which statement?

(a) British industrialists believed that reduced costs and improved worker efficiency would be sufficient to keep Britain abreast of competitive world markets.

*(b) Early British industrial successes fostered attitudes of complacent reliance on proven methodologies and strategies and reinforced entrepreneurial suspicion of new developments.

(c) British manufacturers believed that practical experience and on-the-job training could provide sufficient numbers of skilled workers and technologists to run new or improved machinery.

(d) The burgeoning "informal" empire demanded capital investment abroad rather than at home for the revitalization of various obsolete enterprises.

(e) Pride in the powers of British nationhood was incompatible with the anti-liberal authoritarianism and protectionist policies of united Germany.

5. The technological changes that increased the overall scale of manufacturing after about 1870

   (a) eradicated abject poverty both in the cities and in the country by raising the standard of living throughout the world.

   (b) were able, within a short time, to accommodate and absorb the unemployed, the casual laborers, and those skilled or semiskilled workers who had been displaced by the efficient use of new techniques and machinery.

   (c) facilitated the upward mobility of the working classes by providing a rising scale of earnings commensurate with middle-class standards.

   *(d) forced many skilled workers to relearn the tools of their trade and to accept a concomitant loss of either pay or prestige or both.

   (e) provided concrete evidence that society can progress to its final "positive" stage by means of industrial expansion and consolidation.

6. New materials and new power resources generated new technologies, a cycle that resulted in all of the following *except*

   (a) an increased standard of living, which in turn spurred a rapid growth in the manufacture of consumer goods.

   (b) the transformation in the work patterns in factories that made possible the enormous increase that followed in the volume of manufactured goods.

   (c) alterations in the scale of production that differentially effected various industries: small workshops in some industries could purchase inexpensive machinery and thus turn a profit through reduced labor costs, while the expense of equipment needed in heavy industry encouraged a syndrome of expansion and consolidation in that sector.

   *(d) the phasing out of the working class in an industrial environment utterly dominated by machines.

   (e) a proliferation of corporate cartels and combines, which were believed to represent a natural stage in that progress of industrialization expected to provide eventually the greatest happiness to the greatest numbers.

7. The theory of scientific management of labor is best summarized in which statement?

   (a) Replacing hourly wages with piece rates will give workers an incentive to produce more in order to share proportionately in the increased profits flowing from the enlarged scale of production.

   *(b) Worker output, if measured scientifically, provides a precise method of worker payment.

(c) By observing the typical movements of workers engaged in various tasks, efficient production norms can be established and all workers should be expected to maintain a similar rate of output.

(d) If procedures are rationalized and controls established in all areas of production and distribution, profits will increase.

(e) Requiring that the workers produce as much as the owners think them capable of producing will raise the workers' earning power.

8. What might *best* explain Britain's success in maintaining, however tenuously, its industrial and commercial lead among nations in the late ninteenth century:

(a) the dogma of free trade that Britain alone maintained well into the twentieth century, while other European nations had been forced to institute tariffs aganist foreign competitors.

(b) Britain's investment of $20 billion overseas, one-half of which was in territories under British influence.

(c) the shifting of resources to the service sector of the economy, e.g., shipping, insurance, and banking, which produced far greater profits than that of any other country.

(d) British determination to maintain naval superiority, which stimulated and strengthened the British steel industry.

*(e) a considerable volume of "invisible" exports, in combination with the continued export of manufactured goods.

9. Industrial and commercial competition resulted in all of the following *except* a

(a) search for markets on a global scale, which brought industrialized states into direct competition with each other.

(b) less than satisfactory relationship with less developed areas, from which the industrial nations imported their raw materials.

(c) struggle between Britain and Germany, whose cartels outproduced and undersold British manufacturers in a number of areas.

(d) global system maintained by the balanced military and economic powers of the industrialized nations, the world's masters for the time being.

*(e) rise of mammoth corporations that eliminated unemployment, reduced costs, and provided manufactured goods at stable, low prices.

10. Which of the following institutions is *not* representative of the new capitalist organization:

(a) corporations that combined several industries—vertical incorporation—in order to control either or both the sources of raw material and the markets for manufactured goods.

*(b)   an international monetary organization that controlled the gold standard for the purpose of achieving the orderly growth of an interlocking, world-wide system of manufacturing, trade, and finance.

(c)   a reorganization of several individual companies in the same industry—horizontal incorporation—for the purpose of controlling competition by charging identical, low prices.

(d)   institutions of "finance" capital, which provided money for investment in various enterprises.

(e)   corporations with limited liability for their stockholders.

11.   Which of the following is the best reason for the onset of late-nineteenth-century imperialism?

(a)   A need to invest surplus capital in the nonindustrial nations, whose people assumed the role of an unskilled working class under the hegemony of Western capitalism.

*(b)   National security and the need for preservation of an international balance of political and economic power among industrialized nations.

(c)   A global competition among European powers for claims to or treaty relations with the less developed areas—potential providers of raw materials and markets for manufactured goods.

(d)   The acquisition of territories that promised economic or strategic benefit in the fiercely competitive world-wide marketplace.

(e)   Missionary activities intended to civilize and Christianize the "barbaric" areas of the world.

12.   Britain's informal empire is *best* described by its

(a)   willingness to use tariffs and military power to maintain the international balance of industrial powers.

*(b)   policy of leaving local rulers in charge of their states, yet insuring that the affairs of such states would be conducted to Britain's advantage and within Britain's sphere of influence.

(c)   success in penetrating India and the subsequent extension of British protection over Egypt and the Suez Canal.

(d)   readiness to build the Capetown-Cairo railway and thus dominate the entire continent of Africa.

(e)   concern over German and Russian expansionistic policies, which were perceived as a challenge to British leadership in the global marketplace.

13.   Which statement is *incorrect*? The Boer War

*(a)   was sanctioned by all participants of the Berlin conference and opened Transvaal and the Orange Free State to commercial exploitation.

(b)   precipitated a general censure of the British, reducing Britain's status in the eyes of its own citizens and those of the world.

(c)   forced British military commanders to resort to brutal policies to control the populations of the two enemy republics.

(d)   was initiated by British economic adventurers, whose attempt to exploit the diamond and gold deposits in Boer territory was inhibited by Boer laws.

(e)   lasted three years before British regulars could force the defiant farmers to conclude an armistice.

14. The most significant effect of British direct rule in India was the

(a)   establishment of a British-controlled administration that had the full cooperation of Indian upper classes.

(b)   declaration of the various principalities to be protectorates and their incorporation into a unified British scheme of government.

(c)   development of a school system in which the language of instruction remained English, but that emphasized Indian traditions.

*(d)   appearance of a westernized Indian literate elite, having admiration, perhaps, for their tutors, but loyal, nonetheless, to India. This cadre would provide leadership when a bid was made to gain independence from Britain during the twentieth century.

(e)   realization in British governmental circles that the "informal" rule of the commercially motivated East India Company was detrimental to national security and the maintenance of the balance of global powers.

15. Which statement is *most* satisfactory? As an imperial power, the United States

(a)   defended the rights of underdeveloped countries in the Western Hemisphere from threats by European capitalists.

(b)   could carry out the stipulations of the Monroe Doctrine only because of British maritime support.

(c)   purchased territory from France and Mexico in order to build its nation and insure sustained economic growth and further expansion of capitalism.

*(d)   played a double game: it both protected its neighbors and preyed upon them, either formally or "informally," through its selective encouragement of rebellions, extension of protection to less developed nations, or annexation of territories.

(e)   did not hesitate to intervene militarily to protect its investments and maritime security.

IDENTIFICATIONS

Crucible technique	Méline Tariff
Puddling process	Gold standard
Bessemer method	Fashoda
Alessandro Volta	International Congo Association
Ernest Solvay	"The Indian Mutiny"
Taylor's three-step system	Frederick and William Siemens
"Rentier" class	and Pierre Martin
Sherman Anti-Trust Act	Sidney Gillchrist Thomas
	and Sidney Gilchrist

TRUE OR FALSE

T   1. Prussia's educational system was greatly strengthened by the continuity in curriculum between primary and secondary schools and the University of Berlin, a full-scale system of public education legislated in 1808.

F   2. Cecil Rhodes, prime minister of the Cape Colony, succeeded, after three years of war, in concluding an armistice with the republicans of Transvaal and the Orange Free State.

T   3. The processes that revolutionized the production of steel determined that by 1890 steel would overtake iron as the principle building material in the British shipbuilding industry.

F   4. With the rise of heavy industry in France, cartels became particularly strong there.

T   5. Defenders of cartels argued that the reduced cost of production lowers prices, eliminates foreign competition, and guarantees continuous employment for unskilled or semiskilled laborers.

T   6. The practice of so-called horizontal corporate reorganization in the United States was not curbed until the trust-busting presidency of Theodore Roosevelt, 1901-1908.

F   7. Hoping to stabilize Russia as an ally, the Germans had more capital invested in Russia than in all their colonial possessions combined.

T   8. The Berlin conference declared that European nations with holdings on the African coast had first rights to territories in the interior of Africa, behind thier coastal colonies or claims.

T   9. Japan was the only non-Western nation able to modernize in the nineteenth century.

F   10. Nineteenth-century investment patterns clearly show that investment of surplus capital is a tool in the exclusive service of either formal or informal imperialism.

DISCUSSION AND/OR ESSAY QUESTIONS

1. What were the reasons for expansion of the consumer market between 1870 and 1914? How did this new brand of consumerism change industrial production, manufacture, and daily life?

2. How did the emphasis on efficiency change industrial relations and worker payment patterns between 1870 and 1914? Who determined workers' "potential" and established standards for worker output? How did workers react to these measures?

3. "The achievements of the first Industrial Revolution . . . were the result of what might be called creative tinkering; those of the second revolution were the product of a close and fruitful union of pure science with technology."

   Giving examples, illustrate the differing motive forces for achievement referred to by this quotation. Contrast the role of the inventor during the Industrial Revolution and the later period of industrial progress.

4. What are the political and economic motivations of imperialism? How did the various industrialized nations channel these motivations to construct particular national economic and political policies? Include examples of the ascendancy of one or the other—i.e., political or economic—motivation for Europe's development of colonies, treaty relations, or large-scale investments in particular areas.

5. What effects did global competition between the principal economic powers of the world have on peoples of the less developed areas in Africa and Asia between 1870 and 1913?

SUGGESTED FILMS

Andrew Carnegie: The Gospel of Wealth. 26 min. Color. Learning Corporation of America (1975).

Europe the Mighty Continent: The Glory of Europe, 1900—Hey-Day Fever. 2 parts, each 26 min. Color. Time-Life Films, Inc. (1976).

Europe the Mighty Continent: The Ruling House, 1900—Day of Empire Has Arrived. 2 parts, each 26 min. Color. Time-Life Films, Inc. (1976).

Henry Ford. 27 min. B/w. McGraw-Hill Films (1962).

The Wizard Who Spat on the Floor: Thomas Alva Edison. 41 min. Color. Time-Life Films, Inc. (1974).

Outline

MULTIPLE CHOICE
Choose the best response.

1. The dominant late-nineteenth-century Western intellectual and cultural trends
    supported belief in

    (a)   the expansion of capitalism, according to middle-class precepts of morality
          and economics, and the inevitability of continued material progress.

    (b)   society as a reflection of the continually changing control of means of
          production and distribution, within a dialectical process that would lead
          inevitably to the establishment of a classless society.

    *(c) the dictates of well-laid, "scientific" theories that promised the continu-
          ance of material progress and the ultimate attainment of happiness for all.

    (d)   the incessant struggle for existence of all forms of life, including human,
          within a universe directed by chance and not by order.

    (e)   a mechanistic, materialistic, and deterministic universal law of development,
          decay, and extinction.

2. The so-called labor theory of value

    (a)   is a detailed analysis of the process of production and exchange and distri-
          bution of goods within the capitalistic system.

    *(b) determines the value of any manufactured item by considering the value
          of the worker's labor, which, as it is exploited in the capitalist system, is
          sold as an economic commodity.

    (c)   posits a natural level that wages seek, which will just enable workers "to
          subsist and perpetuate their race, without either increase or diminution."

    (d)   advocated abolition of the wage system and called for the creation of
          workers' cooperatives, which would own factories and elect factory
          managers.

    (e)   was the rallying cry for the wider distribution of private property when,
          in March 1871, the volunteer citizens' army in Paris proclaimed the
          Commune as the true government of France.

3. The political program envisioned by Karl Marx

    (a)   emanated from his passionate moral outrage at viewing the plight of the
          industrialized working classes, and his meticulous, scholarly research that
          resulted in reliable predictions of the future of humanity.

    (b)   was first expressed in his articles in the *Rhineland Gazette* and later
          incorporated into the bylaws of the Communist League in Brussels.

    (c)   was based on his "scientific" theory of history, most clearly set forth
          in the *Communist Manifesto.*

    (d)   was often altered according to the dictates of political events. But, as
          leader of the socialist movement, Marx was likely to decide a course of
          action by referring to his dogmatic principles.

    *(e) was predicated on all of the above.

4. According to the theories of Marx, socialism is all the following *except*

    (a)   an interim period in the dialectical process of historical evolution, called
          the "dictatorship of the proletariat," which will occur after the overthrow
          of the bourgeoisie but before the formation of the classless society.

    (b)   a system in which workers' wages would be determined by the value of
          the work they produce.

    (c)   the result of the inevitable victory of the proletariat, which will only come
          about when society resembles a vast pyramid—with an ever-increasing and
          ever-debased working class at the bottom, in opposition to a few capitalists
          in whose hands economic power is concentrated.

    *(d) a world-wide struggle of the proletariat against the bourgeoisie that can
          transfer the benefits of capitalism to the working classes through parlia-
          mentary maneuvers, making a destructive revolution unnecessary.

    (e)   state ownership of all means of production and of systems to distribute
          and exchange goods.

5. Which of the following is *least* satisfactory as a Marxist theory to explain how
    history would progress if communism were achieved?

    (a)   The dictatorship of the proletariat would be instrumental in the abolition
          of the state and would relegate it to a museum of antiquities.

    (b)   The operation of the means of production and distribution would be
          under the management of voluntary associations.

    *(c) The dialectical process would be stopped for all time, since historical
          evolution would have reached its ultimate goal.

    (d)   Citizens would be expected to work in accordance with their faculties,
          and would be entitled to receive according to their needs.

    (e)   Since no one will own anything, all persons will live solely by working.

6. Which statement expresses the "purist" socialist stance?

  (a) Revolution must abolish both capitalism and the state, and workers must share in the ownership of the means of production through associations that govern their worker members.

  (b) The overthrow of capitalism by violence and the immediate abolition of the state will forestall tyranny.

  *(c) Collaboration with other political parties for immediate, short-term gains will end in the total corruption and demoralization of the proletariat.

  (d) The "inevitability of gradualism," achieved by means of parliamentary democracy, will result in de facto socialism.

  (e) Workers must be made aware of the potential of a general strike by the proletariat to bring about the death of bourgeois civilization.

7. Reread the response alternatives of the previous question. Then mark the list of persons and organizations below whose theories were cited in succession in question 6.

  (a) revisionists, Jules Guesde, Eduard Bernstein, Karl Marx, Georges Sorel.

  (b) George Bernard Shaw, Rosa Luxemburg, Jean Jaures, purists, anarchists.

  (c) Karl Marx, syndicalists, Karl Liebknecht, revisionists, Jules Guesde.

  *(d) syndicalists, anarchists, Karl Kautsky, Fabians, Georges Sorel.

  (e) Karl Liebknecht, Karl Marx, Alexandre Millerand, purists, George Bernard Shaw.

8. The basic thesis of *Origin of Species* is contained in which statement below?

  (a) The hypothesis of natural selection and the implications of the variation factor lead to the conclusion that the human race has evolved from a common ancestor of anthropoid apes.

  (b) Since populations increase more rapidly than do food supplies, the weaker, or less productive, members of society must perish in the struggle for food.

  *(c) It is nature that selects those variants among offspring that are to win out in the struggle for existence and survive as the "fittest."

  (d) Life originated in a spontaneous combination of the essential elements of protoplasm and, through the process of natural selection, gradually evolved into the present multiplicity of complex species.

  (e) Acquired characteristics may be transmitted to offspring. Thus, after a series of generations, a new species will be produced.

9. The moral theory of Social Darwinism is described in which statement below?

    (a) A benevolent God, ruler of the universe, would hardly be imaginable if goodness and evil alike were rewarded in this world by the survival of the fittest.

    (b) No culture can be perceived as "better" than any other, since customs that were formerly seen as "good" or "bad" are now recognized as merely representing "successful" or "unsuccessful" attempts at survival.

    (c) Such traditional virtues as humility, nonresistance, asceticism, and pity ought to be considered vices because they sap the human courage necessary for earning a place in the sun of history.

    (d) Moral values are of little importance in discussing exact, scientific facts of nature or in analyzing deterministic human existence.

   *(e) Religious institutions, as well as ethical concepts of good and evil, are subject to change, since these, too, are governed by the universal law of evolution.

10. Which statement is the *best* explanation for the agnostic position on the existence of God?

   *(a) Neither the nature nor even the existence of the God of the theologians is knowable through science.

    (b) Nothing spiritual exists; the universe consists entirely of matter; and memory, imagination, and thinking are merely functions of matter.

    (c) Religions are nothing more than theories evolved from primitive practices of magic and animism to explain the apparently inexplicable existence of God.

    (d) Organized religion is the only obstacle to natural selection that should be permitted to operate without interference.

    (e) How could a God exist who would watch with indifference the pitiable struggle that humans wage against nature under insurmountable odds?

11. The so-called Social Darwinist offered some comfort to the middle classes of the late nineteenth century by stating that

   *(a) society, just as nature, is a matter of competition, in which the individual or race that can subdue others will survive.

    (b) evolution is a universal law of nature, and natural selection will let the fittest survive.

    (c) not only individuals, but institutions, planets, and solar systems are subject to change in an eternal cycle.

(d)   any assistance given to individuals by the state is against the laws of social evolution and can result in disastrous consequences for society.

(e)   none of the above

12.   Both behaviorism and psychoanalysis

(a)   studied human beings as physiological organisms and reduced their activity to physical responses.

*(b)   attempted to account for irrational human activity by continuing to stress that drives, impulses, and reflexes, over which humans have little control, pattern behavior in ways that can be predicted.

(c)   dismissed "mind" and "consciousness" as vague and meaningless terms.

(d)   interpreted human behavior in terms of the unconscious (the id) being in conflict with the superimposed restrictions of society, which an individual incorporates into personality (as the superego).

(e)   did away with the comforting notion of humanity's superiority within the animal kingdom.

13.   Which attitude supported global imperialism and encouraged industrialized nations to become masters of the world?

(a)   the bourgeois resolve to suppress the entire anticapitalist body, whose criticisms seemed bent on destroying middle-class economic, political, and social security.

*(b)   a belief in the "scientific foundations" of myths that Western civilization was the result of its special fitness, that the white race is superior to the black, the non-Jews to the Jews, and the rich to the poor.

(c)   a reaction against a pessimistic, hopeless view of life in a world where there is "neither joy, nor light, nor certitude, nor peace, nor help for pain."

(d)   the conviction of many governments that policies of brutal oppression were necessary to counteract violence, terrorism, assassinations, or resistance movements aimed at the established power structure.

(e)   increased consciousness of national heritage in less developed areas under colonial rule.

14.   Works by realist and naturalist writers, painters, and sculptors comprise a genre in that they

(a)   expose the greed and baseness of middle-class life and suggest programs for changing the intolerable living conditions of the working classes.

*(b)   provide vigorous criticism of contemporary society, striking chords of protest clearly heard by the middle class and not easily ignored.

(c) break away from middle-class notions of art and beauty, arguing that art is a private matter and supplies its own justification and that the finished product reflects an artist's particular ideation of what is viewed.

(d) try to present elements of nature in an exact, scientific manner, without the intrusion of personal philosophy—although the artists did insist that their characters were victims of heredity, environment, or animal passions.

(e) express great concern over tyrannies perpetrated against the common people by the rich and offer hope that right will triumph over wrong.

15. The artistic declaration of independence from middle-class society was most powerfully annunciated by

(a) the personal, private nature of impressionist painting, which did not set out to teach a lesson or evoke a sentiment. Rather, these works proclaimed the value of a painting as a painting.

*(b) the total repudiation—embodied in cubism—of art as representational "prettiness," intended to express defiance of traditional notions of form.

(c) the expressionists' insistence that paintings of natural objects take into consideration the artist's intensely personal vision.

(d) the powerful caricatures done by Honoré Daumier, which ridiculed the corruption and hypocrisy of bureaucrats and the rich.

(e) the music of Richard Wagner, which interpolated the traditional forms of romantic music with new and fiercely personal melodic patterns.

IDENTIFICATIONS

International Workingmen's
   Association
Revisionists
Syllabus of Errors
Commune
The Civil War in France
Ferdinand Lassalle
Radical socialists

The Riddle of the Universe
Thus Spake Zarathustra
Conditioned reflex
Pragmatists
The Weavers
Symbolists
Paul Cézanne
Reflections on Violence

TRUE OR FALSE

T   1. In Spain, Italy, and Russia, the absence of wide-spread industrialization and the lack of educational opportunity retarded the development of working-class consciousness and socialism as its political expression.

F   2.   As a correspondent to the *New York Tribune*, Karl Marx supported Friedrich Engels while Engels was engaged in writing his *Class Struggles in France*.

T   3.   Malthus's *Essay on the Principle of Population* greatly influenced Charles Darwin's *Origin of Species*.

F   4.   Jean Lamarck's basic hypothesis of natural selection and the factor of variations was clearly proven by Darwin in his *Descent of Man*.

F   5.   Friedrich Strauss and Ernest Renan proved that the first book of the Bible, Genesis, can be fully reconciled with Darwin's account of creation.

T   6.   Most behaviorists believed that every emotion or idea, however complex, is simply a group of physiological responses to some stimulus in the environment.

T   7.   Sigmund Freud believed that mental disorder is the result of a violent conflict between natural instinct and the restrainst imposed upon people by the environment.

F   8.   Henrik Ibsen's *An Enemy of the People* mercilessly satirized middle-lcass order and called for democracy as the only solution to the problems of working men and women.

F   9.   Realist writers also affirmed the possibility of human freedom by emphasizing, like the romantics had done earlier, sentiment and emotional extravagance.

T   10.   Robert Schumann and Felix Mendelssohn are composers of the romantic movement.

DISCUSSION AND/OR ESSAY QUESTIONS

1.   "Artists and public were ceasing to speak the same language, a fact which contributed, as did the ideas of Darwin and Nietzsche, Pavlov and Freud, to the further confusion and fragmentation of Western culture. . . . Their self-imposed isolation served only to increase the general sense of a fragmented world that, despite its material prosperity, was at war with itself."

How did artists, in painting, literature, and music, as well as the ideas of the persons mentioned above, contribute to the fragmentation of Western culture?

2.   What prevented the unification of socialist forces before World War I? What was the role of the middle class in preventing such a unification?

3.   "The time of surprise attacks, of revolutions carried through by small conscious minorities at the head of unconscious masses, is past. Where it is a question of a complete transformation of the social organization, the masses themselves must themselves already have grasped what is at stake, what they are going in for, with body and soul."
          —Friedrich Engels, *The Class Struggles in France, 1848-50*

Describe the sociopolitical movements and organizations that might represent the concepts Engels points out in this passage.

4. Define, and then illustrate with appropriate examples, the theories of relativism, materialism, mechanistic behaviorism, and determinism.

5. Compare and contrast the evolutionary concepts of Darwinism with the progressive theories of social evolution.

SUGGESTED FILMS

Charles Darwin. 24 min. Color. University of California, Extension Media Center (1974).

The Christians: The Roots of Disbelief (1848-1962). 39 min. Color. McGraw-Hill Films (1979).

Darwin and Evolution. 28 min. Color. McGraw-Hill Films (1961).

Europe the Mighty Continent: Social Classes, 1900—a World to Win. 2 parts, each 26 min. Color. Time-Life Films, Inc. (1976).

Karl Marx— the Massive Dissent. 2 parts, each 30 min. Color. British Broadcasting Corporation (1977).

A Third Testament: Tolstoy (1828-1910). 2 parts, each 26 min. Color. Time-Life Films, Inc. (1974).

Van Gogh. 17 min. B/w. Pictura Films Corporation (1953).

MULTIPLE CHOICE
Choose the best response.

1. Internal stability in the European countries and the United States was sometimes promoted by sound political strategies. Which means of enlisting citizens' allegiance was common to all governments?

    (a) An ascendant middle class removed the causes of urban and rural poverty by its leadership in support of vigorous industrial and commercial activity.

    *(b) Participation in governance was extended to segments of the population formerly unfranchised, and occasionally to the majority of citizens.

    (c) National unity was built on the *Volksgeist* of minority groups in the nation and strengthened by toleration of divergent religious opinions.

    (d) Activities of "purist" socialist parties were severely curtailed or prohibited outright.

    (e) All governments succeeded in separating church and state by support of anticlericalism and romantic nationalism.

2. Which factor common to all European countries and the United States made internal stability ultimately impossible:

    (a) the inability of the middle class to eliminate class distinctions and to cope with the democratic aspirations of the masses.

    (b) the cost and public reaction to conscription and universal military training.

    *(c)' the dissatisfaction of some segments of the population with the slow pace of reforms and with the repressive measures used by governments and/or industrial management to suppress protest.

    (d) sympathy for jailed or exiled socialists and trade-union leaders.

(e)   a general lowering of the standard of living due to the control that profiteering international cartels had over world prices.

3.   International stability before 1914 is *best* characterized by

   (a)   the buildup of strong military and naval forces that could maintain the balance of power on a global scale.

   (b)   the very occasional use of the military that, except for the Crimean War, prevented a multinational war for a hundred years.

   (c)   the acceptance of the gold standard, which forced international cooperation between manufacturers and commercial entrepreneurs.

   (d)   alliances that promoted stability and the cause of peace among industrialized nations.

   *(e)   the belief of the middle class in continuous progress through industrialization, which was expected to bring the greatest happiness to the most people.

4.   The worsening of already unstable intranational and international political conditions is *best* indicated by

   (a)   accelerated economic rivalry that nearly thrust the world into catastropic warfare on several occasions.

   (b)   the direct result of Bismarck's imperialistic policies that clearly aimed to isolate France and that strained the international balance of power.

   *(c)   the so-called diplomatic revolution, which resulted in a realignment of European powers within an alliance opposed to German and Austro-Hungarian ambitions.

   (d)   the growth of national consciousness among European minority groups that did not have sovereignty, resulting in uprisings and demands for self-rule.

   (e)   most people's tacit acceptance of successful aggression in the conduct of world affairs as a mark of progress.

5.   A fear that domestic or international instabilities would interrupt peaceful progress was *least* assuaged by

   (a)   the hope that diplomatic activity would solve international problems.

   (b)   the belief that equally matched alliances would create a standoff of the world powers.

   (c)   the political allegiance of the working class won through the enactment of beneficial social-welfare legislation.

   *(d)   increased production of armaments and expansion of standing armies.

(e) the evidence of general prosperity and a higher standard of living for the working class.

6. The inability of the great powers to maintain stability on the Balkan peninsula led to

 (a) Alexander Ypsilanti's rebellion, which, in turn, led to Greek independence and the dissolution of Ottoman rule over the Balkans.

 (b) the Berlin Congress of 1878, which transferred various Ottoman provinces in the Balkans to Russia, Greece, and Austria-Hungary.

 (c) Italian hopes for national aggrandizement by the acquisition of *Italia Irredenta* and territories in North Africa.

 (d) Serbian nationalist agitation among peoples of similar race and culture against Austria-Hungary, one of the Pan-Slavistic movements, which the Russian government supported in its official policy.

 *(e) —in combination with all of the above—the ignition of the First World War on July 28, 1914.

7. Motivated, in part, by fear of socialism as anarchy and by the need to achieve stability within the empire, Bismarck convinced the Reichstag to enact which measures of repression:

 (a) *Kulturkampf* against the Roman Catholic Church, whose activities appeared to be a threat to national unity as Bismarck envisioned it.

 (b) May Laws, which regulated theological seminaries and the appointment of bishops.

 (c) the institution of civil marriage, which was made compulsory even though a religious ceremony might have been performed.

 *(d) the abolition of workers' rights to meet and to publish, and the expulsion of socialists from Berlin, Breslau, and Leipzig.

 (e) the limitations put on the power of the individual states, placing them under the authority of the emperor and his chancellor.

8. In order to gain popular support and loyalty for the central government, Bismarck's social legislation included which of the following:

 (a) conscription of all adult males and universal military training.

 *(b) workers' insurance against sickness, old age, accidents, and incapacity, and fixed hours of labor.

 (c) unemployment insurance.

 (d) a constitutional amendment that permitted control of the chancellor by a simple majority in the Reichstag.

(e) protective tariffs, which continued to exclude competitive manufactured goods.

9. William II put German national stability on a collision course with rebellion when he

(a) granted the demands of Social Democrats after they polled 4,250,000 votes in the election of 1912 and elected the largest single block of representatives to the Reichstag.

(b) dismissed Bismarck because of old age and began to act as his own chancellor.

*(c) proceeded in his plan to act as a divinely appointed ruler, and had the support of the upper and middle classes in doing so.

(d) reasserted Bismarck's international alliances and secured peace during the first score of years of his reign.

(e) actively cooperated with the powerful Catholic or Center party in drafting a new constitution.

10. Leftist activities during the early Third Republic in France are *incorrectly* described in which statement?

(a) Socialists represented a political force that could function in France without fear of repression.

(b) One of the greatest concerns of the government was continued attack from monarchists, Bonapartists, and aristocrats.

*(c) The Radical Socialist party, representing small shopkeepers and lesser propertied interests, initiated and passed labor legislation such as had been granted to German workers.

(d) Two separate laws of 1881 abolished "crimes of opinion," creating a freer press, and waived the need for prior official approval of public meetings.

(e) Hardly any positive social legislation was passed before 1904, and even then it was passed grudgingly.

11. Rightist pressure on the Republican government of France was applied by

(a) radical socialists, who were willing to maintain a compulsory educational system but who did not live up to promises made to labor.

*(b) General Georges Boulanger and his followers—disenchanted citizens looking for a quick, dramatic solution to all problems through a *coup d'état.*

(c) disgruntled workers, who, impatient with the time lag of parliamentary, democratic reform, hoped for progress through the direct action of strikes.

(d)   those whose romantic beliefs in the superiority and stability of French institutions comprised a Republican majority after 1875.

(e)   citizens of humanitarian and liberal leanings, such as those who espoused the views of Émile Zola and Anatole France.

12.   Domestic stability in England was due to all of the following *except*

(a)   a strong belief that Britain had a workable system of government—one that could respond to the growing political power of the working class.

(b)   the extension of suffrage in 1884 beyond the limitations set in the second reform bill.

*(c)   the general prosperity increasingly enjoyed by laborers and unskilled workers.

(d)   the legalization of trade unions, which would later evolve into an independent Labour party.

(e)   compulsory education for all children and the opening of Oxford and Cambridge universities to those who did not necessarily profess the Anglican faith.

13.   The mood of unrest that prevailed in England on the eve of the First World War was *not* evoked by

(a)   the decline in real wages after 1900, which produced the strikes of 1911 and 1912.

*(b)   a compromise between the leaders of the Liberal and Labour parties, who formed a coalition against the policies of Prime Minister Herbert Asquith and sought to oust him from office.

(c)   a liberal plan to grant home rule to Ireland, and the resultant panic among Protestants in Ulster.

(d)   the agitation by militant suffragettes, who disrupted parliamentary meetings, burned politicians' houses, and created an aura of violence throughout England.

(e)   refusal of the House of Lords to accept progressive income and inheritance taxes.

14.   The revolutionary movement to which the tsar yielded in the October Manifesto was initiated by

(a)   Nikolai Lenin, whose treatise *What Is to Be Done?* preached a relentless class struggle and called for an immediate revolution directed by trained leaders of a disciplined party.

(b)   the Menshevik branch of the Social Democrats, who saw themselves as part of the international working-class movement and representatives of the Russian masses.

    (c)   general dissatisfaction with the policies of Nicholas II, who continued his father's vengeful repressionist and russification policies.

  *(d)   the brutal killing of demonstrators on January 22, 1905, which resulted in a general strike of protest by the urban, middle-class population as well as the working class.

    (e)   the defeat of the tsar's army and navy by the Japanese, who proved themselves to be the military superiors of the Russians.

15.   Which response best explains why no effective countermeasure had been found to quell domestic strife in Russia by the eve of the First World War?

    (a)   The tsar remained aloof from the daily problems of the working class and ignored the plight of the peasants.

  *(b)   Peter Stolypin's reforms, implemented between 1906 and 1911, were too modest and, in view of the rising cost of living, too late.

    (c)   Most pledges made in the October Manifesto were negated by sweeping decrees of the autocratic tsar in 1906 and 1907.

    (d)   Nikolai Lenin's activities from abroad proved especially effective in inciting the rural population to violence.

    (e)   Disaffection among large numbers of the bourgeoisie drove them to cooperate with working-class organizations.

IDENTIFICATIONS

Drang nach Osten	Duma
Entente Cordiale	Cat and Mouse Act
Industrial Workers of the World	Emmeline Pankhurst
Progressive movement	Nihilism
Eastern Rumelia	"Go to the country"
Young Turks	Alfred Dreyfus
Slovenes	Marshal MacMahon
Mirs	

TRUE OR FALSE

F   1.   The U.S. Greenback and Populist parties—mildly Marxist-socialist parties—failed to appeal to American workers, who generally believed in economic mobility.

T   2.   The Dual Monarchy, established in 1867, consisted of two equal components, Hungary and Austria, under a single Hapsburg monarch—the Emperor-King Francis Joseph—several common ministries, and a super parliament.

T   3.   The Treaty of San Stefano, concluded in 1878, settled the second Russo-Turkish War and required the sultan to surrender all his European territory except a small enclave around Constantinople.

F   4.   Alexander III of Russia granted a constitution to the Finns, permitted Polish as the language of instruction in Poland, and stopped the persecution of the Jews in his territories.

F   5.   Suffragette violence in England forced the Parliament to grant women voting rights before the outbreak of the First World War.

T   6.   In Britain the prime minister has the actual power to create new membership in the House of Lords, since the Crown, having the designated power to do this, will act on the advice of a prime minister to elevate an unrestricted number of persons to these positions of peerage.

T   7.   As part of a program to gain the support of the working class, the Liberal Lloyd George, chancellor of the exchequer, proposed a budget in 1909 that included progressive income and inheritance taxes.

F   8.   The secret ballot was instituted in Britain with the second reform bill of 1867.

T   9.   After the collapse of Napoleon III's empire, an elected national constituent assembly passed a new constitution in 1875 that made France a republic.

F   10. Neither the Bundesrat nor the Reichstag could veto the proposals of the kaiser or his ministers.

DISCUSSION AND/OR ESSAY QUESTIONS

1.   What were the differences in the contemporary nineteenth-century parliamentary systems of Great Britain and the Third Republic? What were the reasons for relative domestic stability in France and England from 1875 until shortly before World War I, and what forces contributed to instability as world war neared?

2.   How are Bismarck's diplomatic aims and successes reflected in his concept of *Realpolitik*? Choose a viewpoint and defend it: *Realpolitik* depended on the person of Bismarck; world events after 1890 rendered *Realpolitik* obsolete; or a combination of these.

3.   Why did the Dual Monarchy fail in its Balkan policy? How did this policy contribute to international instability? What were the pressures and forces that led to the assassination of Archduke Francis Ferdinand?

4.   How did the new diplomacy after 1890 and the new alignment of nations result in international instability that would lead to war?

5.   What were the aspirations of the various nationalities under each rule: Ottoman, Russian, German, and Austro-Hungarian? How were these nationalities treated by their governors? How did each succeed or fail in its nationalistic goals?

SUGGESTED FILMS

Doomed Dynasties of Europe. 16 min. Color. Film Images, a Division of Radim Films, Inc. (1965).

Europe the Mighty Continent: The Years 1904-1914 – the Drums Begin to Roll. 2 parts, each 26 min. Color. Time-Life Films, Inc. (1976).

Last Years of the Tsars. 19 min. B/w. Films, Inc. (1971).

The Myth of Nationalism. 30 min. Color. International Film Bureau (1975).

Nicholas and Alexandra: Prelude to Revolution (1904-1905). 29 min. Color. Learning Corporation of America (1976).

The Other Russians. 38 min. Color. (Can be leased from the University of Minnesota, which see: *Educational Film Locator*) (1967).

Russian Revolutionism before 1917. 30 min. B/w. Institute on Communism and Constitutional Democracy, Vanderbilt University (1964).

MULTIPLE CHOICE
Choose the best response.

1. African states that withstood conquest and maintained economic independence
    and political sovereignty during the nineteenth century were those that

    *(a)   modernized their political and economic systems according to European
           and American models, which enabled them to fend off potential or real
           invaders.

    (b)   were willing to rely on the economic aid of Dutch industrial magnates and
           financial institutions, given in return for access to African markets.

    (c)   resisted frontier encroachments by Western powers through maintenance
           of strong defensive positions under military discipline of autocratic rulers.

    (d)   forged their own trading operations and successfully competed with foreign
           merchants for access to inland resources of slaves, spices, and ivory.

    (e)   compromised with foreign powers by granting them mutually satisfactory
           concessions in return for ironclad guarantees that their own legitimate
           trade and government activities would not become puppets of the West.

2. All of the following late eighteenth- and early nineteenth-century developments
    except one contributed to the abolition of the slave trade and ultimately to
    emancipation. Which did not?

    (a)   Humanitarian abolitionist sentiments among the Quakers of English speak-
           ing countries were instrumental in the movement to suppress the seaborne
           trade in slaves.

    (b)   A growing number of plantation owners came to believe that output and
           profits would increase if free wage laborers were used instead of slaves.

    *(c)   The cotton gin was invented in America and resulted in the substitution of
           machinery for slave labor and thereby diminished the demand for slaves.

    (d)   Since Africa was still considered "the white man's graveyard" some human-
           itarians concluded that repatriated blacks were better suited to the task of
           "civilizing" the African continent than foreign whites were.

(e)   A growing number of British merchants and industrialists rejected mercantilism and favored policies of laissez faire and free trade.

3.   British imperialism in Africa is best described in which of the following statements?

(a)   Representatives of the British Crown were responsible for stamping out tribalism and illiteracy as well as for ensuring the uninterrupted flow of goods from Africa's interior into warehouses and loading docks for transportation to home industries.

*(b)   British political and military intervention in the African states was primarily designed to prevent interference with British trade.

(c)   Neither Britain nor the European powers pursued a coherent colonial policy to establish African empires until 1813.

(d)   With the termination of slave traffic in 1807, British chartered companies were required to surrender the operations of their fortresses and warehouses to the Crown.

(e)   British colonial officials effectively suppressed the slave trade throughout Africa by the middle of the nineteenth century.

4.   Under the broadening contacts with the western world, both Japan and China did all the following *except*

(a)   suffered various degrees of humiliating infringement upon their sovereignty by the western powers, including external control of customs duties and the assumption of extra-territorial rights.

(b)   adapted western forms of government and framed constitutions in which "Bill of Rights," "democracy," and other western political catch phrases were employed.

(c)   pursued political objectives at the expense of their traditional cultural patterns as international relations became of crucial importance.

*(d)   assimilated western culture and industrial techniques, and thereby won recognition among western capitalist powers as their equals.

(e)   experienced a rise in nationalist sentiment, which prompted them to strike out for control of their own destinies.

5.   Western diplomatic representatives to the Far Eastern countries mainly endeavored

*(a)   to open Chinese and Japanese ports to western traders, to initiate and stabilize diplomatic intercourse, and to place limitations on Chinese and Japanese tariffs.

(b)   to superintend the smooth flow of goods to and from the west, and to help create genuinely democratic, prosperous, and stable societies in both countries.

(c)   to break Canton's commercial monopoly in the East, and to turn Shanghai into the commercial center of China.

(d)   to provide both countries with a western type bureaucratic system by instituting a customs service run by foreigners appointed by European consuls in Peking and Tokyo.

(e)   to combat recurrent anti-foreignism in China and Japan by all available means, including the use of military and naval forces.

6.   The Meiji Restoration can be best described as

(a)   the defeat of the Shogun in 1867 by a popular liberation army and the revival of effective imperial leadership for the first time in 700 years.

(b)   an enlightened era that saw Japan reject Western solutions to the problems of industrialization and develop its own distinctive approach to modernization.

*(c)   a sweeping political, social, economic, and intellectual revolution controlled by the top strata of Japanese society which transformed Japan into a modern state.

(d)   "the last gasp of a fast dying feudal society" that tried to use traditional habits of discipline and docility to unify the country around nostalgia for Japan's early institutions, including Shintoism.

(e)   a revolution initiated by the samurai in 1877 in order to establish a regime that would eliminate feudalism.

7.   The Japanese Constitution of 1899 did each of the following *except*

(a)   set up certain participatory political structures, such as the parliament, although these were to be considered—in the same spirit as the earlier Emperor's Charter Oath—more a gift from the throne than a recognition of human and citizens' rights.

(b)   allowed a previously established cabinet system to function as it had before, accountable only to the Emperor. The Diet had no control over this and other executive matters, including military and foreign affairs, and had only limited control over finance.

(c)   initiated an experiment with constitutional government, which, by the beginning of World War I, had made considerable headway.

*(d)   incorporated what were then largely western political concepts, such as equality, individual rights, government by law, and reformism, in order to bring the greatest happiness to the greatest number.

(e)   reconfirmed the supremacy and inviolability of the Emperor, who retained the greatest portion of national decision-making power and could veto legislation by the Diet.

8.   The role played by the old feudal classes in the transformation of Japan into a modern state is *best* described in which statement?

    (a)   The new capitalist class drew its membership from the old aristocracy, as well as from the bourgeoisie of the Tokugawa era.

    (b)   The Meiji restoration did not appreciably lessen the influence of conservative leaders, whose ideals were shaped by traditions of the feudal past.

    (c)   In 1858 the heads of the four great feudal domains of Japan welcomed foreign intervention in domestic affairs, since they saw in it a chance to discredit the Shogun.

    *(d)   Motivated by a genuine desire to strengthen Japan, as well as by the steady decline in profits from their feudal domains, the feudal nobility willingly surrendered much of its privilege and worked to revitalize the state through assimilation of western culture and techniques.

    (e)   A ruling oligarchy of like-minded members of the "outer" daimyo and their samurai in the Japanese Diet were primarily responsible for the policy of imperialistic expansion in Eastern Asia during the late 1800s.

9.   Which of the following was *not* an aspect of Meiji society?

    (a)   Although total income was rising, the standard of living among the agrarian population was relatively static.

    (b)   The absence of a genuine bourgeois middle class contributed to the maintenance of a gulf between rich and poor that was as pronounced under finance capitalism as it had been under the feudal regime.

    *(c)   Before the outbreak of World War I, former samurai families agitated for universal male suffrage in Japan, so that workers as well as great property owners could effect legislation, and the Diet might begin to find solutions to the political, economic, and social grievances of laborers.

    (d)   An oversupply of cheap labor toiled in small establishments—comparable to the domestic, or putting out system in early modern Europe—and farmers resorted to working in the commercial centers to supplement their insufficient incomes.

    (e)   The Industrial Revolution, in conjunction with scientific knowledge and improved sanitation systems and medical facilities, greatly contributed to the incredible growth of Japan's population after 1867.

10.   Japan's ability to overtake China, for the first time in history, as the leading Asian state was essentially linked to

(a) the opening of Korea to commercial intercourse with Japan, even though the Peking government considered Korea a tributary of the Manchu Empire.

(b) the discovery of massive deposits of mineral resources inthe Japanese islands which provided the foundation for rapid industrialization and for economic hegemony over all of Asia.

(c) Japan's unopposed claim to suzerainty over the Ryukyu Islands in 1881, and China's humiliation in a short war with Japan (1894-95), which led to large concessions of Chinese territory.

*(d) Japan's greater adeptness at mastering the object lessons offered the Asian states by European diplomacy and power politics.

(e) the Anglo-Japanese Alliance of 1902, which assured Japan's acceptance as one of the great powers, and restored, for a time, the balance of power in the Far East.

11. The character of China's contact with westerners between 1757 and 1842 is revealed most clearly by a governmental policy that

*(a) sought to avoid contamination of Chinese institutions by western ideology and practices, while at the same time levying taxes on the legal trade and permitting bureaucrats to exact "commissions" from merchants who participated.

(b) allowed diplomatic contacts with foreign emissaries only reluctantly and considered ambassadors mere tribute-bearers from vassal states.

(c) relied on western nations to carry out many Chinese governmental functions and provide military protection against rebellious groups set to overthrow Manchu rule.

(d) attempted to control trading activities through "security merchants" and confine trading to designated seasons exclusively at the port of Canton.

(e) recognized the opportunism of westerners, especially the opium traders, and, therefore, circumscribed foreign activity to areas where a commissioner of trade and a corps of inspectors could oversee them.

12. Which of the following statements is *incorrect* with regard to Chinese trade in the nineteenth century?

(a) Rulers and upper class scholar-officials considered trade a contemptible business for a gentleman to pursue; thus, they looked down on western traders and entrepreneurs as a low order of humanity, and refused to deal with the reality of a growing western military capability.

(b) Chinese concepts of justice and legal procedure were diametrically opposed to those of the West, since Chinese jurisprudence was based on the premise of group, rather than individual, responsibility for misbehavior.

*(c) Chinese and foreign merchants were unable to establish stable and mutually satisfactory social and trade relationships, and opportunism on both sides was the axiom of early nineteenth century commerce.

(d) Chinese officials complacently believed that the Celestial Empire was superior to "barbarian" governments, and that it would endure the calamities—both internal and external in origin—that burdened China in the years preceding the Opium War.

(e) The moribund, unimaginative, tradition-bound leadership of the imperial government was firmly set against changes that foreign contact seemed to force upon China.

13. As a result of the treaties following the war of 1858-69 between China and the British and French

(a) China successfully barred European merchants from trading in all but four of its port cities where their activities were stringently controlled.

*(b) it was promised that representatives of the Western nations would, for the first time, be received by the Imperial government in Peking.

(c) the opium trade was outlawed once and for all as effective enforcement was made possible with the cooperation of the Europeans.

(d) the principle of extraterritoriality was limited under which Europeans accused of crimes in China could only be tried by their own national courts for certain specific crimes.

(e) Christian missionaries were obliged to terminate their activities and to leave the empire within three months of the Emperor's edict.

14. Which sentence completion best describes those responsible for lasting change in Chinese society? The revolutionaries of China were

(a) mostly conservative southern Chinese who resented—with some justification— the seemingly continuous discrimination against them by the Peking government, and who turned their anti-dynastic revolt into an anti-Confucian religious crusade as well.

(b) preferred by foreign merchants and Christian missionaries to the weak Manchu regime, with its long-standing hostility toward foreign traders, and its overbearing Confucianist doctrines.

(c) supporters of the dowager T'zu Hsi, who restored the prestige of the ruling house after 1861 by reordering the Peking administration, alleviated many of China's trenchant problems, and provided the reformist climate necessary to the success of 1911.

(d) intent on reordering China as a republic, based on Confucian principles of leading Han Learning scholars.

*(e)   vociferous critics of the Manchu government, who drove its rulers to intro-
duce, in 1889, 1905, and 1909-10, such reforms as actually speeded the
coming of revolution.

15.   Among the many factors that contributed to the Chinese monarchy's overthrow,
the most decisive could be considered to be

(a)   the people's resentment of greedy Manchu bureaucrats who, in order to
recover expenses incurred in getting themselves appointed to office,
exacted "commissions" from local merchants and foreigners alike.

(b)   an alarming increase in the illegal opium trade in China, which, unlike
earlier textile trade, brought no revenue to the state while enriching
smugglers, drug pushers, and conniving officials.

(c)   the "unequal treaties," which strengthened the grip of the West on China's
commerce, e.g., treaties that deprived China of the prerogative to set
tariffs, and placed key Chinese coastal cities under foreign control.

(d)   the widepsread internal upheavals directed simultaneously against the
incompetence of the Chinese government and the foreigners who had
taken advantage of it.

*(e)   the frustration and discontent with the general decrepitude and ineffective-
ness of the Manchu administration, which consented to or failed to stop
the changes indicated above.

IDENTIFICATIONS

Hoppo and Co-hong	Chosen ("Land of the Morning Calm")
Lord Napier	Treaty of Shimonoseki
Association for Worshiping God	Anglo-Japanese Alliance
The Treaty of Portsmouth, New Hampshire	House-Canoe
	Dappa Pepple
Alliance Society	Kabaka
Constitutional Compact	Cape Colored
Genro	Battle of Adowa, 1896

TRUE AND FALSE

T   1.   Many capitalist entrepreneurs believed that greater profits could be realized
from trade in African raw materials needed by European industries than
from the slave trade.

F   2.   Africa's major geographical mysteries were insoluble until the discovery
of quinine, which mitigated the deadly effects of malaria.

F   3.   The effectiveness of Japanese political parties after the Constitution of 1889 was ensured by an active daily press, which elicited broad public support for government by publicizing political activities such as parliamentary debates.

T   4.   The Constitution of 1899 and a modern and efficient Japanese military establishment were modeled after that of Germany after 1871.

F   5.   After 1867, the thorough application of western laissez-faire economic practices in Japan supplanted an agrarian economy, strengthened the state, and rapidly secured for Japan the benefits of westernization.

T   6.   Government participation in the economic sphere and the appearance of finance capitalism preceded industrial capitalism in Japan.

T   7.   Shortly after the Sino-Japanese War, Russia, France, Great Britain, and Japan participated in a "battle of concessions" that partitioned China into "spheres of influence."

F   8.   Dr. Sun Yat-sen's "Alliance Society" provided the first president of the new Chinese Republic after the Revolution of 1911.

F   9.   General Frederick T. Ward and Major Charles ("Chinese") Gordon defeated the forces of the Taiping rebellion.

T   10.   The first imperial audience granted to the diplomatic corps in Peking and conducted in a manner acceptable to western ministers did not occur until 1893.

DISCUSSION AND/OR ESSAY QUESTIONS

1. "... humanitarians confidently assumed that repatriated blacks were better equipped to spread the fruits of western civilization to their beknighted brothers in the bush. All these assumptions, while perhaps well-meaning, were deeply rooted in a cultural chauvinism dating back to the heyday of the slave trade."

   What assumptions besides the one noted here were made by Europeans after 1807 in the name of aiding African development? What, then, is "cultural chauvinism," its probable causes, and its results in Africa during the 1800s?

2. Describe the progress of westernization in Japanese economy and culture. What were the similarities of this process to that of western economy and culture? What were the major differences?

3. How and why did the fundamental attitudes and traditional loyalties of old Japan turn into authoritarian, patriotic nationalism that led to a policy of imperialism after the Restoration? Include ample discussion of: (1) the competition of militants and moderates for power; (2) the interplay of economic evolution and political thought; and (3) the roles Japan played in the so-called balance of power in the late nineteenth century.

4. To what extent were the activities of western traders and merchants responsible for the decline of the Manchu Dynasty? What internal forces and events, including the reforms of 1901-11, encouraged its overthrow?

5. "China, it seemed, had gotten rid of the Manchus only to fall prey to greedy and unprincipled warlords."

    Building on question 4, describe in detail the various movements and philosophies influencing Chinese attitudes toward westerners, and the incompleteness of the Revolution of 1911. Also discuss the main reasons China's route to a republic was not particularly straightforward, and the noteworthy non-interference of western governments in these processes.

SUGGESTED FILMS

Imperialism and European Expansion. 14 min. B/w; c. Coronet Instructional Films (1960).

CHINA

The Boxer Rebellion. 21 min. Color. Teaching Film Custodians (1963).

China: Agonies of Nationalism, 1800-1927. 29 min. B/w. Films Incorporated (1972).

China: The Roots of Madness, Part I. 26 min. B/w. Xerox Corporation, Advertising Division (n.d.).

JAPAN

Japan: East is West. 23 min. B/w; c. McGraw-Hill Textfilms (1963).

Japan: New Dawn over Asia. 50 min. B/w. Films Incorporated (n.d.).

The Japanese Economy. 29 min. B/w. Indiana University, Audio-Visual Center (1961).

AFRICA

Liberia, Africa's Only Republic. 27 min. Color. Firestone Tire and Rubber Company (n.d.).

Nigeria: Biafra. 30 min. Color. Carousel Films, Incorporated (1970).

Stanley Finds Livingstone. 28 min. B/w. CBS-TV, producer (1956).

Zulu. 13 min. Color. CCM Films, Incorporated (n.d.).

Outline

MULTIPLE CHOICE
Choose the best response.

1. Responsibility for the First World War rests with

   (a) Germany, because of its attempts to extend the German sphere of influence throughout Europe.

   *(b) no one nation, since all belligerents were most concerned with preventing a modification of the balance of power at all costs.

   (c) public opinion, as expressed in published statements that presented aggression as a legitimate means to exterminate national enemies.

   (d) Russia, for sponsoring—in the spirit of Pan-Slavic cooperation—various Slavic nationalist group insurrections under the leadership of Serbia.

   (e) the government of the Dual Monarchy, which took vigorous action against Serbia as a means of discouraging dissention by minorities residing on Austro-Hungarian territory.

2. The conspiracy to assassinate Francis Ferdinand was apparently motivated by

   (a) the heir apparent's plans to reorganize the Hapsburg Empire into a triple monarchy by the formation of a third, semiautonomous unit composed of the Slavs.

   *(b) Serbian fears that their aim to form a Slav nation under Serbian leadership would be thwarted by the accession of Francis Ferdinand to the throne whose reforms would conciliate the Slavic minorities so that they would accept Hapsburg overlordship.

   (c) Croatian and Slovenian gains on the road to independent status within the Hapsburg Empire.

   (d) popular support of the Union or Death society among oppressed national minorities in Bosnia-Herzegovina and Montenegro.

   (e) middle-class nationalist leaders, who expected that the impending death of the reigning monarch, Francis Joseph, and the elimination of his heir, would give them opportunities to form republican governments along ethnic lines.

3. The actual outbreak of the First World War was due to which of the following contributing circumstances: the

   (a) intransigence of Austria-Hungary in its refusal to settle with Serbian nationalists based on the acceptance of ten of the eleven demands in the July 23 ultimatum.

   (b) uncompromising attitude of the Russian foreign minister, Sergei Sazonov, who succeeded in persuading the tsar to order mobilization of troops.

   (c) attitudes of the kaiser and his chancellor, Bethmann-Hollweg, who wished to punish Serbia without delay and hoped that Russia would not intervene on Serbians' behalf.

   (d) rejection of German ultimatums by Russia, France, and Great Britain.

   *(e) belief of most leaders that it was necessary to take a warlike stance against a potential aggressor who might upset the balance of power.

4. Represented by its spokesmen as a struggle for the protection of the small nations, the avowed moralistic aims of the Entente powers in fighting the First World War are suspect if one considers

   (a) the declaration "Smaller nationalities are not to be crushed by the arbitrary will of a strong and overmastering power."

   (b) the warning issued by Russia's foreign minister that Russia would not tolerate the humiliation of Serbia.

   (c) a statement made by the British foreign secretary that Britain's honor demands defense of international law and protection of small nations.

   *(d) Britain's reversal—on the eve of the war—of its promise to grant self-rule to Ireland, denied on the grounds of national emergency.

   (e) the proposals for realignment of frontiers "along clearly recognizable lines of nationality," and for the autonomous governance for all nationalities.

5. The First World War is well described as a

   (a) gallant effort to safeguard the rights of the weak according to mandates of international law and morality.

   (b) conflict, the only purpose of which was to defend liberty, justice, and reason within the international arena.

   (c) crusade on behalf of a superior culture to protect the fatherland against its enemies and to free the oppressed from the yoke of an autocrat.

   *(d) struggle between rival imperialist countries, who jealously tried to maintain or raise their status internationally at the expense of other countries while jeopardizing the balance of power.

(e) "war to end all wars," "to make the world safe for democracy," and to obliterate autocracy and militarism.

6. The primary reason for the entrance of the United States into the war was

   (a) the threat that German naval warfare posed to British supremacy on the seas, a challenge American economic interests would not tolerate.

   *(b) the belief of the American government that the security of the United States depended on the preservation of the balance of power in Europe.

   (c) a moral ideal, which called for a crusade of good against evil.

   (d) unrestricted submarine warfare, which took American lives, destroyed American property, and violated the rights of a neutral nation.

   (e) American security, which had depended on the defensive shield of the British navy ever since the promulgation of the Monroe Doctrine.

7. The ultimate failure of the Russian provisional government after the revolution of March 1917 was basically caused by

   (a) its failure to understand and alleviate the problems facing the urban proletariat, which was severely weakened and frustrated by domestic troubles before 1914.

   (b) popular reaction to the humiliation of continued defeat at the hands of the Germans.

   (c) the reunification of the Menshevik, Bolshevik, and Radical Socialist factions, who together pressed for a socialist majority in the government.

   *(d) the relative insignificance of a middle-class voice in Russian society, which, if stronger, might have provided educated, prestigious, and possibly popular leadership able to stabilize the government.

   (e) attempts to continue the war according to long-standing tsarist foreign policy in spite of a popular opposition, which eventually forced the government's resignation.

8. The triumph of the Bolshevik coup d'état on November 7, 1917, is best explained by the

   (a) appeal of the slogan "Peace, Land, and Bread," which responded to the needs of war-weary soldiers, landless peasants, and the urban poor.

   (b) lack of resolution in the measures of the provisional government to counteract Bolshevik agitation.

   (c) the strength of the Petrograd soviet under Bolshevik control, and the weakening of all other forms of socialist opposition.

   *(d) organization and discipline under Lenin in carrying out, with hardly a struggle, the overthrow of the provisional government and proclaiming a new, Bolshevist government.

(e)   arming of the Red Guard to oppose tsarist military forces and placing, albeit reluctantly, the guard under the command of the provisional government.

9. The peace settlement drafted in 1919 was mainly influenced by

(a)   Premier Clemenceau, who wanted France to seize this opportunity to impose the strictest of controls over German development.

(b)   representatives of the Entente powers, who either revised or ignored ten of the Fourteen Points.

(c)   David Lloyd George, who was especially concerned about the growth of nationalism on the Continent.

(d)   the stipulations of widely recognized international law, founded upon the natural law principles of liberty, justice, and reason.

*(e)   the belief among victorious soldiers and civilians—constituents of the great triumvirate—that the Entente victory was a triumph of good over evil.

10. One statement below characterizes the essence of the German peace settlement at Versailles.

(a)   The government of the provisional German Republic acknowledged that it was yielding to "overwhelming force" when it signed the document on the fifth anniversary of Archduke Francis Ferdinand's assassination.

(b)   Article 231 of the document clearly designated Germany and its allies as guilt-bearers for the war and, therefore, responsible for war damages.

*(c)   The Treaty of Versailles resembled more closely a punitive sentence against the German nation than a negotiated settlement.

(d)   Germany was dismembered as well as disarmed, and the German nation was forced to pay reparation to the victors.

(e)   The Fourteen Points were consistently and scrupulously applied in the effort to achieve a lasting and just peace.

11. The separate peace pacts with Germany's allies were said to support the principle of national self-determination. But one or the other of these treaties

(a)   created two new states, Yugoslavia and Czechoslovakia, that, far from being ethnically homogeneous, contained large ethnic minorities with strong national aspirations of their own.

(b)   granted the largely German-speaking territories of Tyrol to Italy, the Sudeten mountains to Czechoslovakia, and Danzig to Poland.

(c)   permitted large Greek and Armenian minority groups to be subject to Turkish rule.

    (d)   ceded to Rumania lands having heavy concentrations of Hungarian, Bulgarian, and Bielorussian populations.

  *(e)   did all of the above, in each case flagrantly violating the principle of self-determination.

12.   President Wilson's cherished project, the League of Nations, was *most* seriously handicapped at its outset by

    (a)   Wilson's naïve belief—reflected in the league's operation—that aggressive militarism would dissipate after Germany's defeat and the assumption that control of international relations by a community of powers would be voluntarily accepted by all nations.

    (b)   its structure, owing to the final Covenant of the League of Nations—a document so amended that it impaired the effective functioning of the league within the world community.

    (c)   the exclusion of Germany and Russia from what had been intended as an all-inclusive community of nations.

  *(d)   the repudiation of Wilson's brainchild by the Congress of the United States.

    (e)   its overly idealistic expectation that all nations, regardless of size or power, would be motivated to cooperate by a universal desire to preserve peace.

13.   Among its considerable achievements, the League of Nations did all the following *except*

    (a)   finance agencies to collect pertinent statistics on labor and industry throughout the world, and begin to codify international law.

    (b)   supervise plebiscites in disputed areas, administer internationalized cities, and aid in the resettlement of refugees.

    (c)   provide aid for checking the spread of disease in developing countries, and reduce the international traffic in opium.

  *(d)   resolve tensions that were sources of disputes among small and large nations alike.

    (e)   lay substantial groundwork for a later international organization, the United Nations, which was formed after the Second World War.

14.   The failure of the League of Nations is *most* evident in which of the following statements?

    (a)   Newly independent Lithuania had no choice but to leave unopposed the seizure of Vilna by Poland in 1920, since Poland enjoyed the support of France and the league was susceptible to pressure from powerful nations.

(b) Italy showed that a league member could refuse the league's mediation of its political disputes with impunity when, in 1923, Italy would not submit to the league's intervention in its dispute with Greece.

*(c) The credibility of the League of Nations waned after 1923; thereafter its decisions were repeatedly defied or ignored, especially if the dispute involved a major power.

(d) Manchuria could be conquered by Japan in 1931 and Ethiopia by Italy in 1936 without concern over reprisal or protest by the league.

(e) So little confidence was placed in the league's ability to defend the sovereignty of small states that hardly anyone even thought to appeal to the league during the Czechoslovak crisis of 1938.

15. The results of the Entente victory include all the following *except*

*(a) the gradual abatement of national rivalries and ethnic hatreds, and the accompanying reduction in aggressive militarism and nationalism.

(b) more efficient national management of production and distribution of goods, with governmental control over exports and imports.

(c) changes in the patterns of world trade, following upon the rapid development of industries in Japan, India, and South America.

(d) deficit financing leading to world-wide inflation that severely affected the middle class, whose fixed incomes from invested money were drastically reduced in value.

(e) the emancipation of women, who had shared the burdens of war production in factories and on farms and who were subsequently granted suffrage.

IDENTIFICATIONS

Union or Death	Brest-Litovsk
Raymond Poincaré	Compiègne, November 11, 1918
Trialism	Treaty of St. Germain
Rasputin	Treaty of Neuilly
Alexander Kerensky (1881-1970)	Treaty of the Trianon Palace
Soviet	Treaty of Sèvres
Mensheviks	The Covenant of the League
Easter Monday, 1916	of Nations

TRUE OR FALSE

T   1. The murder of the heir to the throne of the Dual Monarchy was considered in a real sense an attack upon the state.

T 2. General mobilization was translated as "an act of war" in the German, French, and Russian military vocabularies.

F 3. German naval intelligence fabricated reports of war materials being shipped to England aboard passenger ships from the neutral United States.

F 4. Russia's humiliating defeats were caused by the incompetency of the Russian high command, which did not permit the tsar to participate in tactical decisions.

T 5. Italy, technically an ally of Germany, entered the war on the side of the Triple Entente in May 1915 only after its leaders had been bribed secretly by Britain and France with promises of Austrian and Turkish territories to be meted out after the war.

F 6. The provisional government of Russia pledged its support of Entente aims, but refused to expend its material and military resources to capture Constantinople.

F 7. Woodrow Wilson's proposal that negotiations for peace "under any conditions" be suspended until the kaiser no longer ruled Germany was rejected by the rest of the Allies.

T 8. Based on Article 231 of the Treaty of Versailles, German war reparations were established at $33 billion.

T 9. In few cases was the principle of self-determination of peoples based on ethnic heritage more flagrantly violated than in the postwar dismemberment of Hungary.

T 10. Even with all its failings, the League of Nations was at first regarded as the singular worthwhile result of the war intended to "end all wars."

DISCUSSION AND/OR ESSAY QUESTIONS

1. Disillusionment, particularly within the middle class, was a legacy of the war, perhaps best expressed by the British poet Edmund Blunden "when he took as the title for a poem, written to celebrate New Year's Day 1921, the Biblical verse: 'The dog is turned to his own vomit again, and the sow that was washed to her wallowing in the mire.' " Give particular reasons for such despair after World War I.

2. "The struggle was an endurance contest. The victory of the Entente powers came as a result of their continued control of the seas and of their ability to obtain almost unlimited supplies of money, food, and munitions from allies and neutral countries around the world."

   Explain the wartime logistics to which this quotation refers, and illustrate with appropriate evidence.

3. How did the peace treaties assure some opportunities for national self-determination? Describe each area where problems of national consciousness were not eliminated but, rather, were aggravated.

4. Describe the diplomatic maneuverings between June 28, 1914, and August 4, 1914, and explain how these led to the First World War.

5. Describe the various preliminary attempts during World War I to bring about negotiations for peace. Why did these attempts fail?

SUGGESTED FILMS

Europe the Mighty Continent: The Great War—This Generation Has No Future. 2 parts, each 26 min. Color. Time-Life Films, Inc. (1976).

Verdun: End of a Nightmare. 26 min. B/w. Macmillan Films, Inc.

World War I: A Documentary of the Role of the U.S.A. 27 min. B/w. Encyclopaedia Britannica Educational Corp./Films.

The Yanks Are Coming. 50 min. B/w. Films, Inc. (1962).

Outline

MULTIPLE CHOICE
Choose the best response.

1. Movements, policies, and attitudes that stemmed from World War I include all of
    the following *except*

    (a)   the growth of militarism and nationalism in central Europe, and the rise of
           irredenta movements among strong national minorities of the newly created
           or substantially expanded countries of Yugoslavia, Czechoslovakia, and
           Rumania.

    *(b)   the changes in economic policies that otherwise would have meant high
           unemployment, and the drafting of successful social legislation to counter-
           act burdens of inflation, layoffs, and economic depression.

    (c)   disillusionment of the middle class, which materially lost the most due to
           postwar inflation and depression.

    (d)   disgust with the impotence of the League of Nations in dealing with
           aggressions to which major nations were party.

    (e)   the total failure to promote and protect national self-determination, as
           in disappointing decisions rendered by settlement treaties that detached
           certain German and Austro-Hungarian territories from areas of similar
           ethnic heritage.

2. Which of the following concepts of Bolshevist philosophy was put forward by
    Lenin, but is not found in Marx's writings?

    (a)   The exploited industrial working class will rise in a revolution and will
           overthrow the bourgeoisie.

    *(b)   The "dictatorship of the proletariat" will be directed by an elite with
           jurisdiction over the bulk of the proletariat as well as over the bourgeoisie.

    (c)   Capitalism will inevitably destroy itself through intensified market compe-
           tition and the incorporation of industry into ever larger industrial and
           financial units that become less and less responsive to the needs of workers.

(d) As feudalism and manorialism yielded to capitalism when the exigencies of production changed, so too will capitalism be vanquished by communism in an inevitable, historical progression.

(e) The violence characteristic of the revolutionary victory is deplorable, yet in certain countries peaceful means might secure the goals of the working class.

3. Stalin's reforms after the death of Lenin included all of the following *except*

   (a) an economic plan based on a scheme of national priorities for industrial production and commerce.

   (b) the establishment of an extensive bureaucracy to plan, organize, and supervise economic and social activities at all levels.

   (c) agricultural collectivization—reorganizing small land holdings into larger units communally operated by the peasants—that affected all privately owned lands including those of the kulaks, farmers who had been permitted to retain their lands after the revolution in 1917.

  *(d) the organization of the Third International for the purpose of lending moral and monetary support to revolutionary leftist movements across the globe.

   (e) a revival of militarism and nationalism, but also a policy of cooperation with the League of Nations.

4. Considering the constitution of communist Russia and all the channels of post-Stalinist government, the real power in the Soviet Union lies with

   (a) the citizens, who are guaranteed extensive rights, including universal suffrage and the secret ballot.

   (b) the Supreme Soviet of the USSR, composed of two chambers with equal legislative powers.

  *(c) the Communist party, the only party allowed to exist in Russia, and whose overriding will is expressed through the organs of the government.

   (d) the thirty-seven members of the Presidium, who can issue decrees, declare war, and annul the acts of magistrates that are considered contrary to law.

   (e) the Council of Ministers, the highest executive and administrative agency of the state.

5. The result of the Soviet revolution and the Bolshevik regime's accomplishments are *best* reflected in the

   (a) nationalization of factories, mines, railroads, and public utilities, and the reorganization of stores as government enterprises or consumers' cooperatives.

*(b)   rapid socialization, industrialization, and claims of full employment, though at the cost of enormous suffering to over 20 million persons sentenced to slave labor camps.

(c)   reduction of illiteracy, and the opening of educational and cultural opportunities to the common people.

(d)   day-care centers for the infants of working mothers, and free medical care and hospitalization for Soviet citizens.

(e)   indoctrination to make certain individuals were willing to work for the good of society, the fatherland, and socialist ideals.

6.   Which of the following responses is *incorrect*? The Fascist movement in Italy

(a)   was derived from Mussolini's apparently contradictory ideas of Marxist socialism and French syndicalism.

*(b)   in its original platform demanded radical political and social reforms and, after gaining control of the Italian government, succeeded in solving the nation's major problems.

(c)   declared that the state is above everything and everyone, for the state incorporates every personal and public interest and earns the loyalty of its members by its service to them.

(d)   rejected internationalism as a reversal of human progress, for, according to Fascism, society has achieved its highest form in the nation.

(e)   gloried in the concept of war, which supposedly exalts and ennobles human beings and regenerates decadent peoples.

7.   The eventual triumph of German totalitarianism may be understood in terms of which set of circumstances?

(a)   Germany's humiliation on the battlefield and its loss of international prestige demoralized a majority of the German people.

(b)   The wild inflation that Germany suffered during the 1920s particularly hurt the middle class, which continued to search for a government that promised to attend to its problems.

(c)   The effects of the depression were keenly felt among the 6 million German unemployed, whose number was equal to the votes cast for the Communist ticket during the elections of 1932.

(d)   Fear of a Bolshevik revolution motivated a considerable number of capitalists and property owners to throw in their lot with what they judged the lesser of two evils.

*(e)   All of the above.

8.   Which ideology was shared to some degree by all European nations in the post-World War I era?

(a)   Those "of healthy instincts, race, and will" and "who feel themselves born and called to be masters" will eventually gain possession and power.

(b)   Natural selection of the fittest will eventually produce a race of supermen of physical and moral courage and strength of character.

(c)   Since the achievement of the Jew will forever remain Jewish, it follows that these achievements can never truly represent the culture of Western nations.

(d)   Unfit racial and decadent social groups—Jews, homosexuals, gypsies, and opponents of the Fascist movement—are to be blamed for the world's troubles.

*(e)   The success of Western civilization was the result of its special fitness, since the white race had proved itself superior to the black, the non-Jews to the Jews, and the rich to the poor.

9. Which of the following concepts was *not* integral to both the Italian and German forms of totalitarianism?

(a)   After declaring all other parties illegal, the totalitarian party is to extend its control over all facets of life in the name of the people, since the government knows what will best serve society.

(b)   The nation is the highest form of society ever evolved within human history. It has a life and soul of its own apart from the lives and souls of individuals who comprise it.

(c)   Intellectualism and the complicated problems of industrial society corrupt the inherent purity of the race and can be averted only by a strong leader and not by the idealistic dreams of democracy.

*(d)   Race is the determining factor in history and only the super race has made essential contributions to human progress.

(e)   Strife is the origin of all things. Nations that do not expand will eventually die, and so a policy of rearmament is needed to prepare the nation for war.

10. By following the same prewar policies that were considered to have contributed to their victory, the three Western democracies, Great Britain, France, and the United States,

(a)   assured industrial progress by adopting various policies, among them deflation, which kept the price of manufactured goods low and competitive on the world market.

(b)   ignored a number of deleterious results of deflation, such as reductions in wages and dismissals of employees, some of whom became embittered and sought a redress of their grievances through strikes or participation in politically extremist movements.

(c)   continued to direct their economies and social systems according to patterns rooted in nineteenth-century social philosophy, which the leaders of big business had formulated.

*(d)   were forced to initiate new programs that might stem the tide of rising conflicts between the governing classes and the less privileged majorities of these nations.

(e)   so increased postwar production of grain and other commodities that a lowering of prices and a general slump of agriculture followed in the 1920s.

11.   After the onset of Great Depression, the domestic policies of

    (a)   the United States were dramatically changed by Franklin D. Roosevelt's New Deal government, whose social reforms boldly reconstructed the country's conservative economic system.

    (b)   Léon Blum's Popular Front effectively checked the political rightists of France by advancing a set of policies to ameliorate working-class conditions.

    (c)   coalition governments in Britain and France attempted to distribute the burdens of a depressed economy evenly upon the different segments of the population.

    (d)   the New Deal reduced the number of jobless in the United States from 33 to 9 million persons, who, nonetheless, represented over 50 percent of the Western world's unemployed in 1939.

  *(e)   Western democracies could assure full employment only by directing millions of unemployed into the armies and creating jobs within an insatiable war industry.

12.   The world-wide Depression meant all of the following *except*

    (a)   a vicious circle of layoffs, slowdowns in the manufacture of goods, and increasing unemployment.

    (b)   abandonment of the gold standard to make money cheaper, and thus more available for recovery programs.

    (c)   economic nationalism as delineated in John Maynard Keynes's "managed currency" theories.

    (d)   protective tariffs to guard domestic production from foreign competition.

  *(e)   nationalization of the munitions and heavy industries in all of the Western democracies.

13.   The antimetaphysical attitude prevalent in the early twentieth century is least applicable to which of the following statements?

    (a)   Philosophy is merely an instrument to discover truth, which is in harmony with the observable facts of the physical environment.

(b)   Religion is not a branch of metaphysics; it should be understood as a powerful cultural, social, or psychological force.

(c)   Humanity's destiny will be determined by the revolutionary developments occurring in science and especially in the new science of psychoanalysis.

*(d) There is no such thing as an aesthetic principle, since aesthetic principles are based on reason and the history of man has sufficiently proven reason illusory.

(e)   Aesthetic ideals in musical composition cannot be reduced to a one-to-one correspondence with elements of the physical universe. Atonality or polytonality, though, can express the elemental structure of things.

14. Logical positivists' disillusionment with life in the twentieth century is *best* expressed by which statement?

*(a) Everything that cannot be reduced to a "one-to-one correspondence" with something in the physical universe is meaningless.

(b)   Those who refuse to accept the fact that human beings are "beasts of prey" are nothing more than "beasts of prey with broken teeth."

(c)   Life for the so-called "lost generation" is a tragedy staged in boredom and frustration.

(d)   A fundamental fact of life is the existence of human beings as free individuals; this realization is the chief cause of all human agony and terror.

(e)   All political movements deserve to be mistrusted, since each is to some degree corrupt, and those which profess democracy have in fact destroyed human freedom.

15. Religious concepts were decisively reorganized in the time between the world wars, and conclusions were drawn concerning religion and society. Which attitude most profoundly affected the well-being of nations as well as individuals?

(a)   Religion is a cultural force that directly assists in the development of society by clearly distinguishing what is right from what is wrong.

(b)   Religion is a social and psychological force with great therapeutic value in that it can bring the individual into harmony with the "collective unconscious."

(c)   Modern science has shown that the idea of a benevolent God or of a universe guided by purpose is fictitious.

*(d) Duty to society and loyalty to the nation and the ideals of the new order are the exclusive means by which the individual finds meaning in life.

(e)   The process of natural selection is impeded by the operation of ethical codes found within organized religions, especially Christianity and Judaism.

IDENTIFICATIONS

Positive morality	Deflationary policy
Il Popolo d'Italia	*The Protestant Ethic and the*
Fasces; fascio	*Spirit of Capitalism*
Spartacists	Charisma
Franz von Papen	*Hour of Decision*
The Rome-Berlin Axis	Dada-ism
Aryans	Surrealism
Blut und Boden	Bauhaus

TRUE OR FALSE

F   1. Democracy in the Western world between the world wars functioned well despite an atmosphere of discontent and emerging class conflict because citizens felt free to voice grievances.

F   2. Totalitarian systems succeeded in creating an atmosphere of unified national purpose without sacrificing individual liberties during the time between the wars.

T   3. British, French, and Japanese expeditionary forces assisted the White forces in Russia after 1917, hoping to reinstate a Russian government that would resume the war against Germany, from which the Bolsheviks had withdrawn.

T   4. While the Bolshevik constitution of 1936 was being held up as a sign of extraordinary achievement, mass arrests, executions, and lengthy sentences in slave labor camps were busily purging Russian society of "Trotskyites, spies, and wreckers."

F   5. The Third Reich was proclaimed to be the successor of the Holy Roman Empire and the Hohenstaufen empire of the kaisers.

F   6. The runaway inflation that Germany suffered after World War I was not controlled until Hitler's government succeeded in scaling down reparation payments.

T   7. Raymond Poincaré, the premier of France from 1922 to 1924 and again from 1926 to 1929, had been president of France during the First World War.

T   8. The rapid expansion of the communications media had a powerful impact upon vast audiences and provided unprecedented means for heavily influencing public opinion.

F   9. Expressionism in music is best represented by the school of atonality, which retains the long-standing practices of counterpoint in its combination of distinct keys and harmonic systems.

F   10.   John Maynard Keynes was the first influential economist to abandon the idea of a balanced budget and to advocate continual deficit financing as the primary means by which economic development is sustained.

DISCUSSION AND/OR ESSAY QUESTIONS

1.   What are the essential features of Italian and German totalitarianism? How do they compare and what are the differences? What steps were taken by the leaders of the two movements to gain control of their respective governments between the world wars?

2.   What are those elements of social organization and ideology shared by nearly all totalitarian systems?

3.   Why did democracy decline between the two wars, and what were the results of this decline? Try to construct an argument that the totalitarian leaders on the eve of World War II might have used to claim that Western democracies were indecisive governments unable to carry out their objectives.

4,   How did the Bolsheviks succeed in establishing a totalitarian government—i.e., what was the Bolshevik strategy, who were its major personalities, and what were their policies? What were the stipulations of the constitutions of 1924 and 1936? Finally, compare Marx's theories, as expressed in *The Communist Manifesto* and *Capital*, with the actuality of life in Russia under Stalinist social and political systems.

5.   How do architecture, music, and painting represent the disillusioment and anti-metaphysical concepts current in Western culture between the wars?

SUGGESTED FILMS

Ataturk. 35 min. Color. Time-Life Films, Inc. (1971).

Duce. 14 min. B/w. Hearst Metrotone News (1972).

Europe the Mighty Continent: Results of War—Are We Making a Good Peace? 2 parts, each 26 min. Color. Time-Life Films, Inc. (1976).

Franklin D. Roosevelt: The New Deal. 22 min. B/w. ACI Productions (1974).

The Great Depression: A Human Diary. 52 min. B/w. Mass Media Associates (1972).

Great Design. 30 min. B/w. National Education TV, Inc., Indiana University Audio-Visual Center (1960).

The Great War—50 Years After. 25 min. Color. Films, Inc. (1968).

League of Nations: The Hope of Mankind. 2 parts, each 26 min. Color. Time-Life Films, Inc. (1976).

Lenin's Revolution. 20 min. B/w. Time-Life Films, Inc. (1970).

Mussolini. 27 min. B/w. Columbia Broadcasting System (1959).

Overthrow of Social Democracy. 30 min. B/w. National Education TV, Inc. (1960).

The Rise of Hitler. 20 min. B/w. Time-Life Films, Inc. (1970).

Stalin vs. Trotsky. 25 min. B/w. Films, Inc. (1964).

Stalin's Revolution. 20 min. B/w. Time-Life Films, Inc. (1970).

Under the Clouds of War. 20 min. B/w. Time-Life Films, Inc. (1974).

Where Are My People? 28 min. Color. Atlantis Productions, Inc. (1966).

Outline

MULTIPLE CHOICE
Choose the best response.

1. Which statement describes the most notable difference in the characteristics of the First and Second World Wars?

    (a) Domestic pressures and economic rivalries had threatened the international balance of power before the outbreak of both wars.

    (b) With a few notable exceptions, both struggles involved a substantial portion of the world's peoples.

    *(c) New machinery and weapons for mass destruction introduced radically new methods of warfare that nullified many formerly recognized distinctions between soldiers and civilian populations.

    (d) Both conflicts arose between nations and peoples, and not merely from disputes between governments.

    (e) Belligerency against foreign enemies was considered in both cases the best method for coping with national disillusionment and the mounting tensions at home.

2. The treaties forced upon Germany and its allies after the First World War failed most significantly to

    (a) uphold the concept of national self-determination among national minorities forced to live behind alien frontiers.

    (b) prevent the formation of irredenta movements, in fact sown by the peace-making efforts, which had designated territories for postwar annexation.

    (c) abolish the reign of passion and hatred begun during the First World War, when peace provisions were dictated which appeared to the defeated more a criminal "sentence" than a negotiated treaty.

    (d) ease German grievances, which many considered to be legitimate protests against the burden of war "guilt" assigned to Germany and its allies according to Article 231 of the settlement treaty.

    *(e) secure a lasting peace, because of continuous discontent based on economic hardship and frustration of national aspirations.

273

3. The attitude of Western democracies in the face of German, Italian, and Japanese aggression after 1931 is *best* represented by

   (a) frustration and disenchantment with broken promises, anger in the face of undisguised tyranny and injustice, and yet a certain sympathy with the efficiency and strength of totalitarian governments.

   (b) pacifism, since another war was unthinkable to those with memories of the useless slaughter of the war that was supposed to have ended all wars.

   (c) a groundswell of demand that the seemingly legitimate grievances of Germany and some of its allies be acknowledged and resolved.

   *(d) the belief and determination of the French and British governments that peace should be maintained by negotiating on whatever terms of appeasement were necessary to avoid conflict.

   (e) fear of communist expansion in view of the proclamations made by the Third International.

4. Which statement describes the most tragic result of the policy of appeasement?

   (a) When he invaded the Rhineland in 1936, Hitler repudiated the Locarno Agreements with impunity.

   *(b) Judging Britain and France by their past performance, Hitler could safely assume that neither country would honor its guarantee of armed assistance to Poland.

   (c) The Munich agreement signed by Chamberlain and Daladier provided for a negotiated peace on Hitler's terms, but resulted in the annihilation of the entire Czech Republic.

   (d) There was no official reaction from the West when Hitler annexed Austria in 1938.

   (e) Britain and France had done nothing to prevent Japanese expansion into Manchuria or Mussolini's invasion and conquest of Ethiopia.

5. Which alliance was *least* effective in checking the expansionist policies of Nazism:

   (a) the Little Entente, strengthened by the Franco-Russian and Franco-Polish alliances, which intended to prevent a revival of Austrian power and to isolate Germany.

   (b) multiple treaties and agreements that emphasized peaceful means as the most acceptable solutions to international problems, and that denounced war as an international crime.

   *(c) the League of Nations, which failed to relieve world-wide tensions or to prevent clashes between nations, and which continued to deny membership to Germany and Russia.

(d)   the alliances of Germany with Italy and with Japan, in 1936 and 1940 respectively.

(e)   the trade agreement of Germany and Russia that opened the way for political and even military collaboration between the two nations.

6.   The most significant contributory factor in the outbreak of World War II is given in which statement:

(a)   expansion of the armaments industry in Germany, as well as the revival of conscription and universal military training.

(b)   the German-Russian agreement in September 1939, which gave Hitler the green light for an attack on Poland.

(c)   Polish intransigence in the face of Hitler's justifiable demand that the Polish Corridor, as an area with a large German population, be returned to the fatherland.

*(d)   the expansionist policies of Germany after its withdrawal from the League of Nations, which were permitted to advance unchecked by Western democracies until after the attack on Poland.

(e)   annexation of the Sudetenland, condoned in an agreement that the French and British governments signed at Munich in 1938.

7.   Which of the following sequels to the depression of the 1930s proved most important to the development of World War II:

(a)   expansion of armaments production on a large scale, which was seen as a means to reduce unemployment.

(b)   the militant expansionism of Japan and Italy, evidenced by their conquests of new territories, which were seen as potential resources for solving national economic problems.

(c)   substantial reduction in industrial production, lowering of standards of living, and unemployment throughout Europe and the West.

*(d)   triumph of the Nazi party, and subsequent German expansionist policy.

(e)   increased emphasis on economic nationalism by once against instituting high tariffs to shield domestic products from foreign competition.

8.   Alliances, pacts, and guarantees of mutual asisstance made by various participants in the war proved most useful in the case of

(a)   Poland, as seen in the successful defense of its territorial integrity and independence with the aid of British and French armed assistance.

(b)   Czechoslovakia, whose sovereignty was guaranteed by the Entente powers in the Treaty of St. Germain and further secured by the establishment of the Little Entente.

*(c)   Great Britain, which was able to sustain its war effort with massive aid from the United States as outlined in the Lend-Lease Act of 1941.

(d)   Germany, whose Axis partner relieved German military forces in the Balkans and North Africa, freeing them for deployment elsewhere.

(e)   Greece, which resisted German and Italian attacks with the aid of British expeditionary forces.

9.   All but one of the following military actions was a decisive turning point in the Second World War. Indicate the exception.

(a)   The battles of the Coral Sea and of Midway in the Pacific during the spring of 1942.

(b)   The defense of Moscow against the German onslaught during the winter of 1941.

*(c)   The D-Day landings of Allied forces in Normandy on June 6, 1944.

(d)   The defeat of General Erwin Rommel's forces in North Africa in 1942.

(e)   The Battle of Stalingrad on the Volga in the winter of 1942-1943.

10.   Among the new methods of warfare used during World War II, which made the greatest impact on the postwar world:

(a)   the Blitzkrieg, or sudden aerial attacks followed by highly mobile ground units.

(b)   coordination of massive land, sea, and aerial forces in concentrated attacks on multiple objectives.

(c)   total involvement of the civilian population in the horrors of the war through the indiscriminate bombing of cities.

*(d)   the use of atomic bombs, whose terrifying destructive power made Japan surrender immediately.

(e)   increased reliance on mechanical means to transport troops and firepower in order to attain battlefield superiority and to effect tactical surprise.

11.   The Atlantic Charter was all of the following *except*

(a)   an idealistic reaffirmation of the abstract principles of freedom based on the cooperation of the peoples of the world.

(b)   an appeal to the Allies to maintain their commitment to the cause of final victory.

*(c)   a resolution of the United Nations to correct mistakes made by the treaties that concluded the First World War.

(d)   a document that manifested a less than adequate awareness of the realities of power politics.

(e)   an essential element within the United Nations Declaration of January 2, 1942, which had twenty-six signatory nations, including the United States, Great Britain, the Soviet Union, and the Republic of China.

12.   Conferences held during the war

(a)   were called for the purpose of discussing technical problems connected with implementation of Atlantic Charter stipulations.

(b)   cemented the United States and the Soviet Union in fellowship and cooperation, preparing these nations for their future roles as guardians of world peace.

(c)   outlined the tentative division of spoils that was to follow an Allied victory.

*(d)   foreshadowed, in the concessions granted to Stalin, tensions that would soon arise between East and West, since Russia's interests seemed over-represented in agreements Stalin had won from Allied leaders.

(e)   were planning sessions for the ultimate reorganization of the international balance of power under democratically principled leading nations.

13.   With *one exception*, the Potsdam declaration on August 2, 1945,

(a)   reconfirmed the decisions of the Yalta conference and annexed large territories to Poland—including the former free city of Danzig—with substantial German minorities.

(b)   established an inter-Allied tribunal in Nuremberg, composed of representatives of the four occupying powers, to try major Nazi leaders for war crimes.

(c)   divided Germany into four occupation zones, which were to be governed by Great Britain, France, the United States, and the Soviet Union.

*(d)   adopted the charter of the United Nations and its principle of "the sovereign equality of all peace-loving states."

(e)   provided for the total dismantling of Germany's military machine.

14.   Which of the following United Nations agencies has the most extensive duties and fullest jurisdiction concerning international relations?

(a)   The Food and Agriculture Organization, which seeks to promote increased food production and more efficient distribution throughout the world.

*(b)   The Security Council, whose "primary responsibility is the maintenance of international peace and security."

(c)   The General Assembly, composed of representatives of all member states.

(d)   The World Health Organization, which attempts to control epidemics and to assist underdeveloped nations in raising standards of health and sanitation.

(e) The Economic and Social Council, which has authority to initiate studies and to make recommendations with respect to social, economic, educational, cultural, and related matters.

15. The major failure of the United Nations is

(a) its inability to cope with the growing distrust that has been a wedge between the Soviet Union and the West since immediately after the war.

(b) the limits placed on the authority of the secretary-general, whose duties are mainly administrative in character.

*(c) its lack of power to enforce U.N. peace-making decisions upon a permanent member of the Security Council determined to make war or to act tyrannically.

(d) its failure to assume control over the proliferation of nuclear weapons or to set pertinent standards.

(e) the poor record it has had of defusing political confrontations before the onset of violence.

IDENTIFICATIONS

Little Entente   Neville Chamberlain
Neutralized zone   Vichy
Treaty of Rapallo   Sitzkrieg
Locarno conference   The Cairo Declaration
Pact of Paris   The Yalta agreement
Francisco Franco   Cold war
Sudetenland   Clement Attlee
Édouard Daladier

TRUE OR FALSE

T   1. The governments of France and Britain allowed Germany to rearm, since armament production was seen as a plausible means to reduce unemployment.

F   2. The newly created state of Czechoslovakia had a national majority of Czechs in 1938, but also contained strong minority groups of Slovaks, Poles, Hungarians, and Germans.

T   3. Many European and American intellectuals' participation in the Spanish Civil War of 1936 was motivated by idealistic determination to resist totalitarianism.

F   4. The Locarno Agreements and the Pact of Paris provided the League of Nations with effective instruments with which to preserve peace.

F   5.   Although he was a liberal during World War I, Churchill, later considered a maverick conservative, formed his war cabinet entirely from the Conservative party.

T   6.   The United Nations' declaration of January 2, 1942, greatly resembled Woodrow Wilson's Fourteen Points.

T   7.   The peace treaty with Japan left the Bonin and Ryukyu island groups under United States control.

T   8.   The United Nations charter did empower the Security Council to "take actions by air, naval, or land forces" as might be required to maintain or restore international order.

F   9.   The stipulations of the peace treaty with Japan, finalized in April 1952, were fully supported by the Soviet Union, who received parts of two island groups as war-restitution settlement.

T   10.   The United Nations Security Council is empowered to take any action agreed upon by the five permanent members—Great Britain, France, the United States, China, and the Soviet Union.

DISCUSSION AND/OR ESSAY QUESTIONS

1. "The President [Roosevelt] and the Prime Minister [Churchill], after a complete survey of the world situation, are more than ever determined that peace can come to the world only by a total elimination of German and Japanese war power. This involves the simple formula of placing the objective of this war in terms of an unconditional surrender by Germany, Italy, and Japan."
   —Franklin D. Roosevelt, Casablanca, January 24, 1943.

   Do you think that this declaration might have strengthened Hitler's resolve to fight to the bitter end?

2. Describe Hitler's expansionist policy before the attack on Poland. What was the logic behind his schemes, and how did Hitler's successes help him gain a surer political hold over Germany?

3. What are the basic elements in National Socialist theories that led to the concentration camps and the brutalization of over 6 million human beings? Are these elements different in other totalitarian systems?

4. What are the similarities and what are the differences in the causes of the two world wars?

5. Compare the League of Nations and the United Nations with reference to their philosophies, organization, accomplishments, and failures.

SUGGESTED FILMS

Archaeology. 14 min. B/w. McGraw-Hill Films (1969).

Chamberlain vs. Hitler. 25 min. B/w. Films, Inc. (1964).

The Christians: The Godless State? (1848-1945). 39 min. Color. McGraw-Hill Films (1979).

†*Decision to Drop the Bomb.* 32 min. B/w. Films, Inc. (1966).

Field Marshall Rommel. 25 min. B/w. Sterling Educational Films (1965).

†*Hiroshima-Nagasaki (August 1945).* 16 min. B/w. Columbia Center for Mass Communication (1971).

Hitler—a Profile in Power. 26 min. Color. Learning Corporation of America (1976).

In Search of Nazi Plunder. 24 min. Color. Pyramid Films (1976).

Memorandum. 58 min. B/w. McGraw-Hill Films (1956).

Night and Fog. 31 min. B/w. McGraw-Hill Films (1956),

The Nuremberg Trials. 3 parts, each 35 min. B/w. U.S. National Audio-Visual Center (1949).

The Remnant. 60 min. Color. Films, Inc. (1969).

Rise of the Dictators: Form! Riflemen, Form! 2 parts, each 26 min. Color. (From the series Europe the Mighty Continent.) Time-Life Films, Inc. (1976).

The Spanish Civil War. 2 parts, 35 and 26 min. B/w. (Can be leased from the University of Kansas; see *Educational Film Locator*.)

†*Ten Days That Shook the World.* 50 min. Color. Films, Inc. (1967).

Total War. 25 min. B/w. Learning Corporation of America (1969).

Uniting the Nations. 20 min. B/w. Time-Life Films, Inc. (1970).

War and Peace in Europe. Each title 20 min. B/w. Time-Life Films, Inc. (1970).
    Hitler's War.
    The New Europe.

---

*Film deals with concentration camps and the Jewish pogroms.
† Film deals with the use of the atomic bomb.

MULTIPLE CHOICE

Choose the best response.

1. Centuries before the conquest of Latin America by the Spanish and Portuguese,
    the Indians of Guatemala, Mexico, and the Andean highlands

    (a) had developed a religious system administered by a priestly class and pre-
         dominated by superstition and the practice of human sacrifice.

    (b) developed a system of pictographic writing having symbols of phonetic
         value, but whose use was evidently confined to religious purposes, with
         no legal or creative writing.

    *(c) had reached advanced stages of cultural development that, but for the
         European invasions, might have become the bases of unique native
         cultures.

    (d) were cultivators of the land and showed no interest in trade and manu-
         facture. They did, however, build elaborate cities in which a leisure
         class of nobles and priests resided.

    (e) established far-flung empires under hereditary monarchs, who ruled their
         peoples according to the principle of collectivist paternalism.

2. Which set of assumptions best represents the colonial policy of the Spanish
    Bourbon rulers?

    (a) Since land in the colonies is the king's personal possession, he is justified
         in dictating what the colonial population can produce and in limiting its
         commercial activities.

    (b) The welfare of the colonies, meaning first of all their peaceful existence,
         is best determined by the king's agents in cooperation with the hierarchy
         of the Church.

    (c) In order to gain riches and increase its international power, the colonizing
         nation must grant a monopoly of colonial trade to its own merchants.

281

*(d)   Granting commercial concessions to foreigners and easing restrictions on trade, industry, and agriculture ultimately secure the loyalty of colonial subjects and increase the flow of revenue into the royal treasury.

(e)   Carefully established restrictions on the power of viceroys will help prevent excessive official misconduct, limit corruption among merchants, and strengthen royal control over the colonies.

3.   The *major* impetus for declarations of independence and revolutionary wars in Latin America between 1808 and 1826 was given by

(a)   reforms instituted by the Bourbon kings near the turn of the century that, while making Spanish-American trade the richest in the world, failed to abolish oppression and discrimination, including censorship and exclusion of creoles from governmental and Church posts.

(b)   the absolutism of Spanish kings and their mercantilist policies, which, ever since the late sixteenth century, had operated on the premise the Crown should have exclusive right to the wealth of raw materials found in the colonies.

(c)   the impact of revolutionary doctrines from Europe and the United States upon two generations of prosperous creole and colonial white middle classes.

(d)   Napoleon's dealings with Charles IV of Spain and his son, Ferdinand, which gave the colonies an opportunity to rise up when both Spain and France were embroiled in European wars.

*(e)   In addition to all the above, a habit of self-reliant political and economic problem-solving that the colonies had acquired during a period of "salutory neglect" by the Spanish government between 1803 and 1808.

4.   Which description fits Benito Juárez?

(a)   A native of Argentina and governor of the province of Cuyo, he successfully revolted against the Spanish in 1821, gained Peru's independence, and was named "Protector" by the new Peruvian government.

*(b)   An outstanding example of a nineteenth century Latin American revolutionary, this reformer, in a brief term as president of Mexico, reduced the size of the army, eliminated blatant waste and extravagance in government, and took steps to significantly extend public education.

(c)   Having solicited British and American aid for his early campaign, he was the first among a number of revolutionaries who helped establish Venezuela as an independent republic that later joined the United States of Columbia.

(d)   Simón Bolívar's lieutenant and the liberator of Ecuador, he decisively defeated Spanish forces in 1822, and soon thereafter joined his country to Gran Columbia.

(e) Grandson of an African king, this leader headed a slave revolt that resembled a guerrilla war, first directed against the slaves' immediate oppressors, and, later, French rule generally. He is considered the Father of Haitian independence, proclaimed in 1803.

5. Reread the five descriptions in question 4. Determine which Latin American revolutionary each represents, then indicate the series below that corresponds to their order of presentation.

(a) Benito Juárez; Bernardo O'Higgins; Simón Bolívar; José San Martín; Ignacio Comonfort.

*(b) José San Martín; Benito Juárez; Francisco de Miranda; Antonio José de Sucre; Toussaint L'Ouverture.

(c) Simón Bolívar; José San Martín; Ignacio Comonfort; Toussaint L'Ouverture; Bernardo O'Higgins.

(d) Francisco de Miranda; Antonio de Sucre; Bernardo O'Higgins; Ignacio Comonfort; Benito Juárez.

(e) Toussaint L'Ouverture; Simon Bolívar; Benito Juárez; Bernardo O'Higgins; José San Martín.

6. The political history of Latin American states ever since the overthrow of European colonialism has been *chiefly* characterized by

*(a) long, often bloody, revolutionary struggles to attain national maturity and political stability, and to earn recognition within the world community of states.

(b) territorial and economic encroachment by foreigners, who frequently exacted political concessions or economic privilege, such as permission to to own large tracts of land, as terms of their investment.

(c) inadequate attempts by government to respond to a nearly 400 percent increase in the population of Central and South America during the nineteenth century, and the continuation of this growth trend in the present century.

(d) increased societal polarization, with tiny minorities monopolizing the benefits of economic and political systems to the disadvantage of an impoverished and underprivileged majority.

(e) continuous struggle between elements in the Church who support aristocratic conservatism and a camp of anti-clerical liberals over such issues as the desirability of extending suffrage and the need for economic reforms to rescue the peasantry from poverty.

7. The politically stable Brazilian empire achieved under Emperor Pedro I and the constitution of 1824 was overthrown in 1889 by

(a) politically inexperienced military adventurers in the employ of unscrupulous foreign investors.

*(b) slave owners dissatisfied with a governmental measure emancipating all slaves without compensation to their owners.

(c) political idealists eagerly bent on putting their programs, including abolitionism and republicanism, into effect immediately.

(d) a faction of landholding, aristocratic elements in union with the Church hierarchy, both reacting against erosion of their traditional authorities.

(e) a faction of anti-clerical, anti-military liberals, supported by the business classes and the free peasantry.

8. Which statement is correct?

(a) Mestizos and Indians played a less significant role in Mexico than in other Latin American countries regarding the direction of their national political development.

*(b) Mexico's basic economic and social problems were not solved under the dictatorship of Porfirio Díaz, whose policies in land and industrial development helped only the favored few.

(c) The plight of Mexican peasants was mitigated after the War of Reform (1858-61) when the victors, a coalition of radicals and liberals, enacted drastic anti-clerical and land reform laws to supplement the constitution of 1857. This allowed many jobless peasants crowded into the cities to return to the land.

(d) Reforms envisioned by Maximilian earned the respect of most segments of society and probably would have succeeded had the French not withdrawn their economic and military support in 1866.

(e) United States intervention on behalf of North American interests, particularly at the beginning of this century, prevented the gradual development of a politically stable and economically independent Mexico based on the Constitution of 1917.

9. Which statement supplies the *best* insight into why no government in power since Mexico's Constitution of 1917 has ever been able to fulfill its revolutionary ends?

(a) The domination of a single political party and the practically unlimited authority of the president has bred inefficiency, complacency, and corruption.

(b) A population explosion has created urban slums plagued by high unemployment and unrelenting poverty, while the Mexican rural population remains neglected, with neither medical care nor educational facilities.

(c) Mexico has yet to develop technology and managerial skills equal to the task of exploiting the enormous oil reserves recently discovered along the western shores of the Gulf of Mexico.

*(d) In this century basic economic and social problems have grown to such proportions and complexity that even the most earnest efforts of several presidents and governments to eliminate the sources of social unrest have been frustrated.

(e) Agrarian reforms, the hard-core issue of Mexican revolutionary programs, have seldom yielded any appreciable benefit for peasants, and, instead, have antagonized large property owners and native business interests, while greatly increasing national deficit spending.

10. Which statement most accurately reflects conditions in Brazil?

(a) Constitutional changes adopted in 1934 gave Brazil the most democratic government in Latin America; it remained an exemplary participatory government until 1964 and the onset of a military dictatorship.

(b) Expansion and diversification of industry in the 1960s turned the new capital, Brasilia, into the largest industrial city in the southern hemisphere.

(c) In an effort to break the pattern of economic dependence on the U. S. and Western Europe, President Geisel proclaimed Brazil a full-fledged non-aligned world power and supported Soviet involvement in Latin America.

*(d) The escalating price of oil has contributed significantly to Brazil's high rate of inflation, which by 1978 exceeded forty percent annually, resulting in a national debt of forty billion dollars.

(e) Brazil's economic independence and its relatively broad industrial base have resulted in general prosperity, evident in improved health care, a radically reduced infant mortality rate, and expanded social services.

11. Constitutional democracy in Chile was overthrown through a series of events that included *all but one* of the following:

*(a) increased political activity by opposition parties, division within the armed forces, and well-organized strikes and boycotts by workers and the unemployed triggered by Allende's ineptitude and Marxist ideology.

(b) opposition reaction to the March 1973 vote of confidence given President Allende's Popular Unity coalition by almost forty-four percent of the voters, which increased the party's representation in the legislature.

(c) methodical "destabilization" of the Chilean government, accomplished with with the aid of the U. S. Central Intelligence Agency, President Nixon, and and Henry Kissinger's "Forty Committee" of the National Security Council.

(d) an undeclared civil war, launched by the military high command, which eliminated all resistance within weeks and instituted methods of oppression that evoked memories of the regimes of Hitler and Stalin.

(e) economic breakdown deliberately engineered by far-right elements with the support of multinational corporations and the U.S. government.

12. What seems to offer the most plausible explanation of Argentina's addiction to authoritarian governments and its extraordinary political instability throughout the twentieth century?

(a) Rapid industrialization fostered bitter antagonisms between urban and rural classes with radically divergent needs and interests.

*(b) Argentine political history in the twentieth century has revolved around a few charismatic and dominant personalities who attracted cadres of fanatical loyalists and provoked equally fanatical opposition. The tendency of such personal regimes to become thoroughly corrupt and to polarize society has resulted in frequent coups by the military.

(c) The General Confederation of Labor had advocated syndicalist programs predicated on the belief that the workers should own the means of production. To achieve this end the Confederation has consistently supported military dictatorships.

(d) An intense national pride and a belief that Argentina was destined to be the leader of Latin American states has led to a seemingly endless quest for a government capable of fulfilling these expectations. An equally intense resentment of U. S. interference in the affairs of the southern hemisphere has resulted in a rejection of democratic forms.

(e) A high foreign trade deficit, chronic unemployment, a tremendous public debt, and a rising cost of living have been the sources of social unrest for most of this century.

13. The most dramatic omen of substantial change in present day Latin America is the

(a) reassertion of national rights against the Colossus of the North, whose corporations control approximately seventy-five percent of Latin America's raw materials.

(b) mounting revolutionary foment to introduce civilian administrations in place of excessively expensive and repressive military regimes.

(c) attempt to break the stranglehold of multinational monopolies and gain economic independence. While recognizing financial and technical assistance are needed to accomplish this, Latin American governments are now more careful to assess whether accepting aid will really help them meet national goals and narrow the gap between rich and poor.

*(d)   support of leftist revolutionary movements by elements of the Catholic and Protestant churches which advocate direct action in order to achieve social justice and relieve mass poverty.

(e)   a nascent regional federation consisting of five Latin American countries, which is working toward the creation of a common market.

14.   Guided by the government of Fidel Castro, Cuba has made significant progress toward bettering the condition of its people by

(a)   accelerating industrial development so dramatically that Castro's boast that every family would own a house or apartment and every farmer would have a Cuban made air-conditioned tractor by the 1980s is on the verge of realization.

(b)   diversifying its export base so that the nation's economic well-being is no longer subject to the whim of a few fluctuating commodity prices as it had been in the past.

(c)   establishing the legal equality of all of its citizens and guaranteeing a wide range of personal freedoms which had been ruthlessly suppressed by the Batista regime.

*(d)   raising the level of public health through a comprehensive program of improved sanitation, hygiene, and medical and hospital facilities so effectively that the infant mortality rate and deaths due to tuberculosis, malaria, typhoid, and polio have declined significantly.

(e)   severing its economic ties with the U.S. and forging a new political, military, and economic alliance with the Soviet Union.

15.   Current governmental policies and practices in Latin America are correctly portrayed in which statement?

(a)   Whether reactionary or progressive in policy, military juntas and one-party civilian governments rely on the support of the local oligarchy and the help of foreign capital, and any reforms undertaken must receive the tacit approval of these groups.

*(b)   Nearly sixty percent of Latin America's people now live under repressive military regimes or governments directed by the military which are notoriously unresponsive to their nation's economic needs.

(c)   Use of terrorism, assassination, and political imprisonment is the only realistic strategy for present Latin American governments if they are to win out against anarchy and the socialist threat.

(d)   The response of Latin American governments to organized internal opposition rests on counterinsurgency forces, specially trained by the United States Army Southern Command in the Canal Zone.

(e) If multinational corporations, U. S. business interests, and the U. S. Central Intelligence Agency had not interfered in domestic politics of Latin American states, most of these would by now have gained political stability, economic independence, and stature in the community of nations, especially since they have been found to possess vast reserves of precious natural resources.

IDENTIFICATIONS

Bull of Demarcation	The War of Reform
Audiencia	The Andean Group
Asiento	Sandinista National Liberation Front
Bernardo O'Higgins	*Descamisados*
Father Hidalgo	Porfirio Díaz
Republic of Gran Columbia	DINA
Personalismo	
The War of the Pacific	

TRUE OR FALSE

T   1.   Portuguese colonial policy differed significantly from that of Spain and assured a unique pattern of political and economic development for Brazil.

T   2.   By the close of the eighteenth century the Spanish-American trade as a whole was the richest in the world.

T   3.   Without British maritime support the "Monroe Doctrine" would have remained a dead letter.

F   4.   Because of chronic poverty and lack of education, Mestizos and Indians were confined to a passive role in Mexico's political development.

T   5.   Mexican nationals in the United States remit to Mexico approximately $3 billion annually, a figure larger than the profits from tourism in Mexico.

T   6.   Women in Cuba have achieved legal equality with men and have made substantial progress in the professions.

F   7.   Brazil's current economic prosperity is attributable to the rising price of the nation's major export commodity—oil.

F   8.   A revolution in El Salvador resulted in the overthrow of the government of Anastasio Somoza in 1979.

T   9.   President Kennedy's "Alliance for Progress" actually widened the gap between rich and poor in Latin America, and kept governments dependent upon foreign investments.

F   10.   In spite of a very liberal immigration policy, two-thirds of Argentina's population are Indians or the descendants of slaves.

DISCUSSION AND/OR ESSAY QUESTIONS

1.   Define the terms "culture" and "civilization." Apply these definitions in an evaluation of the western hemisphere's oldest civilization before the arrival of white men. Give reasons for the author's statement: "Indians in Guatemala, Mexico, and the Andean Highland had developed superior cultures which bore almost all the characteristics of civilizations."

2.   "What is the oligarchy? It consists of the great landowners—the *latifundistas*—their political and military henchmen, and their financial allies (the bankers and the capitalists, in the old sense of the word) . . . The oligarchs form a true caste, with aristocratic impulses, racist attitudes, and a profound contempt for their own countries."

> —Victor Alba, *Alliance Without Allies:*
> *The Mythology of Progress in Latin America*

If the oligarchy is all things ascribed to it by Alba, what social and political resources does it command? What social and political forces press upon it? Identify groups and persons that comprise the Latin American oligarchies, using historical data to highlight specific countries. Discuss the roles oligarchies have played in Latin America from European colonization through the present.

3.   Discuss circumstances that affected the development of political maturity and stability in Latin America. Is it accurate to compare this process with that of English-speaking North America? Concentrate on similarities and differences between nineteenth century developments in the United States and the pre- and post-independence eras in Latin American states.

4.   Trace the course foreign business interests have taken in Latin America since the nineteenth century. When and how did these interests advance or retard economic growth and political stability? Construct a hypothetical policy you think could avoid disrupting the process by which strong, autonomous economies must evolve, while maintaining the cooperation that would benefit emerging nations.

5.   Describe the main features of Spanish colonial policy. Under the Hapsburg monarchs, how did this policy represent mercantilist theories? What changes did the Bourbons introduce? How did these affect economics and politics in both the homeland and the colonies during the eighteenth century?

SUGGESTED FILMS

Brazil. 15 min. B/w. U. S. Department of Defense, producer (1953).

Brazil: The Rude Awakening. Parts I and II. 27 min. B/w. McGraw-Hill Textfilms (1961).

Castro. 26 min. B/w. McGraw-Hill Textfilms (1963).

Cuba: Bay of Pigs. 29 min. B/w. Films Incorporated (1965).

Communism in Latin America. 29 min. B/w. University of Southern California (1962).

Eva Peron. 26 min. B/w. Sterling Educational Films (1963).

Excavations at La Venta. 29 min. Color. University of California, Extension Media Center (1963).

Focus on Argentina: A Country at the Crossroads. 9 min. B/w. Hearst Metrotone News (1962).

Footprints of the Mayan Gods. 29 min. Color. Hartley Productions (1969).

The Incas. 11 min. B/w; c. Coronet Instructional Films (1961).

Juarez. 29 min. B/w. Teaching Film Custodians (1971).

Latin America. (2 parts) 26 min.; 33 min. McGraw-Hill Textfilms (1964).

Maya. 11 min. Color. Geoffrey Bell (1970).

Paraguay and Uraguay: Contrast on the Plata. 17 min. Color. McGraw-Hill Textfilms (1968).

Peron and Evita. 30 min. B/w. Columbia Broadcasting System, TV (1958).

The Spanish Conquest of the New World. 11 min. B/w; c. Coronet Instructional Films (1954).

Toltec Mystery. 28 min. Color. Henson Films (1964).

Venezuela Moves Ahead. 36 min. Color. Julien Bryan, producer.

Outline

MULTIPLE CHOICE
Choose the best response.

1. The Commonwealth of Nations might be best described as

    (a) an alliance of dependent and independent member states within the British Empire.

    (b) an organization of self-governing states united by their common allegiance to Britain and by their recognition of the British monarch as head of state.

    (c) an irrevocable association of former British colonies tied to Britain by strong economic and political incentives.

    *(d) national communities whose voluntary union is generally symbolized by the British monarchy, but whose autonomy is preserved in that no member is subordinate or answerable to any other regarding its domestic and foreign policies.

    (e) an organization of former British colonies which have been granted the status of semi-autonomous states. Self-governing in domestic matters, the members are committed to a common foreign policy dictated by the British government under the terms of the Statute of Westminster.

2. The Dominion government in Canada as we now know it was established

    (a) in 1847 by Lord Elgin, who, as governor of Canada, chose a cabinet from the assembly's majority party, and set the precedent of signing into law bills that often conflicted with interests of the mother country.

    *(b) in 1867, when the separate colonies of New Brunswick and Nova Scotia united with Quebec and Ontario to form a confederation.

    (c) by the Quebec Act of 1774 through which the British Parliament, seeking to correct certain organizational defects in the Empire, granted Canadians the right to elect a representative assembly.

    (d) in 1837 after friction between the British population of Upper Canada and the predominantly French population of Lower Canada erupted into open rebellion.

291

(e)   in 1931, when the British Parliament enacted a law requiring royal governors to act as diplomatic liaisons to Britain, and not as agents of the Crown.

3.   The British North American Act, passed by the British Parliament in 1867, incorporated *all but one* of the following concepts in creating the Dominion of Canada:

(a)   a federal system, with a clearly defined division of powers between governments of the provinces and the central government.

(b)   the same Constitution Canadians had themselves adopted three years earlier.

(c)   the principle of "responsible government," with power over local affairs vested in a Dominion cabinet, responsible to elected representatives in the lower house of the legislature.

*(d)   a bicameral legislature in which both houses exercised equal powers in all areas.

(e)   responsible government in the provinces, based not on British formulas but, instead, on the Canadian Constitution.

4.   Social and political policies formulated by the Australian government may be traced back to

(a)   the exclusion of Asians from Australia in response to accusations by white workers that these laborers threatened the stability of hard-won wage scales and living standards.

(b)   demands by an agricultural proletariat of the pastoral "stations" that government intervene in economic affairs and provide farmers with benefits comparable to those collectivized industry guaranteed its workers.

*(c)   governmental initiative in the development and diversification of industry and agriculture, particularly after the short-lived gold rush of the mid-nineteenth century.

(d)   awareness that, given the limits of agricultural technology in the early nineteenth century, geographic and climatic conditions precluded the development of Australia as a nation of independent farmers, and that, therefore, it would be necessary for industry to generate products suitable for large-scale export.

(e)   government-financed public works projects intended to increase food production and speed up the development of transportation to and from marketing centers.

5.   Australians' apparent willingness to have government make economic and social decisions that might otherwise fall to the private sector may be credited principally to what feature of their national history?

(a) The failure of collectivistic social welfare legislation, including compulsory arbitration and wage controls, to satisfy both labor and management and to maintain a reasonably high level of industrial productivity.

*(b) The success of consistent, far-reaching, and expedient governmental policies based on comprehensive social and economic planning. These promoted social cohesion, intercepted some developmental problems before they became overbearing—as during the decade after the gold rush—and maintained a high standard of living for the white majority.

(c) The White Australia policy, which has rigidly excluded inhabitants of Asia from immigration since 1906.

(d) The united front capital and labor have formed in demanding government protection against the spread of laissez-faire economic philosophies and the shifting trends of an international market.

(e) Public ownership of a wide variety of economic enterprises—an arrangement business and industry have welcomed, and which, therefore, has reduced the traditional friction between management and labor.

6. In reviewing the development of Australia and New Zealand after 1860, one of the following statements *incorrectly* implies that both nations

(a) pioneered social welfare legislation that was in some respects more innovative than that of the mother country.

(b) imposed tariffs, solidified unionism as a vital economic force, and set out on a path to collectivization. These measures have helped government control the excesses of private business, modulate prices charged for goods and services, and keep industries vital to the general welfare—transportation, energy production, and banking—from control by private interests.

*(c) fostered economic development that was by necessity agriculturally-based, favoring traditionally conservative, small farmers and independent herdsmen, with less investment in the vitality of urban industries.

(d) have—as much by exclusionary legislation as by initial British immigration—homogenized their populations, so that since about 1870 they have been overwhelmingly British in origin. Likewise, they have persevered in maintaining British national character, not hesitating to use the law to set the direction of society.

(e) —exposed to Chartism and traces of socialism by British immigrants—have constructed political and economic democracies where liberal and radical programs, but not violent revolution, seem to flourish.

7. The British East India Company is correctly portrayed in which statement?

*(a) The Company, a chartered, privately owned joint stock corporation, functioned as a British governmental agency from 1834 to 1858 and its trading

posts were gradually and unsystematically transformed into regional centers of colonial administration.

(b) From its inception the Company showed an appreciation for the complexities of Indian trade relations by selecting its agents for their expertise in dealing with the country and its people, and requiring them to report regularly and directly to the Company Court of Directors in London.

(c) Before 1858 Parliament had no jurisdiction over Company agents, and the chief agent in Calcutta was left to integrate administrative activities of separate British holdings as he saw fit within the general framework of directives from the Company's governing body.

(d) Although an 1814 act of Parliament opened commerce in India to all British subjects, it renewed a Company trade monopoly in China and other Far East regions and did not keep the Company from ruling India as if it were a private estate. In fact, the Company enjoyed commercial hegemony in the Far East until 1932 when it became a pseudo-agency of the British government until it was permanently disbanded in 1958.

(e) When, after the Great Mutiny, Britain revoked the Company Charter and set about transferring responsibility for government to the Crown, large-scale military operations were initiated throughout India to unify principalities not previously "opened" by commerce or primed for British rule.

8. The preservation of English supremacy in India during the second half of the nineteenth century was *primarily* made possible by

(a) the generally effective actions taken by English colonial officials to check crime, protect property, introduce modern methods in agriculture, and build an extensive network of railroads that eventually proved beneficial to all the provinces.

(b) the loyalty of native troops, which were fiercely protective of their officers. An objective of British training had been to instill in servicemen pride in the corps, while it cautiously intermingled minority interest groups to minimize chances of a nationalist rebellion.

(c) a taxation system that exacted less revenue than those of former autocratic regimes, was borne mainly by the merchant classes, was legally bound to reinvest the proceeds in Indian enterprises, and helped provide relief, social welfare, and educational benefits.

*(d) the tacit support of the hereditary princes, who in return for an assurance of continued local power ignored the progress of events outside their principalities, plus the extraordinary efficiency of Indian Civil Service operations.

(e) English educational efforts in India, which ensured that many educated Hindus and Muslims serving in the National Congress sympathized with the English cause.

9. Among events that triggered an Indian nationalist movement, the most important was

   (a)   Italy's defeat by Ethiopia, Russia's defeat by Japan, and the difficulty Britain had in subduing the Boers in South Africa, all of which shattered the myth of European invincibility.

   (b)   the fear that India's Muslim minority would be subjected to Hindu domination which led to the establishment of the Muslim League in 1905 as a rival to the Indian National Congress.

   (c)   a split in the Indian National Congress between moderate and extremist elements and among various sectarian and special interest constituencies.

  *(d)   the formation of the Indian National Congress in 1885 as an "unanswerable reply to the assertion that India is still wholly unfit for any form of representative institutions."

   (e)   the uncompromising stand taken by the British government in the face of violent demands for *purna swaraj*, with increased censorship of the vernacular press and arrests and deportations of suspected nationalist agitators.

10. Which statement represents Jawaharalal Nehru's concept of an independent Indian government?

   (a)   While a program of non-cooperation with the British government will eventually gain India its independence, only a radical reordering of Indian attitudes with respect to the "Untouchables" will uproot social injustice and keep Hinduism from losing its credibility.

  *(b)   If independence and the establishment of democracy are to be maintained in India government must take direct action to alleviate poverty, to rehabilitate village economies and the peasantry, and to protect industrial workers.

   (c)   Indian Muslims are not merely a religious minority at potential disadvantage in Indian politics but a distinct nation.

   (d)   "Islam is our faith, democracy is our policy, socialism is our economy, all power to the people."

   (e)   Although the Constitution clearly sets up areas of state jurisdiction, local privilege can be suspended and the "disciplined democracy" governed by emergency rule if conditions threaten to subvert law and order. This should allow needed reforms to be carried out even during times of political factionalism.

11. Reread the choices in question 10. Then mark the list of persons below whose concepts were presented there in succession.

   (a)   M. A. Jinnah; Mahatma Gandhi; M. Nehru; Indira Gandhi; Ali Bhutto.

   (b)   Ayub Khan; M. A. Jinnah; Indira Gandhi; J. Nehru; Mahatma Gandhi.

   (c)   Ali Bhutto; Ayub Khan; Yahya Khan; Indira Gandhi; J. Nehru.

*(d)   Mahatma Gandhi; J. Nehru; M. A. Jinnah; Ali Bhutto; Indira Gandhi.

(e)   Zia al-Hag; Yahya Khan; Mahatma Gandhi; Mujibur Rahman; M. A. Jinnah.

12.   Which statement may best explain why the Indian nationalist movement gained momentum and eventually attained India's complete independence?

(a)   The Amritsar massacre of 1919 focused Indian attention on the repressive aspects of British policy in India and antagonized many Indian leaders who had previously been consistent defenders of Britain.

(b)   Britain's efforts to assuage Indian nationalism through reform were regarded as self-serving and insincere; they favored propertied interests, fostered divisiveness, and offered the impoverished masses nothing at all.

(c)   The Indian National Congress was able to reach a nearly unanimous decision to set out for complete independence from Britain in 1929. Moderates and radicals enlisted the support of the general population and firmly resolved to resist the government with a mass campaign of civil disobedience.

*(d)   The British controlled educational system in which classes were conducted exclusively in English and were dedicated to the proposition that the Indian population could be indoctrinated to accept Britain's tutelage. The British sought to achieve this end by strictly regulating the educational materials used in the schools and by limiting the skills acquired by their subjects.

(e)   Indian nationalists considered the Government of India Act of 1919 to be a wholly inadequate step toward the goal of representative government that was to be India's reward for joining the Allied war effort. Rather than preparing India for responsible government, in the British sense of the term, it seemed to be designed to perpetuate divisive sectarianism and splintered interests.

13.   Mahatma Gandhi's program for a better world included each of the following, *except*

(a)   non-violent mass action as a means to defend a moral principle against repression by a superior physical force.

*(b)   India's cultural heritage as represented by the strictest adherence to traditional Hinduism.

(c)   the progress of religious and ethical values in human society through purposeful cultivation of spiritual resources.

(d)   devotion to helping the poor, the downtrodden, and the disadvantaged, regardless of race, religion, or social status.

(e)   the belief that in any action undertaken the means used will largely determine the quality of its consequences.

14. The Indian Republic's current problems are *best* represented by which of the following statements?

    (a) The government is unable to keep abreast of an inexorable population growth rate by increasing agricultural production, job opportunities, and social services.

    (b) Indira Gandhi has ruled in an increasingly arbitrary and inflexible fashion, which belies India's liberal Constitution and its democratic electoral process.

    (c) The National Congress has permitted the formation of a government that, while democratic, operates in effect under a one-party system.

    (d) A Hindi-speaking Indian leadership and rapid forced absorption of some 500 princely states into a new republican political structure after 1948 stirred up old linguistic rivalries and sectional and social prejudices.

  *(e) All the above, in conjunction with bureaucratic ineptitude and lack of vigorous leadership that could put to good use the country's extensive resources to support a prosperous, industrialized, and educated society.

15. Which of the following did not contribute to the move by Bangladesh for independence from Pakistan?

    (a) Vigorous agitation by the Awami League around the time of the 1970 elections, creating a platform for regional autonomy of territory controlled by Urdu-speaking Punjabis.

    (b) The geographic, economic, and social separation of East and West Pakistan, with the only common bond between them being espousal of Islam.

    (c) A genocidal war against a Bihari minority, initiated, perhaps, by the Bengalis, but later relentlessly carried out by West Pakistani troops.

  *(d) Indian governmental policies designed to incorporate East Pakistan as a defensive buffer zone against Chinese expansionism to the south.

    (e) The inability of president Yahya Khan to solve problems of widespread poverty, joblessness, and the steadily rising rebellious mood of the East Pakistanis.

IDENTIFICATIONS

Statute of Westminster

British North America Act

Parti Quebêcois

The Official Language Act of 1969

W. B. Griffith

Australasian Federal Council

The New British School of
    Systematic Colonizers

Swadeshi campaigns

Satyagraha

Purna Swaraj

Nizam

Lok Sabha

Harijans

Amritsar Massacre

Suttee

TRUE OR FALSE

T   1.   The century-long commercial rivalry between France and England that climaxed in the French and Indian War was resolved when France surrendered most of its once magnificent American Empire to Britain.

T   2.   The only apparent prerequisite for membership in the Commonwealth of Nations is the desire to belong.

F   3.   Even though the Commonwealth of Nations has assumed the appearance of economic and political independence, it remains a necessity and a boon to Great Britain's well-being.

F   4.   The largest minority population in Canada is of Central and East European origin.

T   5.   Both New Zealand and Australia were discovered by the Dutch a century before the arrival of Captain James Cook.

F   6.   By 1859 the various Australian colonies had established themselves as an organized state with a responsible central government and a unified economic system.

T   7.   In 1906 thousands of Melanesians and Polynesians, who were initially brought to Australia from the Pacific islands as workers, were deported to their homelands.

T   8.   New Zealand was the first Commonwealth nation to bestow suffrage upon women, permitting them to vote in national elections as of 1893.

F   9.   The same legislation that dissolved the British East India Company revoked stockholders' rights to dividends and provided only tentative assurances that the stock would be redeemed by government purchase.

F   10.   Declaring himself a citizen of the Indian Republic, Sheikh Mohammed Abdullah of Kashmir demanded that Pakistan cede his province to India.

DISCUSSION AND/OR ESSAY QUESTIONS

1.   James Arthur Balfour's famous report on governance of the British colonies in 1926 and subsequent enactments by the British Parliament set the stage for the successful formation of the Commonwealth of Nations. Does the report have any precedents in British political history? Why might this investigative report have been coolly received in 1837 at the time of the Canadian rebellion? Why would it have gained wider acceptance throughout the century that followed? Discuss how the persistence of mercantilism may have slowed down colonial reform, but ultimately bowed to Balfour's liberal notions. What argument could be offered that mercantilism rather than responsible government would have been the more expensive policy for Britain? Was Britain the only interest to resist "federation"?

2. What are the problems Canada has faced in its relations with the United States since the end of World War II? What measures has it taken in international trade to protect its economic autonomy? Discuss the role natural resources have played in the economy of Canada, and how they appear to be shaping the nation's future.

3. Describe and compare the political systems of Canada, Australia, and New Zealand. Compare them to the U. S. political system. Consider how the form a government takes may constitute a statement on prevailing attitudes toward the relative importance of individual freedom, the power of the state, and consensus of national goals. Discuss these concepts fully.

   Often the form of federation a nation finally accepts will reflect the experience of its early local government. Using Australia and other pertinent examples, discuss this trend, and any benefits or pitfalls it seems to bring to national governmental organization.

4. Australia and New Zealand "developed institutions of political and economic democracy surpassing those of the mother country." Illustrate this statement with specific examples, and include a discussion of why former British colonies could move more quickly on certain issues than the parent state.

5. What were the benefits and shortcomings of British rule in India before independence? In what ways is the British influence on India still apparent?

SUGGESTED FILMS

CANADA

Canada in Crisis. 59 min. B/w. National Educational TV, Inc., producer (1964).

Canada: Unity or Division. 23 min. B/w; c. Encyclopedia Britannica Educational Corporation (1959).

Canada's History: Colony to Commonwealth. 16 min. B/w; c. Coronet Instructional Films (1962).

AUSTRALIA

Australia. 11 min. B/w. Encyclopedia Britannica Educational Corporation (revised) (n.d.).

Australia: The Land the People. 16 min. B/w; c. Coronet Instructional Films (1957).

Exploration 1770: Reviewed 1970. 10 min. Color. Australian News and Information Bureau (New York) (1970).

NEW ZEALAND

New Zealand. 22 min. Color. New Zealand Government Travel Commission (Los Angeles) (n.d.).

INDIA

Ghandi's India. 20 min. B/w. Peter M. Robeck and Co., Inc. Time-Life Films, Inc., distributor (n.d.).

India's History: British Colony to Independence. 11 min. B/w; c. Coronet Instructional Films (1956).

Nehru's India. 20 min. B/w. Peter M. Robeck and Co., Inc. Time-Life Films, Inc., distributor (n.d.).

The Population Explosion. 43 min. B/w. Carousel Films, Incorporated (1960).

PAKISTAN

A Land Divided: India and Pakistan at War. 15 min. B/w. Hearst Metrotone News (1972).

Nefa. (2 parts) 15 min. Color. National Education and Information Films, Ltd. (Bombay, India) (n.d.).

Pakistan: Its Land and People. 17 min. B/w. Edward Levonian, producer (1955).

MULTIPLE CHOICE

Choose the best response.

1.   Which of the following inaccurately portrays the events that aided the establishment of the Turkish Republic?

    (a)   The Treaty of Sievres broke up the Ottoman Empire and restricted Turkish holdings to Istanbul and the northern and central portions of Asia Minor.

  *(b)   The autonomous national states in European Thrace, the Christian Republic of Armenia, and central and northern Anatolia—inspired by the principle of national self-determination—voluntarily united as the Republic of Turkey.

    (c)   In 1923, after a military campaign to re-establish their primacy in Asia Minor, the Turks extracted the Treaty of Lausanne from western powers under which they were permitted to retain lands then occupied in place of of the harsh War settlement.

    (d)   A group of nationalists obliterated the Armenian nationalist movement, frightened the Italians into withdrawing from Anatolia, and reconquered most of the European territory awarded Greece in post-War negotiations.

    (e)   Mustafa Kemal, by persistence and imaginative leadership, managed to depose the Sultan, reconquer territories lost between 1829 and 1922, and transform Turkey into a modern and progressive state.

2.   Which of the following actions taken by Anwar Sadat contributed to the alienation of Egypt's Arab neighbors?

    (a)   The continuation of Nasser's domestic policies, including suppression of all political parties that might have challenged the dominance of the Arab Socialist Union, the only legal political party in Egypt.

    (b)   The expulsion of Soviet advisors from Egypt in 1972, which led to a radical change in Egypt's international position.

    (c)   The reopening of the Suez Canal in 1975 to merchant ships of all nations, including Israel, which had been denied its use since 1956.

  *(d)   The bold reversal of an uncompromising foreign policy bent on Israel's destruction following the 1973 war.

(e)   The loss of the October 1973 war against Israel in which Egypt and Syria attempted to take over the Sinai Peninsula.

3.   Egypt's willingness to accept the Anglo-Egyptian Treaty of Friendship and Alliance in 1936 was triggered by its fear of

    (a)   Zionist agitation which had kept Palestine in turmoil since it was made a mandate of the League of Nations in 1918.

   *(b)   invasion by the Italians, who were then engaged in a war in Ethiopia.

    (c)   the French, who were intent upon expanding their already substantial colonial empire in Africa.

    (d)   the fundamentalist Islamic brotherhood known as the *Wafd* who were intent on overthrowing the government of King Farouk.

    (e)   diplomatic and economic isolation caused by its expulsion from the League of Nations.

4.   Jewish and Arab hostility in the country now known as Israel was generated by

    (a)   Zionist agitation to convert Palestine—with its approximately seventy percent Arab population—into a national homeland for the Jewish people.

    (b)   Arab resistance against a steadily increasing and culturally alien Jewish population in Palestine.

    (c)   the American Zionists' adoption of the Biltmore Program, which demanded the establishment of a Jewish state and a Jewish army in Palestine.

    (d)   the opening of Palestine to Jewish immigrants after 1933, which only increased tensions there and resulted in bloody violence between Jewish and Arab extremists.

   *(e)   all of the above, exacerbated by Britain's inability to maintain order and to devise a plan for establishing either a unified homeland, acceptable to both Jewish and Arab nationalists, or dual independent national territories.

5.   Which of the following is the most significant result of independence movements in sub-Saharan Africa?

    (a)   Soviet Russia, the United States, and their allies lent support to African rebellions and changes in government in order to extend their spheres of influence without directly confronting one another.

    (b)   Nigeria, one of the richest countries in Africa, was devastated by civil wars, which resulted in the loss of over one million lives.

   *(c)   African nations became engaged in a prolonged struggle to establish black majority rule in countries where white minorities exercised real power.

    (d)   Jomo Kenyatta's theory of African socialism helped prevent the domination of government by those with economic power and guaranteed full and equal participation of every mature citizen in Kenyan political affairs.

(e)   A reign of terror was instituted by the Mau Mau organization aginast white settlers and immigrants in Kenya between 1952 and 1958.

6.   Which of the following statements most effectively sums up the nature of the problems confronting Israeli society today?

    (a)   Enormous defense spending, which, in spite of massive U.S. economic and military aid, consumes about half the national budget.

  *(b)   A web of complex internal pressures and a constant external threat have precipitated serious economic and psychological problems among Israel's citizens.

    (c)   A steadily growing popular demand has arisen within Israel for accommodation and compromise with the Arab countries, in spite of the belligerently nationalistic stance of the Likkud bloc.

    (d)   By 1980, excessive urbanization and rampant inflation had reached an annual rate close to 100 percent in sharp contrast to the prosperity and agricultural development that occurred between 1948 and 1967.

    (e)   Social discrimination and disadvantages are suffered by Israeli citizens of Arab descent and Sephardic or "Oriental" Jews from Arabic and North African countries.

7.   With *one exception*, it can be said that in the twentieth century Saudi Arbaia

    (a)   is a theocratic state created by the union of the kingdoms of Hejaz and Nejd, ruled by an absolute monarch, and governed by members of the royal house, numbering about 3000 crown princes.

    (b)   pursues an anti-Israeli policy and subsidizes other Arab states, but at the same time remains staunchly anti-communist and generally aligned with the United States, trading oil contracts for western technology.

    (c)   controls the world's largest known oil reserves and, in union with the Organization of Petroleum Exporting Countries, potently influences international politics.

  *(d)   is a striking illustration of the compatibility of socialism and capitalism, a blend seen in the modernization of its cities and the assuagement of rural poverty through welfare programs, all financed by the accrued interest on foreign investments.

    (e)   rigidly follows the principles of Muslim traditionalism by banning alcoholic beverages, secluding women, and providing enviable welfare benefits to its citizens.

8.   All of the following contributed to the resentments of the regime of Muhammad Riza Pahlavi which pervaded Iranian society in the 1970s. Which statement most effectively sums up the problems that actually triggered the Iranian Revolution

which resulted in the overthrow of the Shah and the establishment of an Islamic republic?

(a)   The extravagant and militaristic use of wealth—accumulated from revenues of the nationalized petroleum industry—to embellish the trappings of an absolute monarchy seemed to scorn the national constitution.

(b)   The subversive activities of the *mullahs*, rankled by their diminished influence under the Pahlavi dynasty, and intellectuals and professionals, alienated by corruption in the government and the use of repressive tactics, including terror and torture, against opponents of the regime, singlehandedly turned the people against the Shah's regime.

*(c)   An economic slump in the late 1970s, accompanied by unemployment and a fifty percent rate of inflation, set off a wave of strikes by oil field workers and riots by university students which effectively stalled the economy.

(d)   The support of the U. S. and other western governments which were blind to persistent problems in Iran's economy, the nearly universal hatred the population bore towards the Shah, and the logical outcome of SAVAK operations antagonized the populace.

(e)   The meagre results of the "White Revolution" left sixty percent of Iranian adults illiterate, the majority of farmers with tiny, unprofitable holdings, and ten percent of the population in control of half the national wealth.

9.   Which of the following statements concerning the new states of Africa is *incorrect*?

(a)   Libya was the first of the one-time colonies to achieve independence after World War II.

(b)   Ghana could probably be described as the leader of the African colonial revolt.

(c)   Algeria was the scene of the most violent colonial revolt in North Africa.

*(d)   The Congo was the scene of the most peaceful transition from colonial status to independence.

(e)   In the late 1960s Nigeria experienced a bloody civil war with a great number of casualties.

10. The modern countries of the Middle East

(a)   without exception, were once part of the Ottoman Empire, whose social and political system sought to cope with proliferating domestic problems at the time by encouraging ethnic groups to cultivate peaceful relations with their neighbors. This was done by setting up territorial states as homelands for each group.

(b)   gained political independence after World War I by appealing to the League of Nations in the name of the principle of self-determination. In the case of Turkish ethnics after 1923 this assured their development as autonomous nations.

(c)   are finally approaching effective union in the Arab League, which was founded in 1954 for mutual defense and economic development, has a multinational parliament, and was the successful arbiter of the Lebanese civil war (1975-76).

(d)   established their own national governments, often against the wishes and in defiance of religious authorities, yet fully in accord with the tenets of Ayatollah Khomeini's *Islamic Government.*

*(e)   have not yet eliminated illiteracy, disease, high mortality rates, and widespread poverty in spite of ambitious programs of modernization and industrialization.

11.   Short of an internecine racial war, the greatest hopes for South Africa's black majority to gain equal status with the white minority lie in

(a)   passive resistance, acts of defiance, and demonstrations opposing the Bantu Self-Government Act (1959), which envisioned the creation of a number of independent Bantustans, each with its own tribal identity, and, therefore, with little sense of African national identity.

(b)   the Anti-apartheid policy of the Progressive Federal Party, recently formed by a small group of white liberals, remnants of the opposition United and Progressive parties of 1959.

(c)   the programs of the *verlighte*, a group of white Afrikaners who demand an easing of the rigid Apartheid laws, especially in the area of cultural traditions.

*(d)   intensified militancy, stimulated by the articulate leadership of the Black Peoples' Convention (1972) and the South African Students' Movement, and the increasing isolation of South Africa from the world community of nations.

(e)   the Organization of African Unity, which intends to resolve inter-African disputes, prevent external interference in African affairs, and lay the groundwork for majority rule in South Africa. Its chief emphasis is identifying the forms of local government best suited to each region and allowing these to operate within the federal structure of the Organization.

12.   The roots of South Africa's present difficulties might be traced to

(a)   its policy of anti-Semitism, clearly recognizable by 1938 and maintained by fanatic whites, who resented alleged Jewish ownership of the gold and diamond mines of the Rand, and demanded that no Jews be allowed to immigrate to South Africa.

(b) the Nationalist Party, formed in 1912, which strove to preserve the cultural independence of the Afrikaners, opposed fusion with the British—who regarded it as imperialist—and worked to change the Dominion into a republic.

*(c) attempts by victorious Britain to reach reconciliation with extremist Boers after the war (1899-1902), and its refusal to address itself to the plight of the African majority, and its reluctance to impose upon South Africa a universal and non-racial franchise.

(d) the efforts of the Vorster government to seek a rapproachement with the black African nations to the north and to devolve more autonomy on the newly created Bantu states within South Africa.

(e) the withdrawal of South Africa from the Commonwealth of Nations in 1961, with the intent to turn South Africa into an Afrikaner nation.

13. Which of the following statements *best* describes neocolonialist tendencies in Africa?

*(a) European technocrats and capitalists continue to play important roles in the political and economic sectors of many African states.

(b) Reliance on the western nations for advanced technology and development loans puts most African states terribly in debt to the International Monetary Fund, to which they have surrendered to a considerable degree their fiscal autonomy.

(c) Presently, inter-African warfare and internal instability are the result of growing militarism, which some industrialized nations have made possible or consistently supported through their armaments industries, and failed to discourage on diplomatic grounds.

(d) Although local governments are remarkably responsive to the masses, the process of governmental centralization and the diminishing importance of popularly elected legislative bodies continues in most African countries.

(e) Ethnic conflicts and the colonial legacy, embodied in European settlers and and their communities, impede a return to authentic African values, and, thus, realization of Pan-Africanist ideology.

14. The concept of African socialism that Julius Nyerere promoted is summarized in which of the following statements?

(a) People should not assume self-government unless they first acquire a sense of responsibility to the state and liberate themselves from the prejudices of the past; until these things are accomplished, the head of state must be the enlightened director of government.

(b) The essence of democracy and socialism in Africa cannot be based on a dictatorship of the proletariat nor any other form of class rule. Rather, it should be based upon full and equal participation of every mature citizen in political affairs, a condition that should prevent seizure of power by those who wield economic power.

*(c) Society is an extension of the traditional, communalistic family form of social organization, and must be rooted in recognition of the dignity of work and sustained through national self-reliance.

(d) Since all secular power is the work of the Satan, it remains the duty of Muslims to organize a theocracy that will carry revolutionary Islamic policy to its final worldwide victory.

(e) The natural condition of national authority is that it rest in a single person, for the ruler governs by divine and ancestral right, holding in his person the sum of all executive, judicial, and legislative power.

15. Reread the specific views of government held by statesmen of the Middle East and Africa as presented in question 14. Which list below properly orders these historical figures to correspond with their theories?

(a) Seko Mobutu; Mustafa Kemal; Jomo Kenyatta; Julius Nyerere; Ayatollah Khomeini.

*(b) Mustafa Kemal; Jomo Kenyatta; Julius Nyerere; Ayatollah Khomeini; Jean Bedell Bokassa.

(c) Ayatollah Khomeini; Seko Touré; Seko Mobutu; Mustafa Kemal; Jomo Kenyatta.

(d) Julius Nyerere; Ayatollah Khomeini; Seko Touré; Seko Mobutu; Mustafa Kemal.

(e) Jomo Kenyatta; Julius Nyerere; Ayatollah Khomeini; Jean Bedell Bokassa; Seko Mobutu.

IDENTIFICATIONS

Treaty of Lausanne
Wafd
Biltmore Program
Likkud
Fagan Commission
General Law Amendment Act
Ujamaa
Kurds and Baluchistani

Camp David Accord
Baath Socialist Party
Treaty of Vereemiging
Transkei
Steve Biko
Balfour Declaration
Zionists

TRUE OR FALSE

F   1.   Mustafa Kemal's successors supplanted his benevolent dictatorship with a democratic republic after World War II.

T   2.   By the 1930s most Arabs had come to believe that the Jewish presence in Palestine threatened the Arab way of life and endangered the rights of non-Jewish communities, even though sectarian courts were invested with power to settle many disputes within the ethnic communities rather than through federal structures.

F   3.   The Islamic concept of society as held by Iranians can accommodate Western concepts of civilization and social order.

T   4.   Israel's economy was greatly strengthened by payments West Germany made in restitution for Nazi crimes against the families and companions of Jewish emigrants.

T   5.   The war of October 1956 was initiated when Israel attacked Egypt with the encouragement of the British and French governments.

T   6.   Between 1967 and 1975 Israeli defense spending escalated tremendously, becoming the world's highest in proportion to population."

F   7.   After establishing the theocratic state of Saudi Arabia, King Abdul Ibn Saud abolished slavery in Hejaz and Nejd.

F   8.   The Israeli constitution of 1949 provides for proportional representation, a unicameral parliament, and suffrage for citizens of Jewish ethinic origin.

F   9.   According to the Constitution of 1909, the Cape Colony, Natal, the Orange Free State and Transvaal were united into a federal state having limited jurisdiction over essentially autonomous member republics.

F   10.   The Balfour Declaration issued by the British government gave the Arabs an equal voice in the determination of the future of Jewish Palestine.

DISCUSSION AND/OR ESSAY QUESTIONS

1.   A former "president of the World Zionist Organization, urged Israel to seek security by fulfilling its destiny as a unique spiritual center rather than striving to be 'a state like all other states'. He recommended Israel's neutralization—returned to its pre-1967 borders but with independence and sovereignty guaranteed by the the two superpowers—and a gradual demilitarization of the states of the Middle East."

       —Nahum Goldmann, in the article "True Neutrality for Israel."

   Discuss the viability of Nahum Goldman's program for future Israeli policy in the Middle East. What difficulties may be encountered in implementing such a program?

2. "All secular power, no matter what form it takes, is the work of Satan. It is our duty to stop it in its tracks and to combat its effects . . . It is not only our duty in Iran, but it is also the duty of all the Muslims of the world, to carry the revolutionary Islamic policy to its final victory."
   —Ayatollah Ruholla Khomeini, *Islamic Government*

   Discuss fully the Ayatollah Khomeini's concept of a universal Islamic government in view of present problems in the Middle East, particularly the differential rate at which the various national economies are developing. Does Pan-Africanism offer any object lessons for the Islamic nations of the Middle East?

3. Why does Africa depend to some extent on the industrialized nations? What are the political and economic implications of this dependency (e.g., its effect on the the evolution of domestic political structure, foreign policy, internal fiscal policy, and international trade)? How could Africa bargain for more equity in international trade? Discuss, among other topics, issues surrounding price-fixing for natural resources and access to international waterways, such as the Suez Canal.

4. Why is the Middle East a "scene of confrontation between the superblocs" and also "the focal point in the growing tension between advanced industrial nations and underdeveloped countries of the Third World?"
   Using sources other than the text, examine the concept of nonalignment. What potential does it have for improving international relations? Conversely, how might it raise anxiety among advanced industrial nations?

5. What are the origins of Apartheid policy? How was it implemented? In your discussion detail the legislation that created and heightened racial tension in South Africa. How have such laws prompted world criticism? How has South Africa's rejection of such criticism led to its isolation from the community of nations?

SUGGESTED FILMS

Africa. (Nigeria). 25 min. B/w. Hearst Metrotone News (n.d.).

Africa Awakens. 29 min. B/w. United Nations Films and TV Distribution Officer (1958).

Africa: Colonialism. 29 min. B/w. National Educational TV, Inc.; Indiana University Audio-Visual Center (n.d.).

Africa: The Belgian Congo. 29 min. B/w. National Educational TV, Inc.; Indiana University Audio-Visual Center (n.d.).

Afrikaner. 40 min. Color. Time-Life Films, Incorporated (1971).

Ataturk: Founder of Modern Turkey. 35 min. Color. Time-Life Films, Incorporated (n.d.).

Decolonization in Africa. 19 min. B/w. McGraw-Hill Textfilms (1969).

Iran: Between Two Worlds. 15 min. B/w; c. Encyclopedia Britannica Educational Corporation (1954).

Iran: Brittle Ally. 54 min. Columbia Broadcasting System (1959).

Israel: Exodus to Independence. 29 min. B/w. Films, Incorporated (1972).

Mau Mau. 20 min. B/w. British Information Service (New York) (1955).

Nasser vs. Ben-Gurion. 25 min. B/w. Films, Incorporated (1964).

Road to Independence. (Africa). 27 min. B/w. McGraw-Hill Textfilms (1958).

Turkey: Emergence of a Modern Nation. 17 min. B/w; c. Encyclopedia Britannica Films (1963).

White Africa. 40 min. B/w. Peter M. Robeck and Company, Inc.; Time-Life Films, Incorporated, distributor (1969).

Outline

MULTIPLE CHOICE
Choose the best response.

1. The aims of the present Japanese government in economic and foreign affairs are accurately reflected in which of the following statements?

    (a) To give Japan a military leverage as formidable as its economic competitiveness, the government is working to convert the Southeast Asia Defense Agency into a force with offensive capability as well as a defensive nuclear arsenal.

    *(b) Reminiscent of the Japanese business community and liberalism of the early 1920s, the government and opposition parties in general agree that Japan depends for its survival upon peaceful relations with many other countries. As Japan's gross national product increases so also does its need for new markets, and statistics of essential imports to Japan attest to its great need for raw materials and foodstuffs from all over the globe.

    (c) Favorable balance of trade with high income areas and the OPEC countries is seen as a way to counterbalance the inflationary cost of industrial raw materials and energy and to retain Japan's economic superiority in Southeast Asia.

    (d) Natural resources have become a focal point of diplomacy as Japanese leaders continue in their efforts to reach conciliation with the Soviet Union; among their goals are to regain the Kuril Islands and conjointly develop known oil and gas reserves in Siberia.

    (e) Japan's leaders, with popular support of the Japanese people, have worked to carry out the Security Treaty as renewed in 1970, which binds Japan to follow the United States' lead in cultivating relationships with non-Communist nations in Asia and, recently, with China.

2. Contemporary Japanese society can be characterized in each of the following ways, *except*

    (a) although once highly literate and traditionally hierarchical, it is now stratified on the basis of earned rank in a group or organization and personal educational credentials.

    (b) as simultaneously traditional and innovative: just as equal opportunity is assumed in politics and economics from the Japanese viewpoint, so a person's social status is considered to be determined by merit.

311

*(c)   that it is not discriminatory toward women, who hold significant positions in political and economic life as an outgrowth of progressive ideals articulated in the national constituion.

(d)   that it represented a nearly complete turnabout from an antiquated feudal mentality and class structure, in which inherited noble rank and family pedigree were of utmost importance.

(e)   that it is still paternalistic and patriarchal; individuals can enjoy a great deal of security, although not individuality, and social harmony has priority over legalism.

3.   One of the following statements *incorrectly* implies that Japan's participation in World War I

(a)   demonstrated its adeptness at mastering the object lessons offered by European diplomacy and power politics, and at taking action both at home and abroad to become a credible force in the emerging world order.

(b)   had the short-term effect of reaffirming its position as a great power among the "Big Five" at the Paris Peace Conference in 1919. However, in the long run Japan's "equal partner" was obscured by the prejudices of western nations, which penalized Japan with high tariffs in the name of protectionism and betrayed racism in exclusionary immigration laws.

(c)   was rewarded in the peace settlements with German concessions and occupied territory on the Shantung peninsula and north Pacific islands. Even though the League of Nations mandate of the islands and Japan's hold over Shantung was imperialistic, Japan was actually in transition to a period of anti-military and pro-conciliation sentiment, as its voluntary return of Shantung to China four years later illustrated.

*(d)   reasonably assured that Japan would have equal status with the U. S. and Britain in terms of rearmament; this was specified in the Naval Limitation Agreement, conlcuded in 1921-22 during the Washington Conference.

(e)   impelled Japanese leaders to implement liberal democratic policies, mainly because they perceived democracy as an integral part of twentieth century progress, and wished to cooperate with the victorious governments toward a prosperous future.

4.   The failure of liberal democratic trends in Japan prior to World War II is probably *best* explained by

(a)   the negative impressions projected by the western democracies whose political and economic failures stood in stark contrast to the dynamic performance of the major totalitarian states.

*(b)   the rise of militant ultra-nationalism which was exacerbated by a tradition-bound social system and an economic system that had failed to cope effectively with an expanding population at home and escalating competition abroad.

(c)   inability of liberal politicians, who had no cultural or institutional experience in the democratic process, to resist international trends toward virulent nationalism.

(d)   Japan's taking up the challenge to surpass the West economically, one of the psychological and social reactions against long-standing racial and economic discrimination against Asians. This challenge was foreshadowed when the Peace Conference of 1919 turned down a declaration on the equality of nations, and it was very clear during and after the worldwide Depression.

(e)   the intensely nationalistic foreign policy of both principal political parties; although the first was supported both by farmers and capitalists and the second mainly by industrialists, they did not differ significantly in the methods chosen to advance Japan's interests, and not until 1931 did moderation of the jingoist spirit show itself in Japanese foreign policy.

5.   The post-World War II recovery and transformation of Japan's political, economic, and social life has been impressive but not all pervasive. The nation continues to be troubled by vestiges of its past. Which of the following *cannot* be regarded as a long standing problem?

(a)   Japan continues to be utterly dependent on external markets for a wide range of raw materials—oil, coal, iron ore, lead, copper, zinc, etc.—which are absolutely essential to the continued high performance of its industrial complex and, therefore, to its economic well-being.

*(b)   Japan's economy continues to be disrupted by labor unrest and prolonged and crippling strikes. The failure of Japanese management and labor to achieve good working relations is attributable to the traditional class distinctions that separate them.

(c)   Despite improvements in their constitutional and legal status, Japanese women continue to be victims of an antiquated feudal mentality. They have not been extended equal opportunities within the economic and social structures; they have not attained positions of leadership in significant numbers; they have not achieved wage parity with male workers; nor have they received benefits comparable to male workers.

(d)   Japanese society continues to be hierarchical although status is now dependent upon identification with a group, rank in an organization, or educational credentials rather than upon accidents of birth.

(e)   Japanese political habits and psychology carry overtones of an earlier tradition characterized by strong local loyalties and personality cults which have resulted in a preference for government by men rather than by law. The persistence of this tradition has prevented the rise of national parties with clearly defined policies or even the development of a national political consciousness.

6. Japan's remarkable post-War recovery was *mainly* due to

   *(a) the ability of the Japanese to adapt foreign institutions to their own social and cultural traditions and turn these to their advantage.

   (b) the willingness of the emperor to accept terms of surrender and to serve as a symbolic link to the past at a time when so much of the past seemed to have been destroyed forever.

   (c) the Constitution of 1946, which declared that sovereignty lay in the hands of the Japanese people as a whole, and left the emperor only formal powers.

   (d) the vigorous and consistent promotion of Japan's long-term interests by General Douglas MacArthur, Supreme Commander for the Allied powers, who directed Occupation operations (1946-1951).

   (e) the policy of demilitarization and opposition to the decentralization of industry, which freed military expenditures for reconstruction and prevented the reestablishment of monopolistic commercial interests.

7. Japan's Constitution of 1946 contained all of the following, *except*

   (a) an elaborate Bill of Rights which went beyond the traditional American civil liberties to include such benefits as the right to work and to bargain collectively.

   (b) a parliamentary form of government with a bicameral Diet, and a cabinet responsible to the House of Representatives.

   (c) the principle of separation of Church and State which was, in part, designed to keep religion from ever again becoming an extension of government policy.

   (d) a renunciation of war as a sovereign right of the nation and of a military establishment that might be capable of waging war.

   *(e) guarantees of universal male suffrage on the grounds that it was more in tune with traditional Japanese values than universal adult suffrage would have been.

8. The Kuomintang party's emergence as the leader of the Chinese Nationalist Revolution was primarily due to

   *(a) the organizational ability and initiative of agents sent to Canton by the revolutionary Communist regime of Soviet Russia; they had come as part of the Moscow-Canton detente (1923-27) to aid a small band of reformers headed by Dr. Sun Yat-sen, who insisted that parliamentary democracy was the ultimate goal of the revolution.

   (b) the forcefulness of a body of doctrines worked out by Dr. Sun, providing a political philosophy to inspire the masses and a viable program to organize a strong and free China under a republican constitution.

(c)   the growing internal confusion and increased reliance on Japanese aid during China's participation in World War I, a time when the central government of the "phantom Republic" was unable to control its own territory.

(d)   the failure of the republican government in Peking to control ex-soldiers and bandits in the provinces, where they ruled as tyrannical warlords.

(e)   the success of bold military action taken by the Canton forces under the leadership of General Chiang Kai-shek against northern militarists in 1926.

9.   Which of the following statements describing Communist and Kuomintang relations is *incorrect*?

(a)   Originating as a party for revolution, the Kuomintang had welcomed and benefited from Russian assistance before 1927, but never intended to serve the interests of a foreign power.

(b)   While anti-communist in orientation, the Nanking government of Chiang Kai-shek closely followed the Soviet pattern when it established a dictatorship of the Kuomintang, subordinating popular sovereignty to party tutelage.

(c)   Only by purging radical pro-Russian elements from the party and dismissing Russian advisors in 1927 could Chiang Kai-shek and the conservative faction initiate plans for reconstruction and extend their authority throughout China. Among problems they encountered were the persistence of warlord regimes and the necessity of maintaining a strong army to regulate the "tutelage" of citizens.

*(d)   A believer in the inevitable coming of world revolution, Dr. Sun Yat-sen welcomed the effects of cooperation with Russia, feeling this would help to eliminate traditional elements that threatened to slow the progress of the revolution, to invigorate the Kuomintang with young radicals, and to turn China into an outpost of Soviet Communism.

(e)   Soviet agents' attempts to overthrow the Peking government resulted in the termination of diplomatic relations between the semi-established government operating in Canton and that of Moscow.

10.   The Kuomintang party's failure to unite China under a nationalist government is best explained by

(a)   Communist success in currying popular favor by introducing, under Sun Yat-sen's "Principle of Livelihood," reforms that the Kuomintang promised but never instituted.

(b)   the inability of the Kuomintang regime to solve the massive problems of Chinese society.

(c) the lengthy war with Japan which drained the country's resources, demoralized the population, and promoted generally chaotic conditions which the Communists were able to exploit to their own advantage.

(d) Communist successes in the countryside, where their prestige grew, especially during World War II, until they controlled much of northern China.

*(e) all of the above.

11. Which of the following political theories and programs *cannot* be ascribed to the practical political philosophy of Mao Tse-tung?

(a) ". . . Several hundred million peasants will rise like a tornado or tempest, a force so extraordinarily swift and violent that no power, however great, will be able to suppress it."

*(b) Strengthening "people's loyalty to the nation," "establishing popular sovereignty under the direction of experts," and implementing social reform "to improve the material condition of the entire population" must be the aim of a truly revolutionary republican government.

(c) Ownership by the whole people first calls for the merging of rural cooperatives and collective farms into large communes, so that food production can be significantly increased and a prospective labor force for industrialization can be established.

(d) To achieve an entirely equalitarian society, "hedonists," "revisionists," "anti-party activists," and those who "take the road to capitalism" have to be ruthlessly eliminated.

(e) Education consists of a combination of theory and practice, and must include "half-study, half-work" programs for students and teachers alike.

12. The Communist regime of Mao Tse-tung decided that a high price would have to be paid for transforming Chinese society. Which of the following policy decisions contributed the most to the tremendous cost in terms of individual freedoms during Mao's Revolution?

(a) In keeping with the principles of a "People's Democratic Dictatorship," it claimed to have achieved a willing coalition of peasants, workers, petty bourgeoisie, and "national bourgeoisie," through political education carried on by guerillas before the Revolution and by the Party thereafter.

*(b) Because it is possible to remake human nature through psychological pressure, "thought control" and "reform through labor" are legitimate means to form a new man, who will instinctively serve society.

(c) Legislation and the long course of the Revolution have broken up the traditional patriarchal structure of Chinese society and have emancipated—at least in theory—the women of China. Many women are now in the work force, and the single-unit family is the common mode of residence and association.

(d) The Mao regime worked to restrict the birthrate by providing contraceptives and family-planning clinics, and stopped the growth of cities through programs to control migration from rural areas and to force resettlement of millions of urban dwellers.

(e) Decentralization was emphasized in Mao's economic programs in an attempt to establish a symbiotic relationship between industrial urban centers and the surrounding agricultural areas in order to encourage regional "self-reliance" and a degree of self-determination.

13. The "Great Proletarian Cultural Revolution" launched by Mao Tse-tung in 1966 was designed to

(a) maintain the fervor of the Communist revolution until it had produced a truly equalitarian society.

(b) counter a trend toward a relaxation of effort on the part of the people in the face of the promise of material success.

(c) replace the Soviet's dual system of parallel state and party structures that was developing in China with a flexible but unified system.

(d) purge the party of "moderates" who would abandon the goals of the revolution and reform the party structure.

*(e) all of the above.

14. By the late 1950s the "indestructible friendship" between China and the Soviet Union began to come apart. Differences led swiftly to a deterioration in diplomatic and economic relations between the two nations. Which of the following *did not* contribute to this rift?

(a) The Chinese resented the Russian's failure to fulfill their commitments to provide the Chinese with the technical and economic assistance.

(b) The Chinese accused the Russians of abandoning the cause of world revolution against imperialism and of pursuing a policy of peaceful coexistence and accommodation with the capitalist nations.

*(c) By the early 1960s the Chinese had rationalized relations with numerous capitalist states and found them to be more reliable and less demanding sources of technical and economic assistance than the Soviet Union.

(d) The Chinese regarded the Russians as the complacent heirs of an old revolution who had lost their revolutionary fervor while the Russians regarded the Chinese as ungrateful perverters of Marxist orthodoxy.

(e) Conflicting territorial ambitions generated tensions between the two communist states that were most strikingly demonstrated by the tens of thousands of Chinese and Russian troops who faced each other along the length of their 5,000 mile common border.

15.   The Chinese government in the post-Mao Tse-tung era appears to be

*(a)   more concerned with economic development and less concerned with ideological purity than Mao's government was.

(b)   more concerned with reaching an accommodation with the Soviet Union and less concerned with cultivating better relations with the capitalist nations than Mao's government was.

(c)   more concerned with furthering the cause of world revolution and less concerned with normalizing relations with the industrial states of the east and west than Mao's government was.

(d)   more concerned with developing genuinely democratic forms of governance and less concerned with maintaining a strict, authoritarian party line than Mao's government was.

(e)   all of the above.

IDENTIFICATIONS

Burakumin
Nine Power "Open Door"
   Treaty
Zaibatsu
Seiyukai
Minseito
Oriental Exclusion Law
Michael Borodin
San Min Chu I

Manchukuo
All-China People's Congress
"National" capitalists
The "Gang of Four"
Bonin and Ryukyu
Association of Southeast Asian
   Nations
Taiwan Relations Act

TRUE OR FALSE

T   1.   Although diplomatic relations were restored between Japan and the Soviet Union in 1956, Russia never fully accounted for Japanese World War II prisoners of war.

T   2.   The so-called "hamlet people" and a resident Korean minority of some 600,000 persons have never been completely accepted by or assimilated into Japanese society.

F   3.   Although Japan has contributed substantially to development programs in Southeast Asia, especially since 1966 when the Asian Development Bank was founded, reparation settlements have never been concluded between Japan and the countries its armies overran during World War II.

F   4.   Entirely consonant with the Wilsonian principles, the Japanese convinced participants of the Peace Conference of 1919 to endorse "the equality of nations and the just treatment of their nationals" as a principle of international relations.

T   5.   In spite of Article 9 of the Japanese Constitution that "land, sea, and air forces, as well as other war potential, will never be maintained," Japan's strength in conventional weapons now exceeds what it was at the peak of World War II.

T   6.   In 1925, the Canton government, controlled by the Kuomintang high command, was actually a Soviet-sponsored but not communist regime.

F   7.   The vicissitudes of the Great Proletarian Cultural Revolution (1966-1977) greatly retarded progress toward the Party goals of rapid agricultural and industrial growth.

F   8.   In order to collectivize all agricultural land, Mao Tse-tung used his method of "persuasive reasoning," which entailed the ruthless liquidation of all resisters.

T   9.   The revolution Mao brought to China was the first successful large-scale revolution ever to be founded on peasant support and directed by a leader from the peasant class.

F   10.   Without American and Russian military aid communist guerillas could not have penetrated Japanese lines during the War, nor could they have established control over much of northern China.

DISCUSSION AND/OR ESSAY QUESTIONS

1.   "To some observers the contemporary Chinese Communist regime bears more than a superficial resemblance to the classical imperial tradition of a benevolent government wielding absolute power over an obedient and disciplined population. It follows that as long as the rulers enjoy the 'mandate of Heaven', their position will not be seriously challenged."

Describe the classical imperial tradition of a benevolent government wielding absolute power over a disciplined population. Can you see specific traces of this tradition in the Kuomintang governmental policies? Can you support this passage by citing particular Chinese Communist policies? What connection might any of these have to Dr. Sun Yat-sen's concept of a period of tutelage on the way to popular sovereignty? Finally, if the Chinese people already revered the government and tended to obey its directives, why then were revolutionaries preoccupied with loosening family ties and rechanneling energy into state loyalty?

2.   "Although it has been likened to fascism, the 'Imperial Way' proclaimed by the ultranationalists undoubtedly had more in common with the ancient Japanese concepts of the state as a patriarchal society and of the superiority of government by men to government by law."

Bringing into your discussion material from other chapters of this text, explain the ancient Japanese concept of the state. What prompts the statement that the Japanese acknowledged the superiority of government by men to government by law? How is the government that took Japan into World War II exemplary of of this point of view? How is the post-war Japanese government also a variation of this same theme?

3. "Japan's military defeat and subsequent occupation by the conqueror's troops marked the third time in the country's history that it was subjected to strong doses of foreign influence. Unlike the earlier occasions, the Japanese were not acting voluntarily. But although forced to accept changes, they again succeeded to a remarkable degree in adapting them to their own social and cultural traditions and in using them to promote renewed growth and fresh achievements."

Briefly summarize the two earlier occasions when Japan was exposed to strong foreign influence. Illustrate with specific examples how Japanese adaptability to forced change has manifest itself in post-War Japan. Consider both what has been assimilated from foreign cultures and what has been retained, modified, or directly applied from traditional Japanese institutions.

4. Define the term "Sunyatsenism." What were its principal tenets? How were they applied by the Nationalist regime at Nanking? Why was the principal figure of early Nationalist ideology likewise acknowledged by the opposition Chinese Communist party? Discuss at length the issue of a foreign presence being a prime target for revolutionary propaganda.

5. What were the origins of Kuomintang and Soviet contacts? Chart the course of Chinese and Soviet relations before and during World War II. How and why did diplomacy, direct assistance, and training programs deteriorate to the point of bitter antagonism between these nations? What are the reasons for the present Sino-Soviet split?

SUGGESTED FILMS

China. 18 min. B/w. March of Time: Time-Life Films, Incorporated, producer (1945).

China: Communist Triumph and Consolidation, 1945-1971. 29 min. B/w. Films, Incorporated (1972).

China: Enemies Within and Without, 1927-1944. 22 min. B/w. Films, Incorporated (1972).

China-Russia: Communism in Conflict. 17 min. B/w. Hearst Metrotone News (1963).

Japan: A New Dawn Over Asia. (2 parts). B/w. Public Media, Incorporated (1963).

Japan's Revolution. 29 min. B/w. Indiana University Audio-Visual Center (1959).

Outline

MULTIPLE CHOICE
Choose the best response.

1. Tensions that developed after World War II to threaten world stability and temper hopes for a lasting peace were most seriously escalated by

    (a) a decline of the Western imperial powers, coupled with colonies' nationalistic rebellions for independence.

    (b) changes in world-power relations, which assumed a bipolar character based on the rivalry of the United States and the USSR.

    (c) the mistrust that loomed between wartime allies, which was increased by Stalin's obsession with external security.

    (d) the sudden emergence of the United States as the most powerful nation of the world, controlling the destinies of at least half of the earth's population.

    *(e) the Soviet Union's ideological intransigence, its development of atomic weapons, and the race that ensued between the world's two superpowers to add new and more deadly weapons to their arsenals.

2. Among the effects of the Second World War on the United States, which of the following became the impetus for the so-called Cold War?

    (a) At a time when the people of the United States constituted only 7 percent of the world's population, their incomes represented 30 percent of its estimated total income.

    (b) The unemployment problem of 1939 disappeared, personal income doubled, and savings quadrupled after the war.

    (c) Most Americans came to regard America's strength as incomparable and were convinced that no rival existed that could challenge it.

    *(d) The U.S. government was ready to counter any belligerent move on the part of the Soviet Union that might have upset the precarious alignment of powers along Eastern communistic and Western democratic lines.

(e) Since, of the Big Five powers, only the U.S. homeland was not ravaged by war, the U.S. economy could provide the surplus of goods necessary for reconstruction of the postwar world.

3. Which Soviet policy decision caused the major intensification of the Cold War?

(a) Russia's mistrust of capitalism, the dogmatic enemy of the prerevolutionary proletariat, was not diminished by the victory it had won as an ally of the Western democracies.

(b) Some of the hostility displayed toward other nations emanated from Russia's resentment over losses it had sustained in World War II.

*(c) Contrary to the Yalta Agreements, Soviet governmental efforts to ensure external security were channeled into the establishment of a buffer zone of "people's republics" in eastern Europe so as to maintain Soviet influence in these areas.

(d) The tremendous losses of the war caused unprecedented poverty and hardship in the USSR, conditions that the government felt would undermine citizens' allegiance to the Communist regime if they continued.

(e) The government attempted to unite the peoples of the Soviet Union by issuing a steady stream of propaganda that warned of an imminent attack on Russia by the capitalist powers.

4. Power relationships among the Big Five powers after World War II were most drastically changed by the

(a) revolution in China, which allied the Soviet Union with the Communist insurgents and brought in the United States on the side of the Nationalists.

(b) loss by France and Britain of their colonial empires, which reduced those two countries to a secondary status and forced them to depend increasingly on the United States.

(c) inflexible Soviet policy of increasing its sphere of influence in eastern Europe and in the Balkans. These actions contradicted the United Nations' declaration, signed by the USSR, that guaranteed all peoples the right to choose the form of government under which they would live.

*(d) polarization of national allegiances around the United States and the Soviet Union after Great Britain, France, and China were diminished as world powers by their own domestic difficulties and insurgencies in their colonies.

(e) United States' decision to strengthen its competitors and former enemies through programs of massive economic and military aid, on the assumption that the relative economic independence of western Europe would lessen its salience as a Soviet revolutionary target.

5. An inheritance of post-World War II power politics, the spirit of United States' foreign policy was *best* illustrated by

   (a) the Truman Doctrine, which provided military and economic assistance to noncommunist countries' governments in order to prevent further communist infiltration.

   (b) a policy of Soviet containment—i.e., the United States seeks allies who are willing to use military force to oppose both Soviet Communist expansion and revolution world-wide.

   (c) the Marshall Plan, which granted economic assistance to countries in western Europe in the belief that communist revolutions cannot be easily precipitated in economically independent nations.

   (d) the North Atlantic Treaty Organization (NATO), a military alliance able to call up an army composed of divisions contributed by its members, whose principal aim was to discourage or resist expansionist policies, primarily those of Soviet Russia.

   *(e) All of the above.

6. That tensions between the United States and the Soviet Union could begin to ease during the late 1950s and 1960s was the result of all the following *except* the

   (a) accession to power of Nikita Khrushchev, who sympathized with the discontent in the Soviet sphere concerning restrictions and rigidities that had been imposed by Stalin's regime.

   *(b) Brezhnev Doctrine, which asserted that the Soviet Union has the right to interfere in the affairs of any "socialist" country that falters in its loyalty to Soviet leadership.

   (c) principle of "peaceful coexistence," predicated on the "scientific" concept that capitalism will inevitably collapse without force of arms and will be followed by a dictatorship of the proletariat.

   (d) agreement of the governments of Great Britain, France, the United States, and the USSR to iron out differences at a "conference at the summit" in 1955.

   (e) program of de-Stalinization and the doctrine of "more than one road to socialism."

7. An important concomitant to the U.S. policy of "containment" after 1945 is seen in which of the following:

   (a) the division of Germany into a nominally independent German Democratic Republic under Soviet control and the Federal Republic of Germany supported by the Western powers.

(b) collapse of the Four Power administration of Germany and the blockade of Berlin by Russia in retaliation for uniting the western zones of control under one authority.

*(c) a painfully learned lesson that superpowers are unable to exercise their power fully, nor can they impose their will upon another unless they are ready to destroy civilization, including their own.

(d) massive intervention of the U.S. forces in Vietnam, which proved to be a failure and resulted in the total victory of the Viet Cong, Vietnamese communists.

(e) a major war in Korea, which contributed greatly to the deep-seated hostility between the United States and the People's Republic of China during the next thirty years.

8. Changes in the post-World War II world meant new power statuses and new attitudes. The most important in terms of its promise for continued human progress has been the

(a) decline of Western imperial powers, and the emergence of the Third World nations of Africa, the Middle East, Asia, and Latin America.

(b) hope sustained by many nations that the two midcentury superpowers will accommodate their national goals to the limitations under which their power must be voluntarily placed if a catastrophic atomic war is to be avoided.

*(c) growing recognition that the burden of finding solutions for vast economic, racial, nutritional, and political problems cannot be limited to one country, nor can programs focus on one area of need, for the problems are often interrelated and affect all peoples of the world.

(d) emergence of a new, and important, power block, the European Common Market, more sympathetic to the United States than to the Soviet Union but, nonetheless, independent in its actions.

(e) rejection by some thinkers of the West's predominant theory of "progress" —the twin goals of industrialization and urbanization—which may in practice interfere with efficient attainment of national aspirations.

9. The dissolution of long-standing power structures is *incorrectly* described in which of the following statements?

(a) The British colonial empire was expediently surrendered to governments rising from nationalist movements.

(b) Mao Tse-tung's communist revolution succeeded in spite of massive aid from the United States to the Nationalist government, which had little popular support.

(c) A bitterly fought, lengthy conflict could not secure France's control of its colonial possessions in North Africa.

(d) Decades of political struggle established national governments in Africa, with black majority rule in all nations except South Africa.

*(e) According to Soviet leaders, multiparty, nationalist governments, supported by popular majorities, were established in all Soviet Socialist Republics and People's Democracies.

10. The most fundamental factor contributing to the conflicts in Indochina in the late 1970s was

(a) the continued interference by the great powers in the affairs of the nations of the region.

*(b) the resurgence of old ethnic and national rivalries that had been held in check during the common struggle against French and American imperialism.

(c) the chronic instability of Cambodia which invited invasion by the Vietnamese and the Chinese.

(d) the desire of the Chinese to develop a series of client states in the region, much as the Soviet Union had in Eastern Europe.

(e) the Vietnamese goal of unification of all of Southeast Asia under the direction of Hanoi.

11. The future well-being of Third and Fourth World nations is least likely to be assured through

(a) the establishment of international associations that will facilitate regional interdependence, promote economic assistance programs and the achievement of favorable balances of trade, so that their collective weight is readily felt in international affairs.

*(b) the creation of police states maintained by military forces well trained in counterinsurgency techniques, which will promote economic progress indirectly by centralizing planning and defending national sovereignty.

(c) international meetings of Third and Fourth World nations dedicated to the cultivation of friendship and economic cooperation without interference from the superpowers, and the solidarity these efforts foster among the non-aligned states.

(d) increased economic assistance to the dispossessed nations by the industrialized nations.

(e) reliance on one or another superpower, whose military and economic patronage often provides security, relative independence, and material prosperity.

12. The vital interest of the Soviet Union to extend its sphere of influence throughout the world is most effectively summed up in

*(a) Nikita Khrushchev's statement "We will bury you," based on an unrelenting belief in the global triumph of communism.

(b) Soviet intervention in the affairs of the newly emerging nations of the Third World—in Africa, Asia, and Latin America.

(c) the ruthless suppression of revolts in the satellite countries: Poland, Hungary, and Czechoslovakia in particular.

(d) Soviet support of communist revolutionaries everywhere via military and economic aid.

(e) educational opportunities offered at the University of Moscow to potential leaders of developing countries with the aim of familiarizing them with the trappings of Soviet communism.

13. The antimetaphysical or materialistic concepts prevailing in industrialized Western society were most seriously challenged by

(a) the communist insurgents of China under the leadership of Mao Tse-tung, who overthrew the Nationalists by 1949.

*(b) Ayattola Khomeini, who wished to reverse westernizing trends in Iran by establishing a government based on the religious concepts of the Koran.

(c) leaders of the Indian National Congress party, who achieved autonomy of the subcontinent by noncompliance and civil disobedience.

(d) the often violent nationalist revolutions in Africa against Belgian, French, and British colonial rule.

(e) the revolutionary leaders in Poland and Hungary whose rebellions in 1956 were directed against the oppressive rule of atheistic Soviet communism, which had been installed through imperialistic tactics.

14. Recent attempts to ease world tension between the superpowers are *least* helped by

(a) the policy of detente, intended to diffuse rivalries that could occasion conflict through negotiations and discussions that stress common interests.

*(b) ideological differences in the notions about the nature of human development and the future.

(c) attempts to limit the expansion of armaments and the spread of nuclear weapons.

(d) the Camp David agreement between Israel and Egypt that appears to have initiated a break in the Israeli-Arab deadlock.

(e) the accommodation reached between the United States and China in the early 1970s.

15. In the development of new power relationships, world war has been avoided so far for which of the reasons given below:

   (a) the unwillingness of the U.S. government to extend the Korean War into China and thus risk a nuclear war.

   *(b) recognition among all nations that self-interest and attempts to change the balance of international power is severely limited by the possession of nuclear weapons and the fear that their use might destroy the world.

   (c) the Soviet government's agreement to withdraw offensive missiles and bombers from Cuba after John F. Kennedy ordered a naval blockade of the island in October 1962.

   (d) determined action by the United Nations Security Council, which has succeeded in its primary responsibility of maintaining international peace and security.

   (e) the Third World nations in the United Nations General Assembly which often empowered, by an overwhelming majority vote, the secretary general to use any means to compel belligerent nations to solve their problems by peaceful means.

IDENTIFICATIONS

The "thaw"
De-Stalinization
"More than one road to
   socialism"
Summit conferences
Common Market
Achmed Sukarno
Shmer Rouge
Kampuchea

Fourth World
Bandung Conference
Colombo Plan
Asian Development Bank
Association of Southeast Asian
   Nations
Ho Chi Minh
Tet offensive

TRUE OR FALSE

T   1. In the mid-1970s the United States ranked thirteenth in the world in the number of teachers per school-age population; seventeenth (after Poland) in the ratio of physicians to population; seventeenth in infant mortality rate; and twentieth in life expectancy.

T   2. In foreign aid contributions to dispossessed nations in 1975, Western European industrialized nations averaged .36 of one percent of their GNP; the United States only .27 of one percent, while the Soviet Union gave only one-tenth as much as the U. S.

T   3.   Soviet troops supporting Soviet puppet rulers overthrew the Czechoslovakian government in 1968 on the grounds that Soviet hegemony was threatened by the economic and social privileges granted to Czechoslovak citizens.

F   4.   During the 1960 summit conference with Russia, the United States government would not acknowledge the fact that reconnaissance flights had been dispatched over the USSR to discover the location of military targets.

T   5.   The Soviet Union, some European nations, the United States, and China are today prepared to engage each other indirectly through the medium of the Third World adversary nations.

T   6.   The Greek monarchy was restored in 1949 with the aid of certain Western nations after a bitterly fought civil war between loyalists and communist insurgents who received Russian support.

F   7.   The peoples of India have come to believe that only a democratic form of government will afford their nation the means by which trenchant poverty, illiteracy, overpopulation, and near starvation can be routed.

F   8.   Having lost its North African colonies, France voluntarily turned over its naval and air bases at Bizerte to the government of Tunisia in the late 1950s.

F   9.   The conflicts of Indochina in the late 1970s were the result of the ideological differences between the superpowers and their client states.

T   10.   Kwame Nkrumah of Ghana and Patrice Lumumba of the Congo were assassinated with the apparent knowledge and/or aid of the American Central Intelligence Agency.

DISCUSSION AND/OR ESSAY QUESTIONS

1. "An ability to accommodate goals to limitations was a talent difficult for superpowers to master. Yet it remained their best hope for a continuing, if uneasy, peace."

   Why are the superpowers forced to develop such an ability of accommodation? Do you think that the present goals of world powers endanger the existing status quo?

2. What are the reasons for the bipolarization of the world during the ten years after 1945? What role did China play in this process? What have been the results?

3. What are the reasons for the disappearance of Western civilization as it has been described and analyzed in previous chapters? Why do we speak of a "world civilization" today?

4. "Political power may change hands, but the power of money remains a prime mover in the affairs of the world."

Illustrate this proposition with appropriate examples, focusing on the twentieth century and briefly indicating nineteenth-century roots of this era's money power.

5. "However much power has shifted since World War II, power politics remains a game nations believe themselves compelled to play, if necessary, in opposition to their ideological commitments."

Supply a satisfactory definition for the term "power politics." Defend the contention made above by citing indicents of covert alliances, intelligence activities world-wide, changed promises, rhetorical threats, and the like in postwar politics.

SUGGESTED FILMS

Africa Is My Name. 22 min. Color. Atlantic Productions, Inc. (1961).

The Aftermath of WWII: Prologue to the Cold War. 24 min. B/w. McGraw-Hill Films (1962).

The Arab Jews. 28 min. Color. Verite Products, Inc. (1976).

Britain and Europe. 20 min. B/w. (From War and Peace in Europe series.) Time-Life Films, Inc. (1970).

Chaos and Conflict. 30 min. B/w. National Educational TV, Inc., Indiana University Audio-Visual Center (1966).

China: The East Is Red. 21 min. Color. Doubleday Multimedia, a Division of Doubleday and Co., Inc. (1971).

The Cold War. 20 min. B/w. Time-Life Films, Inc. (1970).

Crisis in Asia. 20 min. B/w. Time-Life Films, Inc. (1970).

Cuba: The Missile Crisis. 2 parts. 26 min. B/w. National Broadcasting Company, TV, TV, producer (1965).

Europe United. 28 min. Color. (Can be leased from the University of North Carolina; which see *Educational Film Locator.*) (1974).

Gandhi's India. 20 min. B/w. Time-Life Films, Inc. (1970).

History of the U.S. Foreign Relations: Part 4—the Road to Interdependence. 30 min. Color. United States Department of State (1976).

Hungary and Communism—Eastern Europe in Change. 17 min. Color. Encyclopaedia Britannica Educational Corp./Films (1964).

Indonesia: Land and People. 14 min. Color. Coronet Instructional Films (1957).

Indonesia: Words and Deeds. 10 min. B/w. Hearst Metrotone News. (n.d.)

Inside Red China. 51 min. Color. Carousel Films, Inc. (1966).

Iran. 18 min. Color. Pyramid Films (1972).

Israel-Nation of Destiny. 27 min. Color. Atlantic Productions, Inc. (1972).

Khrushchev and the Thaw. 20 min. B/w. Time-Life Films, Inc. (1970).

Khrushchev Era. 29 min. B/w. National Education TV, Inc., Indiana University Audio-Visual Center (1960).

Korea: The Link. 26 min. B/w. CCM Films Incorporated (1965).

Let My People Go. 54 min. B/w. Films, Inc. (1965).

Mr. Europe and the Common Market. 51 min. B/w. Carousel Films, Inc. (1962).

The New China. 20 min. B/w. Time-Life Films, Inc. (1970).

Nuclear Forces. 30 min. B/w. Associated British Corporation (London) (1966).

Nuclear Power in World Politics. 20 min. B/w; c. Films Incorporated (1967).

One Man's China, No. 5—One Nation, Many Peoples. 25 min. Color. Time-Life Films, Inc. (1973).

Problems of the Middle East. 22 min. Color. Atlantic Productions, Inc. (1967).

Revolution in China: From War to Revolution. 20 min. B/w. Time-Life Films, Inc. (1970).

Roots of the Cold War. 28 min. Color. Association—Sterling Films (1973).

Russia. 24 min. Color. International Film Foundation (1958).

Search for Unity: A European Idea. 2 parts, each 26 min. Color. (From the series Europe the Mighty Continent.) Time-Life Films, Inc. (1976).

The Story of Ghana. 20 min. B/w. Time-Life Films, Inc. (1970).

The Story of Modern Egypt. 20 min. B/w. Time-Life Films, Inc. (1970).

Vitenam Epilogue. 15 min. Color. Hearst Metrotone News (1973).

Vietnam: Why—A Timely Report. 15 min. B/w. Hearst Metrotone News (1964).

Outline

MULTIPLE CHOICE

Choose the best response.

1. The growth of centralized governments throughout the world—in some instances before World War I, but in most cases thereafter—was *mainly* caused by the

   (a) initiation of social programs to protect the population from the depredations of unemployemnt, sickness, and old-age dependency.

   *(b) motivation to improve or, at any rate, stabilize the nations' international position, which politicians hoped could be accomplished by tightening governmental hold over the economy and over the investment of enormous sums in up-to-date armaments.

   (c) convictions held by supporters of these governments that dissatisfaction and internal unrest would contribute to national decline and loss of effective power in the international community.

   (d) expansion of bureaucracies to manage comprehensive, nationwide programs established by the legislators.

   (e) genuine desire of most politicians to support programs providing a decent life style for their constituents.

2. The most serious consequence of centralization of government power is

   (a) the growth of a total welfare state, advocated by most post-Stalin socialists, instead of collective ownership of the means of production.

   *(b) the increasing control over the lives and decisions of all citizens by ponderous government bureaucracies that threaten to contribute to individuals' alienation from society, lack of self-direction, and feelings of helplessness.

   (c) continuous economic development from which the majority of citizens will benefit, and that has derived from the harnessing of new energy sources made possible by government-financed research.

331

(d) the probability of lasting world peace, because ideologies—both capitalist and socialist—were dulled by bureaucratic administration under both types of rule.

(e) distribution of the profits of capitalist economies to the needy through government agencies and managed monetary systems.

3. Critics of bureaucratic centralization and control over citizens' lives have done all the following *except*

(a) urge governments to moderate national goals and trim bureaucracies on the realistic grounds that government programs had not alleviated poverty and misery despite enormous expenditures.

*(b) put an end to the growth of big government.

(c) elect conservative governments in several Western countries since the mid-1970s, and curb government programs by limiting taxation.

(d) raise a powerful voice against both the notions of socialist "progresss" and the biased interests of the "military-industrial complex," regardless of their ideological position.

(e) urge the adoption of revolutionary measures against the "one-dimensional society" of industrial capitalism, wherein the interests of the individual were to be subordinated to corporate interests.

4. Which of the developments of events listed below is likely to have the *greatest* impact on current and subsequent generations of Americans:

(a) the escalation of the war against North Vietnam on the grounds of "evidence" most likely manufactured by President Lyndon Johnson and his advisers.

(b) the subversion of leftist Third World governments by the United States Central Intelligence Agency.

(c) the disregard of American citizens' constitutional liberties by President Richard Nixon when he authorized domestic spying in the name of national security.

*(d) the loss of confidence in "democracy" experienced by many Americans, and disillusionment about their ability to control the processes of government.

(e) the intervention of multinational corporations, with the cooperation of the C.I.A., in assisting the overthrow of the socialist government of Chile.

5. One of the following philosophies, current in black civil rights movements, differed from the others by advocating violence. Which statement contains the exceptional viewpoint?

(a) Black Americans are descendants of the "greatest and proudest race who ever peopled the earth."

(b) Islam, the truth faith of Africans, will overcome the feelings of helplessness that blacks have experienced by restoring pride to black peoples.

(c) "Love of God and man" must be translated into specific crusades against injustice, as Gandhi taught.

*(d) Power must be gained by revolutionary means before society's wrongs against black people can be corrected.

(e) America will be destroyed by the racism that pervades white society.

6. The response options for question 5 give the major theses of five philosophies of the black civil rights movement. Indicate below the correct order of individuals and/or groups who maintained those views.

(a) Marcus Garvey; Elijah Muhammad; Martin Luther King; Eldridge Cleaver; Nat Turner.

*(b) Marcus Garvey; Malcolm X; James Farmer and Martin Luther King; Black Panthers; James Baldwin.

(c) W. E. B. Du Bois; Elijah Muhammad; James Farmer; Black Panthers; Harriet Tubman.

(d) James Baldwin; Malcolm X; Martin Luther King; A. Philip Randolph; Nat Turner.

(e) Marcus Garvey; Elijah Muhammad; James Farmer and Martin Luther King; Nat Turner; Black Panthers.

7. Which of the following statements is *incorrect*?

(a) Black Americans are convinced that the battle for equality is justified and is as yet unwon.

(b) The emerging independence of African and Caribbean nations offers exemplary strength to black people in their fight against discrimination and disadvantage.

(c) Many who emigrate to Great Britain from former colonies are faced with substandard housing and extreme discrimination in jobs.

*(d) The civil rights laws enacted in the United States in the 1960s have brought black Americans to full equality with other segments of the population as regards voting and school desegregation.

(e) Most black civil rights leaders in the United States advocated the use of nonviolent methods in fighting for equality and justice.

8. The upheaval by the younger generation, especially in the 1960s, may be best described as a

(a) protest against the war in Vietnam and the idea that it is a "duty" to preserve what are actually the masked goals of a military-industrial complex and not those of the nation as a people.

(b)   rebellion of students, exempt from military service and attending colleges and universities, who protested against the institutions of the Establishment long before adult liberals spoke out against the devastations of the war in Vietnam.

(c)   movement that forced the retirement of President Johnson of the United States in 1966 and of President de Gaulle of France in 1967.

*(d)   function of the emancipation, in a few individual cases, from the formalities of older value systems, but, in the majority of instances, an expression of uncertain and impatient adolescent behavior.

(e)   dedication to the principles of counterculture based on the concept of "relevancy."

9.   In the 1970s, when the U.S. government was called to task by its citizens for rejecting popular control and accountability, many movements were afoot. Which *did not* take place?

(a)   Based on a record of widespread discrimination, women and blacks won sizable popular support in their attempts to gain rights.

(b)   Black movements declared their willingness to work for reform within the existing system.

*(c)   Civil rights laws and affirmative action programs prepared the way for passage of an Equal Rights for Women Amendment to the Constitution.

(d)   Groups of blacks, women, and the young began to assert demands for equality.

(e)   Based as it was on the disaffections of one generation and without a substantial support base in the general population, the youth movement faded away by the 1970s.

10.   The justification for blacks, women, and youth, in particular, to participate in agitation for equal rights is *not* central to

(a)   Gunter Grass's *Local Anaesthetic*, which analyzes protests against the Establishment and the motivation for political involvement.

(b)   Richard Wright's portrayal of the working class during the time of the New Deal in his *Black Boy*.

(c)   Lorraine Hansberry's story of a family living under the burdens of Northern white racism in the play *A Raisin in the Sun*.

*(d)   Boris Pasternak's *Dr. Zhivago*, in which the author is preoccupied with the Soviet system and its regulation of the lives of all citizens.

(d)   Simone de Beauvoir's study of *The Second Sex*, and its denunciation of the male middle class.

11. The work of the majority of postwar artists *cannot* be described as

   *(a) having an ideological commitment to the renovation of society or concern over its direction, while supplying "meaning" or "message" for reflection.

   (b) a revolt against the abstract expressionists that pressed art to the ultimate question of choice of medium.

   (c) new experiments in abstraction that depicted everyday objects, such as soup cans or comic-strip characters, yet were not intended as any protest against the trappings of industrialism.

   (d) representative of "nothing but content—no association, only sensation."

   (e) a collective perception that painting is a somewhat isolated, mechanical operation—i.e., "the treatment of canvas with paint."

12. Ecology can be *best* described as

   *(a) a discipline that studies the interrelationships between living things and their environment within the context of the entire chain of life.

   (b) a term made popular during the 1960s by young revolutionaries, who protested industry's destruction of natural resources and life cycles, and its disproportionate use of the world's resources for commercial rather than humanitarian purposes.

   (c) people's growing awareness of how so-called civilized society taxes nature, a problem whose solution might be found in scientific methods to harmonize human activities with natural cycles.

   (d) a lack of management of natural resources that now makes it impossible for science to cope with the multitude of pollutants from cheaply manufactured synthetic materials that answer only immediate commercial needs.

   (e) a special concern of the United Nations Economic and Social Council, which now has the financial means and authority it sees as necessary to half the world-wide wastage of land.

13. The main cause of the population explosion since the mid-century has been the

   (a) refusal of some Third World leaders to limit population growth either by sterilization or contraceptive devices, because they believe that such a limitation amounts to a subtle form of genocide, encouraged by industrialized nations that refuse to voluntarily lower their own expectations and standards of living.

   (b) ability of the rapid industrialization of Third World countries and the rise of scientific food production to overturn Malthus's theory of subsistence and to make the transformation to modernity surprisingly manageable.

   *(c) considerable birth-rate increase concurrent with the reduction of the death rate due to advancements in medicine.

(d)   widespread social welfare programs that provide security and health care, and that anticipate many of the fatal complications people met with in former times due to hazards of industrial life, disease, and poverty.

(e)   general rise in the standard of living that has enabled most people to secure adequate housing facilities and sufficient food.

14.   Achievements of science and technology in the latter twentieth century are described in each statement below. Which contention might be *least* supportable?

(a)   Electronic devices have aided the development of automation, which can process, handle, and control production scientifically with minimal human intervention.

*(b)   The careful application of scientific discoveries has become a panacea for the practical problems of human existence, and most science-oriented thinkers see such a process of refined applied science as the chief hope for the world's future.

(c)   Insecticides, especially DDT, have practically eliminated malaria-carrying mosquitoes in Malaysia, thus explaining why its use was once sanctioned, even though evidence of its disastrous side-effects is not freely admitted.

(d)   Discoveries in the health sciences have revolutionized the treatment of patients and increased life expectancy.

(e)   Most Americans can hardly imagine a life style without the internal combustion engine.

15.   The drawbacks of science and technology are *best* indicated in which of the following?

(a)   The discovery of viruses, "miracle drugs," and vaccines have contributed, in part, to a dramatic population increase.

(b)   The internal combustion engine and the chemical DDT have created more problems for society than they have solved.

(c)   Automation has proven a mixed blessing since it creates technological unemployment in the modern world each time it refines the manufacturing process.

(d)   The harnessing of nuclear energy for peaceful use and the disposal of nuclear wastes are frought with incalcuable risks due to deadly radiation.

*(e)   Science and its application to technology seem to continuously create new problems each time they offer a workable solution to an old problem.

IDENTIFICATIONS

DNA
$E = mc^2$
Herbert Marcuse
NAACP
Harlem Renaissance
Albert Camus
The Castle
Henderson the Rain King

Native Son
Their Eyes Were Watching God
Right-to-life movement
Abstract expressionism
Hyper-realists
Eniwetok Atoll
Gulag Archipelago

TRUE OR FALSE

T 1. Knowledge of the genetic processes in DNA could lead to dangerous attempts to produce artificially a breed of "perfect" humans.

F 2. Lieutenant-Colonel John H. Glenn, Jr. was the first man launched into orbit around the earth.

T 3. By 1970 not only the United States, but the Soviet Union, China, Britain, France, India, Israel, and other nations either possessed atomic weapons or were in the process of developing the technology to do so.

T 4. The atomic bomb was the achievement of scientists working for the War Department of the United States, many of whom were refugees from Nazi or fascist oppression.

F 5. Since most Americans in the North did not share the predominant southern attitudes toward black people, many blacks emigrated from the South to the North during the twentieth century.

T 6. Over 400,000 blacks were made to serve during the First World War.

F 7. As a response to the political program of the National Urban League, racist southern whites initiated the movement of black emigration from America to Africa.

T 8. The Aswan High Dam of Egypt incresed the water supply of the country, but irreparably damaged Egypt's fishing industry by reducing the flow of algae nutrients to the Mediterranean.

F 9. By mid-century the population and the land areas of the underdeveloped portions of the globe were equal to that of the developed portions.

T 10. Development in nuclear science evoked disturbing questions as to capabilities, limitations, and implications of science and technology.

DISCUSSION AND/OR ESSAY QUESTIONS

1. How do you see the role of historians who are called upon to analyze their own society? What might be the lesson of history for the modern age? How can one plan intelligently for the future?

2. "This conjunction of an immense military establishment and a large arms industry is new in American experience. The total influence—economic, political, even spiritual—is felt in every city, every statehouse, every office of the federal government. . . . We must guard against the acquisition of unwarranted influence, whether sought or unsought, by the military-industrial complex. The potential for the disastrous rise of misplaced power exists and will persist."
   —Dwight D. Eisenhower, "Farewell Address"
   Why did President Eisenhower warn his country of the growing might of what he called "the military-industrial complex"?

3. How and to what degree were women's rights and black rights advanced by the literary work of women authors? Name these authors and place their works into historical perspective.

4. What were the reasons for the doubt and pessimism about the human condition that prevailed among the world's creative thinkers of the postwar era?

5. What are the causes of the "demographic revolution"? If there are not changes in these factors or the influence they have upon current population trends, what results could be expected?

SUGGESTED FILMS

Acid (LSD). 27 min. Color. Encyclopaedia Britannica Educational Corp./Film (1970).

Anatomy of Violence. 30 min. B/w. National Educational TV, Inc., Indiana University Audio-Visual Center (1967).

And Who Shall Feed the World? 54 min. Color. McGraw-Hill Films (1974).

Arena. 10 min. Color. Pyramid Films (1970).

Assembly Line. 30 min. B/w. Macmillan Films, Inc. (1961).

The Black Community and the New Deal. 30 min. B/w. (From the Black History series, section 16.) Holt, Rinehart and Winston, Inc. (969).

Black Roots. 60 min. Color. Impact Films (1970).

Bulldozed America. 25 min. B/w. Carousel Films, Inc. (1965).

Casals Conducts: 1964. 17 min. B/w. Encyclopaedia Britannica Educational Corp. Films (1965).

CBW: The Secrets of Secrecy. 49 min. Color. Films, Inc. (1969).

The City and the Future. 28 min. B/w. Sterling Educational Films (1963).

The City of Necessity. 25 min. Color. Assocaition of Instructional Materials (1962).

Einstein. 42 min. B/w. Time-Life Films (1969).

An Essay on War. 23 min. Color. Encyclopaedia Britannica Educational Corp./Films (1972).

Footnotes on the Atomic Age. 46 min. Color. Films, Inc. (1970).

The Futurists. 25 min. Color. McGraw-Hill Films (1967).

Genetics: Man the Creator. 22 min. Color. Document Associates, Inc. (1971).

The Great Divide. 20 min. B/w. Time-Life Films, Inc. (1970).

Information Explosion. 11 min. Color. AIMS Instructional Media Service, Inc. (1973).

Into the Jet Age. 20 min. B/w. Time-Life Films, Inc. (1970).

The Laser Beam. 16 min. Color. Handel Film Corp. (1968).

Man and the "Second" Industrial Revolution. 19 min. Color. McGraw-Hill Films (1970).

Oh! Woodstock! 26 min. Color. Films, Inc. (1969).

Picasso is 90. 51 min. Color. Carousel Films, Inc. (1972).

The Population Explosion. 42 min. B/w. Carousel Films, Inc. (1960).

R. Buckminster Fuller: Prospects for Humanity. 30 min. Color. National Education TV, Inc., Indiana University Audio-Visual Center (1979).

The Shrinking World. 20 min. B/w. Time-Life Films, Inc. (1970).

Target Moon. 24 min. Color. ACI Productions (revised, 1974).

Universal Machine. 29 min. B/w. National Education TV, Inc., Indiana University Audio-Visual Center (1962).

A Woman's Place. 52 min. Color. Xerox Films (1973).